CONSTITUTIONAL AND ADMINISTRATIVE LAW

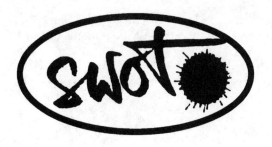

CONSTITUTIONAL AND ADMINISTRATIVE LAW

Fourth Edition

Robert G. Lee, LLB

Professor of Law, Cardiff Law School

and

Mark Stallworthy

Director, Centre for Professional Legal Education,
University of East Anglia, Norwich

Series Editor: C.J. Carr, MA, BCL

BLACKSTONE
PRESS LIMITED

This edition published in Great Britain 1995 by Blackstone Press Limited, 9-15 Aldine Street, London W12 8AW. Telephone: 0181-740 1173

© Robert G. Lee, 1985

First edition, 1985
Reprinted 1988
Second edition, 1989
Third edition, 1991
Fourth edition, 1995

ISBN: 1 85431 337 1

Typeset by Montage Studios Limited, Tonbridge, Kent
Printed by Bell and Bain Limited, Glasgow

CONTENTS

11 *Public order*   179

Freedom of association — Public order offences under the 1986
Act — Other public order offences — New statutory develop-
ments: trespass — Revision — The examination — Conclusion
— Further reading

12 *Police powers*   212

The Act and the codes — Arrest — Stop and search — Entry and
search — Seizure — Detention and questioning — Revision —
The examination — Conclusion — Further reading

13 *Conclusion*   241

Index   245

PREFACE

The guidance and assistance of Mark Stallworthy was acknowledged in the preface to the third edition of this book. This edition goes one step further. Mark has been largely responsible for the production of the fourth edition. Ten years have passed since work began on the first edition of the book — the first in the SWOT series. Robert Lee is no longer the angry young man of the first edition — the Preface to which is reproduced on the following pages. He has become a tired old practitioner who now only teaches in the rarefied atmosphere of postgraduate law study — and then only occasionally.

What was needed was a fiery young teacher to revitalise the book — but Mark did it instead. He has the advantage of being involved in day-to-day contact with undergraduate students. Given the nature of the book this is a crucial advantage. The subversive intention of the book remains. Read the Preface to the first edition and find out.

Two main developments to this latest edition will be apparent. First, we have sought to offer guidance on how to cope with the more varied form of assessment to which students are now subjected. Secondly, we have produced a guide to further reading in the hope that this will prove helpful. This is in addition to the many texts referred to in the substance of the chapters. With the passage of time, the need to record our gratitude to the staff at Blackstone is undiminished.

Robert Lee
Mark Stallworthy
Various Adnams houses in East Anglia
May 1995

PREFACE TO THE FIRST EDITION

No one with any faith in the examination system of assessment could have written a book quite so cynical as this one. But then, I have no faith left. The values attributed to the system — and objectivity is the most obvious of these — are far outweighed by the inefficiencies and the resulting pressures placed upon candidates. That the candidate may fail to reflect his or her true abilities under such circumstances is hardly surprising. It is staggering that the testing of a full year's work in a three-hour period can be suggested with any seriousness. Indeed not only do I doubt the wisdom of those teachers who continue to defend the process of assessment by unseen examinations alone, I doubt also their motives. For we cannot pretend that this process, when compared with other patterns of assessment, is not the cosiest and most convenient of the options — notwithstanding the pain it causes students.

If it was simply that an examination caused the student a good deal of hard work, or in some way challenged the candidate to resolve problems under severe time constraints, then I should have no complaints. The deficiencies in the system are of a different nature. By allowing the student such limited scope to be heard, and by testing such a restricted range of abilities (thus excluding, e.g., lingual skills totally) the tendency is to penalise particular students and give an undue advantage to others. If asked to describe this trend, then I should say that it is the harder working students that tend to lose out. By lessening the opportunities to prove one's worth, the more worthy candidates are disadvantaged.

Not only do we allow the continued existence of this unfair and inadequate system, but we do nothing to minimise its capricious nature. The fact that there is so little available coaching in examination technique only reflects a reluctance to admit that a whole range of skills unconnected with law might be necessary to succeed. This book makes no apology in attempting to redress the balance and provide some much needed guidance — even though it is clear there are those who might frown upon the attempt.

At no point is this book seeking to provide a simplification of the legal material, or a set of notes to cram. In one sense it decries the existence of such easy solutions. At the same time it does explain that any three-hour examination will carry inherent flaws as a system of assessment. Therefore it will point out that the material to be learnt can be slimmed down, that it may be possible to take short cuts or to leave an impression of possessing a greater knowledge than is actually the case. As a consequence, the material in the book is itself limited and incomplete. Any attempt to use the book as a standard textbook is destined to failure. The material is selective in two ways. First, it is unlikely to cover the whole of the syllabus since the chapters deal with subjects by way of examples. Second, the substantive law in each chapter is supposed to provide the basis for answering sample questions later in the chapter. This material too, and the case law upon which it draws, is highly selective.

Hopefully none of this ought to detract from the merits of the book since these lay in the guidance given on revision and examination technique. If I had been wishing to write a text on constitutional law, it would have been a very different book indeed. I would go further and say that I should not like to study a syllabus as sterile, and in particular, as devoid of theoretical analysis as the one projected in the book. In fairness to my colleagues, I do not think that it represents the course taught at my present institution. Having said that, the book is written for a particular market: students upon a typical first-year degree course in constitutional law, who realise that they are going to find the examinations a struggle. It may be that, because of the manner in which it is written, it will be useful to students at a level below law degree studies. So be it — may it help them all.

Which brings me to the people who helped me. I should like to thank the staff at both Lancaster University and Lancashire Polytechnic who have taken time to discuss the project with me and advise me upon it. I am most grateful to Alistair, Heather, Jonathan and Juliet of Financial Training. It is inconceivable that one could be given greater support and encouragement in the course of any publication than I received in writing this book. I should like Joan to know that even in my view (though she might not believe this) typing a manuscript with a broken arm goes beyond the call of duty. To her and to Helen I am most grateful — especially for their patience. Drawing the cartoons is the thing that I am least grateful to my wife Anne for, but the others would fill a separate book. Finally I should like to thank generations of my students without whose totally inane questions and abysmal examination answers I should never have become sufficiently frustrated to write the book.

Robert G. Lee
Down the Duke
Still not Spring 1985

TABLE OF CASES

1 SURVIVING IN THE ASSESSMENT JUNGLE

There is only one sure way to pass an examination and that is to cheat. If this sounds improper then consider that after a full year of work on a subject, countless hours of teaching, endless reading of case law and textbooks and days and nights of fretful revision, many law schools still assess the students in a single, three-hour examination. That is hardly a fair process. Only the most moralistic of students would have qualms about taking a short cut by a careful attempt to cheat the system. On the other hand it is important to be careful since many traditional methods of cheating during examinations have proved to be inefficient, leading, when discovered, to the failure of the paper rather than the desired pass. For this reason it is wiser to dispense with cheating inside the examination room and to take sufficient steps to guarantee success in advance of the examination itself. This could be described as cheating at exams rather than cheating in exams.

CHEATING AT EXAMS

It is because examinations are an inadequate form of assessment that students worry about them so much. Comments such as 'I never do myself justice' or 'I can't possibly learn all this' are common, and they are not without justification. All teachers know of students who underachieve in examinations; sometimes these are the better students in the year. Equally some characters manage surprisingly well on a limited amount of work. How can this be? If we focus on the shortcomings of the written examination, it is obvious that there is a limited amount of material which can be written down in the time-limit. Paradoxically this is why the lazy student can be comparatively successful in comparison with hard-working students who often achieve only marginally better results. This accounts for some of the demoralisation on the part of those students who say 'I never do myself justice'.

A more positive approach would be to say 'They can't possibly ask me that much in a single examination'. This might prevent two major problems which commonly undermine your efforts. First you would not be so intimidated by the sheer bulk of material (and especially case law) when undertaking revision. Secondly, you would be less likely to produce answers which contain every available element of the year's learning (kitchen-sink answers) but which fail to address the point of the question, and often lead to a problem with time. The ideal solution would be to gain access to a copy of the examination paper in advance and to prepare the requisite number of answers which clearly and concisely dispose of the questions set. Unfortunately on most courses, security arrangements and the possibility of criminal charges, make this impossible or undesirable. This does not mean that there is nothing you are able to do to place yourself as near as possible to our ideal solution of knowing the questions and having answers prepared. The notion of cheating at exams means taking every possible opportunity of arriving in this favoured position, but if possible you should begin in the first week of the course to lay the foundations of examination success.

SYSTEMATIC STUDY

It is indisputably the pattern that students who perform well throughout the year tend to achieve the better examination results. On the other hand we have all heard of the student who was bright enough to gain a first-class degree without bothering to work. But how many of us have met this mythical student? It is simply not possible to cope with assessments in law or any other subject except from a basis of knowledge. Imagine sitting an examination in Russian or zoology tomorrow. Irrespective of your IQ, without some study of the materials, you would fail hopelessly. The only truth in the exceptional student myth is that there are students with a sufficient capacity and study skill to achieve good results with an economy of effort, but that is rather different from achieving results without work. On the contrary good results are invariably a product of efficient study — possibly spread evenly throughout the year.

Unfortunately, however, it is true that certain students work hard throughout the year and underachieve in assessments. So hard work alone may be insufficient, and with some students, the harder they work, the more the work seems intimidating or even impossible. This seems especially true of first-year law students faced with a new subject and vast lists of references to cases and statutes. Those reduced to tears are not the lazy students (who do not bother enough to cry) but those who are almost too conscientious.

Little information is given on coping with study, and it is impossible to know how to organise study time in order to meet the demands of lecturers, tutors, and the course work. Hard work seems to place one even further behind schedule. Yet it is possible to cope with your course. Thousands of students have done so in the past, but how on earth did they manage it?

All law degree courses require examinations. This is because law degrees can lead to a professional qualification, and the professional bodies still require a substantial examination element. The object of your study ought to be a comprehensive set of notes from which you are able to revise. It is alarming, as a tutor, to see students with files and files containing thousands of words written on backs of envelopes, cigarette packets, and enough notepaper to have lasted Shakespeare a lifetime. Included is every last seminar comment (however unhelpful), a full transcript of the lectures including the jokes, and clippings of the most recent and controversial litigation to have been reported in the *Sun*. After the first year as a lecturer in constitutional law one of the authors sat down with some enthusiasm to mark the scripts. One question on parliamentary privilege had been answered by a large number of students, and some three-quarters of these essays began with the words, 'At the commencement of each parliamentary session, the Speaker declares several ancient and undoubted privileges'. After the first couple of scripts he began to wonder where such drivel could have come from, before eventually realising that they were the first words of his lecture! The most disconcerting feature was that so many students had used their lecture material as the sole basis of their revision.

GOOD HABITS

In a course which operates a system of lectures, seminars based upon set reading, and a number of written assignments during the year, it is not wise to become too dependent on the lectures. Often the seminars or tutorials will increase your understanding to a greater extent. However, lectures do form a short cut in learning if you use them wisely. Concentrate therefore on the structure of the lecture as a guide to how to approach the subject, and to how the argument or explanation of the topic is developed. This may be done by writing down the key issues. Even if you fail to understand the material, jot down why you are puzzled — then the issue may be clarified later by reading or asking questions. Above all listen to the lecture even if this means keeping a minimum of notes. This is better than making a longer set of notes but without ever fully concentrating on the words spoken. More can be gained from a lecture if it is not the student's first contact with the subject. A little prior reading on topics for forthcoming lectures will make the subject-matter more intelligible and allow you to listen to the argument being advanced rather than take first-time notes. Take notes by all means, but not a copy of every word spoken, and do not expect your notes to form a complete and final set. In a subject like constitutional law, the lectures will contain little original or obscure material since most of what is said will be available in books, articles and primary material, such as law reports.

The lecture will place you in a position to do further reading, and this may be necessary for seminar work. Again you will wish to make notes of what you read. Some law students keep a card index with the details of the cases which they have read. Making notes on reading may help you to concentrate on and understand the material. Remember, however, that if you are preparing for class discussion the important thing is to familiarise yourself with the area of law in advance. Too many students arrive at seminars totally dependent on the notes they have taken and unable to discuss subjects with any spontaneity. Knowledge consists of the accumulation of information which can be applied in new situations. The accumulation of information alone is worthless unless it is capable of application. So making notes on reading is not sufficient. Seek to answer the questions on the seminar sheet. These are often previous examination questions. Discuss the issues if you have the opportunity. Try to relate your new learning in constitutional law to what has gone before, especially as themes are often interrelated.

When the lectures and tutorials on a particular topic are finished, you ought to be in a position to write a complete set of notes on that topic. Most students do not do this and in consequence find themselves at the start of their revision with several sheets of notes on a point, none of which fit well together, and some of which are downright confusing. A couple of hours at the end of a topic will allow you to prepare a final version of your information whilst it is fresh in your mind. Books can be used to clarify misunderstandings, and you can close your file with confidence knowing that you have laid solid foundations for when you return at the revision stage.

Save your other 'raw material', but this final set of notes should be kept separately. Because you will use it for learning, it should have a particular style. Pages and pages of closely written sentences are impossible to remember. Lots of headings listing the main points will help. Keep these logical and give them numbers or letters. Thus if we are discussing delegated legislation, a side heading might read: 'C. SAFEGUARDS AGAINST ABUSE', and below that, '1. PARLIAMENTARY' and '2. JUDICIAL'. There might then be further headings, e.g., '(a) The Scrutiny Committee'. Lists are extremely valuable. If you can remember that there are four major parliamentary safeguards in your notes, then you are half-way to remembering what they are. Use lots of new paragraphs and indentations. Use colour—perhaps a different coloured pen for case names. Sometimes in recalling facts during an examination it may be possible to build a picture in your mind's eye of your notes. Having got that far, it will usually be possible to fill in the details, but only if your notes are distinctive and not long boring pages of unintegrated, and largely illegible, handwriting.

Even if you are not using notes for examination revision but for course work, careful structure will help a great deal. Law is very much about analysing problems. The better your notes are structured, the better informed your analysis will become.

It will be clear that there is a great deal to be done and that the effort must be spread over the whole of the course. We shall see later that semesterisation of courses has tended to increase the pressure on students. No one will work well unless sufficiently motivated to do so. In the short term, however, immediate targets can be extremely valuable in making progress. In higher education where there is plenty of free time for study, often you have to set your own targets. One way of doing this is to work to a timetable during which certain pre-arranged tasks ought to be completed. This approach has two advantages. It encourages regular study habits and it saves wasted time at each session deciding upon what should be done next.

Law lecturers comment frequently upon the success of mature students in comparison with standard A level entrants. One reason for this may be that mature students have grown used to regulating their work activity. They regard, say, 9 a.m. to 6 p.m. as their working day and waste less of this time chatting or drinking coffee, but study consistently for much of this period. Often family commitments reduce their time for study and force them to make best use of time. Each student must consider an individual timetable. There is no reason to worry if it proves difficult to follow at first since the development of good habits takes time, and it is not unusual for keen students to be over-optimistic as to what can be achieved. On the other hand, there are 168 hours in a week and even allowing for sleep, meals, travel etc., a good deal of time is available for both socialising and study. It is for you to decide which hours should be spent on which, but very late study or study beginning after a night out may well prove counter-productive. Blocks of study built into your timetable ought not to be too long — certainly no more than a couple of hours as a maximum without a significant break.

The key to study is habit. It is important to devise a programme that you can invariably keep to. Remember that it is always more difficult to begin a period of study, but once you begin it is relatively easy to continue. In order to establish a routine, you may wish to consider where you study. Most law students are forced to do a great deal of work in the library because of the necessity of access to legal materials. Some law students sit at the same desk in the law library day after day. The regular use of the same desk has a number of advantages. It becomes theirs and they leave books there all day returning as a matter of custom.

It is helpful to build rewards into your timetable, even if it is only last orders at the bar. Enforced breaks — such as a regular commitment to sports — may be helpful. It is useful to know how other people operate, and even watching your fellow students can help you to decide your own pattern. In the end, however, you must devise a system which is realistic and right for you. But what if you have not done any of this and you are now coming up against a deadline? It does not matter, you need a systematic approach just as much, and maybe more. Often, coming up to examinations, more study time will be needed. Consider the gaps in your programme, and be imaginative — an hour before breakfast might make a great difference.

COURSE WORK

Before moving on to deal with revision, one final comment on course work. A growing number of courses include course work within the final assessment. This will generally take the form of a number of essays (or answers to legal problems) during the year. But whether or not there is a significant element of course work, it ought to be used as an opportunity to prepare for the examination. Essays provide a vehicle for in-depth study of particular issues. They also offer (or should offer) an opportunity for direct and relevant feedback from the tutor.

Essays offer the chance to practise legal writing techniques. Written work clears up problems of legal terminology, forces the student to evaluate legal concepts, and helps eliminate grammatical errors. Perhaps the most significant advantage is that the law student begins to understand the workings of legal authorities, by introducing case law and statutory provisions to support the development of an argument. So treat course work seriously whether or not it counts towards the assessment. Moreover, because examinations come around infrequently it is hard to adjust to them, but the more adept a student is at legal writing the easier examinations will become. For both examinations and course work you must show that you think conceptually; that you apply the legal principles in a concise, accurate and relevant way; and that you can show critical judgment.

An examinee's desperation under pressure can often result in a descent into imprecise and irrelevant areas; in course work too there is a temptation to throw everything in, in an uncontrolled descriptive stew. These approaches threaten the impression you want to create for the marker. Markers look for a logical thinker, applying principles and supporting information, in a coherent fashion, and able to apply the conceptual material in such a way as to show an analytical mind.

CHANGING PATTERNS OF ASSESSMENT

Assessment creeps up upon the student in a number of guises. The standard examination format remains on the majority of courses. Yet the 'course work' element of most courses has undergone something of a tranformation in recent years. Because examinations require careful thought and pre-planning, much of these introductory chapters is about how to achieve a pass. But we concentrate on course work too. Continuous assessment helps develop your ability as a lawyer, and achieving a good grade will require concentrated effort on your part throughout the course.

It is increasingly likely that you will have to prepare yourself differently according to the task in hand. The lot of the law student is not always a happy one. In the remainder of this chapter we aim to set the scene by looking at assessment, the techniques and approaches which you will need to think about, and some guidance to help decide what works best for you.

An increasing number of universities now split their academic year into semesters. If your course is not semesterised then you may wish to skip this section. But be warned. It may be heading your way.

The benefits of the introduction of semesterisation seem to many to compare unfavourably with the Schleswig-Holstein question, about which only three people ever knew the answer. Unfortunately, one was dead, another mad, and the third had forgotten the question. As most students will now fall into the arms (or more properly, tentacles) of semesterisation, we shall set out shortly what we think it means. Semesterisation grew out of the extension of modular degree programmes. Under these programmes students are able to accumulate credits and use them to transfer to another degree programme, at the same or another institution.

To create smaller units offering credits the semester system splits, or pretends to split, the academic year in half. Modules are studied and assessed in a single semester. This means that assessment takes place at two points in the academic year.

The first semester is often called the autumn semester, and runs from around mid to late September, to the end of January thereby actually taking up most of an English winter! The second semester, or spring semester, typically runs from the end of January into the early summer. Examinations, or other forms of final assessment, will therefore take place during January, and (rather more traditionally) in May and June. It will immediately be apparent that the traditional festivals fall rather inconveniently. The longish Christmas and Easter breaks, useful for revision, in particular tend to restrict the study time available in the second semester. New students who cannot start until A-level results are known simply cannot arrive any earlier in the autumn than they do, and this is one of the reasons necessitating January assessments. There is therefore the relatively novel task of preparing for examinations that take place during January. The assessment process can be quite prolonged. For instance, if the autumn semester assessment in (say) contract consists of course work, for submission to your tutors either prior to the Christmas break or upon the New Year restart in around mid January, there may be little time to revise for an examination in (say) constitutional law towards the end of January.

Moreover the autumn semester makes way for the spring semester literally overnight (bring a raincoat), offering little recovery time from the rigours of assessment. There follows a frantic dash to cover most of the material of the new modules by the Easter break. Unsurprisingly, you may be faced with new material after the Easter break, although by then examinations are only three to four weeks distant. This seems not so much a semesterised course as an obstacle course.

A simple guide to semesterised assessment is as follows:

(a) *Examinations*. You will still be required to sit examinations. Indeed in the so-called 'core subjects' (or 'foundation elements') examinations are a compulsory part of the assessment process in order to gain exemptions from professional examinations.

(b) *Course work*. This element becomes increasingly prevalent and may take a variety of forms. The increased frequency of the assessment process has heightened the emphasis upon results. You may find that the opportunity for course work to be an exercise in feedback has been adversely affected.

Many law subjects are naturally resistant to the semester format. The preferred solution has been to create a split in traditional course subjects. Therefore, do not be surprised to find courses with meaningful titles such as 'Constitutional and Administrative Law I and II'. The interdependence of such courses is obvious, but note that many modular schemes require both assessment and subject-matter to be mutually exclusive. In the real world a solicitor or barrister could hardly say 'Sorry, I can advise on the public order offences, but the way the police arrested you is part of another course', but there it is. At least you know that you are likely to be assessed twice in constitutional and administrative law. There may be course work assessment at the end of the autumn semester for a course called 'Constitutional and Administrative Law I' and a three-hour examination at the end of the spring semester for 'Constitutional and Administrative Law II', but there are many other possibilities, including examinations in everything.

Because students still fear examinations so much, they are the subject of chapters 2 and 3. The rest of this chapter concentrates on course work.

FORMS OF COURSE WORK

Course-work assessment has grown in most law courses using enticing problems or an essay question, linked to dire warnings as to length. Given the fact that the quality of your analytical approach will determine your class of degree, one of our objectives in this book is to stimulate you to improve your approach to these tasks. The review of different areas of constitutional and administrative law contained in later chapters attempts to help you with this.

Over time the methods of course work have changed. Not all course work is written. A few words are necessary here concerning oral presentations. This may even extend to the use of the video camera. We do not unreservedly welcome every development in the assessment process, and students often have enough pressures without worrying about the kinds of criticism — as to style and especially mannerisms — which a videotape will emphasise. However, the simple presentation does have some merit of enabling the well-prepared student, with a coherent and thoughtful set of arguments, to carry and convince the (admittedly captive) audience in an emphatic way.

We will spare you advice on how to appear more photogenic (especially as the assessment is not concerned with seeing whether you can come over as Sue Lawley or David Bellamy). The important factor in such an assessment will be your ability to present your arguments cogently and coherently. The approach which you should adopt should not be so very different from that which applies to your written work. Indeed, that is the basis of any presentation.

We suggest that the particular features which you should bear in mind from the beginning are: first, there is the obvious element of time constraint and this will influence how the presentation is to be approached; secondly, there is no going back and therefore the presentation must be as complete as you can make it; thirdly, you must concentrate upon the impact of what you say upon the listeners and assessors, especially in the sense of carrying them with you; and, finally, you must be aware of the need to establish credibility, and structure your presentation accordingly.

Put crudely, there are fewer hiding places when you have to present arguments to an audience. The disadvantage for the student is that you are there to be questioned. In a written paper you may be given the benefit of the doubt if you are vague on a point. The marker may assume that you know what you mean. In a presentation you will be questioned and the questioning may lead to greater exposure of your ignorance or uncertainty.

How should you approach this type of assessment? In our experience, believe it or not, students too often fall into the trap of undervaluing themselves and their arguments. Remember that you already will have a good record of academic achievement. All you are required to do is to make your case in a more structured way. One great advantage that you have is that the nature of the exercise allows you a degree of control to choose what to cover. Stick to a number of limited themes, but prepare them carefully and rehearse their presentation.

The way to blow any such advantage is to prepare insufficiently. You must know your stuff: the facts of the case, or analogous cases; authorities which are useful, or threatening, to your argument; likely grounds of challenge; and strengths and weaknesses of your case. Law schools generally offer oppor- tunities to attempt, or to watch, the oral development of such structured arguments, in mooting programmes. If you watch a moot (or, even better, go into court) try to avoid getting too entangled in the detail of the law. Look at how arguments are being developed — how they are structured. Consider whether you are persuaded by the arguments presented. Listen to how weaknesses are defended. Look at how speakers manage to persuade the judge or other listeners. If you get the chance to take part in moots, you should do so. It can be a great learning exercise. It helps build confidence and you begin to understand the nature of legal argument.

Whether you are performing in an oral presentation or are writing a standard essay, there are some common rules which are obvious, but very important. The traditional pattern of scholarly aargument is as follows. You present a thesis (or hypothesis); you gather evidence which is relevant; you apply that evidence to the thesis; you present your conclusion as to whether or not the thesis is borne out. This may sound complex, but it is actually relatively straightforward. In the case of most course work, the thesis will be contained in the question which you are set. For example, you are often given a quotation from a book and asked to discuss it. That quotation will present a particular view. Your task is to show whether that view is correct or not. In order to do this, you will research the law and find out whatever you can about the area in question. Using what you have discovered, you will begin to form a judgment as to whether or not the assertion which you are discussing is correct. By reasoned argument, you must apply the evidence which you have uncovered to the quotation itself. Thus in effect you may say, 'This assertion is wrong because . . .' and then you will present a view of the law which runs contrary to the quotation. You can then round this all off by reiterating, briefly, whether or not the quotation can be taken as correct.

This formula immediately offers you a structure. It has a beginning, a middle, and an end. Provided you bear it in mind, you cannot go far wrong. It is still important to emphasise that much will depend on how well-reasoned your argument is, but you need not spend vast amounts of time wondering what it is you are supposed to do. It can also be very useful to bear this structure in mind for the purposes of any examinations. Because it is a ready-made structure, it can be quickly and easily applied in the examination room, and you will not waste vast amounts of time pondering how you should go about answering the question.

CONCLUSION

This chapter has tried to demonstrate that the methods of assessing students are increasingly fragmented. That is to say, they consist of a whole variety of approaches. In one sense, this offers some variety to the student which is rather better than the standard traditional examination format. On the other hand, it can put significant pressures on the student, who is having to cope with a far more varied process of assessment. Nonetheless, we hope that we have shown that the development of good habits will serve you well whichever form of assessment faces you. The two chapters which follow concentrate specifically on preparing for the form of assessment which most students still dread — the examination.

2 PREPARING FOR EXAMINATIONS

Before you begin to prepare for the examination, be sure that you know what is required of you. This should be made clear in the course guide or prospectus. The importance of looking up this material is that, increasingly, there are diverse forms of examination. In many you will sit down with a question paper and an answer book for the requisite period of time. Increasingly, however, it will not be a three-hour examination but one for a shorter period. Also, you may be able to take materials with you into the examination room. Statutes may be permitted, although you will often be told that these must be unmarked. Some universities provide fresh, official copies to you for the purpose of the examination. Others will be happy for you to use *Wallington and Lee's Public Law Statutes* if you have purchased a copy.

Other types of examination are gradually developing, however. This is especially true away from the core subjects, where the Law Society does not make particular demands. Open-book examinations may appear superficially attractive, but examiners commonly observe that a sizeable amount of time seems to be devoted by students to flicking through the materials hoping for inspiration. If you sit an open-book examination, bear in mind that the more material you take into the examination room, the longer your search period is likely to be. It makes every sense to restrict yourself to a small core of significant material, carefully indexed, on the relevant areas likely to be examined.

Because the purpose of the examination is in part to place the student under a time constraint, it is idle to think that you can produce material of the quality of your course work within the examination room. However, answers by students in examinations are often surprisingly good given the limited time available. Your chances of enhancing your performance in the examination must improve with preparation. All students realise this, which is why so long is spent in revision. However, not all revision time is well spent. What will gain you a good examination mark is a relevant, coherent, conceptual analysis of the question which is set. Trotting out lists of relevant points may have served you well lower down the school system, but it is not likely to produce you a high mark in university examinations. What follows in this chapter is a revision guide which will enhance your performance by helping you direct your efforts and spend your time efficiently.

BEGINNING REVISION

Whether or not your study programme has gone well during the course, there will come a point when you will need to start to revise. A common question is 'How early should I start to revise?' Students are worried that if they start too early they will forget the material before the examination. Although, as is explained below, not everything committed to memory can be retained, revision is based on frequent review of the materials, and many students arrive at the examination date thinking 'If only I had two more days'. Our answer is to advise revision at the earliest opportunity on which this may be commenced without damaging first-time preparation for the course. After all, if you are well ahead of schedule you can always take a break for a day or two.

Allocate your time equally to the subjects to be examined. There is a tendency to begin to prepare for the early examinations, and to leave too little time for revision of later papers. The most important feature of revision is to have a clear set of notes from which to work. If you have followed the procedures suggested above, this is unlikely to prove a problem. If not, then the first task will be to produce a set of notes which can be readily committed to memory. Two practices seem to infect some students. The first of these is attempting to learn from the textbook by underlining passages. It is true that by making words prominent on a page they become easier to recall, but not if three-quarters of a textbook is emphasised in this way. In any case it is always easier to recall your own words rather than someone else's. The second is the photocopying of masses of material. The authors can photocopy materials free of charge, but hardly ever bother. This is not just to save money but because we have long since discovered that a seat in the library with the law report and a note pad is the best method of digesting the material.

So even if you are short of time you ought to compile your own set of notes from which to revise. Once you have your set of notes, the next step is to read through the notes in their entirety, two or three times if you can manage it. At this stage you should be aiming at a general level of knowledge of the subject. Thus, you should know what is meant by natural justice, what it mainly consists of, when it applies and what remedies are available if the rules are breached. We shall see later why this approach is vital. As you are reading begin to map out the subject, list the topics which you have covered, and consider the relationship between them. Decide in your own mind which topics you know well and are confident in, and those areas in which you are weak. Iron out any final misunderstandings. At this stage, if your tutors are helpful, it may be sensible to ask for clarification of a particular point.

CONTINUING REVISION AND BEGINNING TO CHEAT

As you read through your constitutional law notes there is a likelihood that you may despair because you cannot believe that it is possible to memorise the whole of the notes. As we shall see later, much depends on what we mean by memorise, but it may be true that there is a great deal to remember. Bear in mind, however, that actors commonly learn scripts verbatim, whereas all you are being asked to do is familiarise yourself in your own words with legal concepts. Nonetheless the first step to learning bulky materials is to break the task down into smaller units. You are likely to find it easier to learn 10 one-page units rather than one 10-page unit, all the way through. This is especially true if the 10 units all have separate identity. It is a good idea, therefore, to split your file of notes into a number of smaller files according to the topics which you have covered in your course.

Depending on the nature of your course you may find yourself with some 10 to 15 such topics. If you have difficulty deciding how your course splits into topics, look at the syllabus, the lecture handouts and the tutorial sheets. For example, if you covered complaints against the police, this material might well be subsumed in your file on police powers. If, however, there were five or six separate lectures on the police complaints system and a tutorial on the topic, then it might well merit a file of its own. On the whole it is better to make the files wider than narrower. A file on freedom of expression may be more advisable than a series of separate files on, e.g., official secrecy, contempt of court etc.

Now for the cheating, although this may be controversial advice: suppose you are left with the 12 files covering a range of broad topics which represent your work on constitutional law for the year. You ought to know that the format of the examination demands, for example, that you answer four questions from a choice of nine. Clearly if you arrive in the examination able to answer all nine questions then you have wasted a great deal of effort. An ideal situation would be that in which you are able to answer five or possibly six questions from which you can choose your best four. If we assume two candidates of similar abilities both of whom have spent an equal amount of time on revision, one of whom has revised six particular topics on a paper and the other one, nine, we should expect the former to perform better if we ask for answers to only four questions and the latter to do much better if we ask for answers to all nine. If we know in advance that nine answers will not be sought then logically we should advise the former student's approach.

The problem is that there are risks involved, but these are not nearly so great as may be imagined. If you cover the whole of your course in 12 chosen topics and revise seven of them, this cuts down your revision by almost half. If you are desperately unlucky all five topics which you omitted may appear on the paper, but so will four other topics which you have revised thoroughly, and then only two problems can remain — either you find one of those questions particularly awkward or topics are mixed together and questions straddle the chosen topics and those not chosen. So, it is not possible to eliminate the risk entirely, but it is possible to minimise it considerably by sensible planning based on a calculated review of the options available.

Moreover, looking at these two problem situations, the first is that the question is particularly awkward. If you have revised that topic thoroughly, it is puzzling to see why this should be so, but remember that a difficult question will pose problems for everyone else sitting the paper. The next chapter will attempt, in any case, to offer advice on awkward questions. The second complication arises if a topic which you have revised mixes with one you know less well. Note the words 'know less well', since no one is suggesting that you abandon the other topics completely. Suppose that there is a problem question on freedom of expression concerned essentially with a newspaper (the *Moon*) found to be in contempt of court, and in the very last line the problem states that the judge has a large shareholding in a rival newspaper (the *Planet*). Your heart sinks, because you have not selected natural justice as one of your chosen topics. But, even in thinking that, you have recognised that the question relates to natural justice — some candidates will fail to do even that. If you have followed the revision strategy this far, you know the requirements of the rules of natural justice, whether they apply here (and of course they do), whether they have been breached (even if you cannot cite case law) and what the available remedies are.

This might not be as complete an answer as you (or the examiner) might wish, but it will suffice bearing in mind we are working upon the worst possible scenario of no alternative question available to you. As is shown in the next chapter, few students have the capability of covering every point in a problem question in detail. In the above example, the major issue to be covered is still contempt of court and the majority of marks will be awarded for consideration of this issue. Moreover, the mixture of contempt and natural justice is an unusual one and not easy to predict, but many issues have obvious links. Thus it would be foolish to cover public order but not police powers, or to cover parliamentary sovereignty and neglect the constitutional implications of UK membership of the European Union.

Finally, if you do opt to revise selectively, choice of subjects ought not to be haphazard. A perusal of past papers is generally informative. It will indicate generally either questions which invariably appear, or some form of pattern of alternating topics from year to year. It will illustrate the type of questions asked — examiners have highly individual styles — and the number of essay or problem questions. If, for example, there are always five problem questions, then that can be a limiting factor when the examiner writes the paper. It is not so easy to devise a problem on the rule of law. Find out which lecturer is setting the paper if possible. Does the person have pet subjects? This will be indicated by the number of lectures spent on topics, and the research interests or recent publications of the person involved.

It helps to keep a sense of perspective if you focus on the examination from the examiners' point of view. They are not indifferent to whether or not you pass. The success rate in examinations reflects inevitably on their ability as teachers, and for this reason, if no other, no examiner positively seeks to fail students. Nor will they devise examination questions designed to catch you out. On the contrary, they are likely to be diligent in ensuring that every single issue on the paper has been thoroughly covered in the teaching.

REVISING IS MORE THAN REMEMBERING

A good examination answer is based on knowledge. Knowledge of a subject comprises a good deal more than a set of facts which have been memorised. Imagine that on the day of the examination, your lecturer is forced to sit the paper rather than invigilate it. Assuming that he or she is relatively competent, the paper would presumably pose no great difficulty. Yet there would have been no revision for the examination. It is no answer that they are lecturers and somehow different. Knowledge is knowledge — so how did they acquire it? They read books, drafted the syllabus, broke it down into topics, prepared lectures, organised seminars, reviewed the course, and wrote an examination paper. Perhaps they did the same last year and the year before. At no point did they memorise the material.

The biggest mistake that most law students make is to spend too much time memorising material, and not enough time attempting to comprehend it. Some time ought to be spent during revision, therefore, analysing past questions and drafting possible answers. This is not merely good practice but it will illustrate the nature of constitutional law in a number of situations presented in previous examinations. Rather than just memorise your own notes, read, or reread some of the shorter textbooks to ensure that you are familiar with the structure and key issues of a particular topic. Try consciously to build links between different topics or even different subjects such as public order in constitutional law and the trespass or public nuisance material from your tort syllabus.

Even where memory work is essential, for example, with topics with a great deal of case law, this can be reduced by a clear understanding of the issues. Students are notorious for working from case to principle, rather than from principle to cases. Lawyers ought to be able to recognise or to state the legal proposition involved, and then to introduce case law as an authority for that proposition. Suppose someone sought your advice as to whether they could obtain an injunction to prevent the passage through Parliament of a Bill which adversely affected them. The way to approach this problem is to recognise that the issue is one of parliamentary sovereignty. The law is that no court can impeach or question parliamentary proceedings and an illustration of the courts applying this principle by refusing an injunction would be *Blackburn v Attorney-General* [1971] 1 WLR 1037 or *MacCormick v Lord Advocate* 1953 SC 396. Simply to search for a relevant case without fully analysing the issue would waste time.

Yet students learn parrot fashion whole lists of cases, the facts and the *ratio*, without even considering the principle which they illustrate. Each case is an individual tree and they fail to realise that there is a wood in the form of the principle which the cases establish. As a result they often learn too many cases. Take an example of the principle outlined above — that courts cannot challenge the validity of an Act of Parliament — there are many illustrations of this. Students faithfully commit to memory a range of cases such as *Edinburgh & Dalkeith Railway Co.* v *Wauchope* (1842) 8 Cl & F 710, *Lee v Bude & Torrington Junction Railway Co.* (1871) LR 6 CP 576 and *British Railways Board v Pickin* [1974] AC 765. These cases are not all the same as they differ in both facts and judgment, yet they all illustrate the one principle. Constitutional law students should ask whether at the level at which their notes are written, all three cases are necessary or whether *Pickin*, the more recent House of Lords authority, does not provide adequate authority for the principle. Why learn three cases when one will suffice?

REMEMBERING ... AND FORGETTING

What is said above suggests that there is more to revision than remembering, but not that remembering is unnecessary. Memory work is part of revision, and it is the part that causes students heartbreak. They commit their notes on a particular topic to memory and go to sleep happily. On returning to their notes at least half of the material has been forgotten. They then decide that their efforts are in vain, and that revision is a hopeless task. It is important to realise that the situation is the same for everyone. Fortunately for our sanity, the human brain does not automatically retain every image and experience. Remembering, like all other aspects of study, has to be persevered with. It is soul-destroying to find hard-learnt material quickly forgotten, but the bright side is that reinforcement will be much quicker than was the original effort.

Reinforcement is necessary for a number of other reasons. First, whilst we tend to remember facts recently revised, because not everything can be learnt at the last minute, recapping is vital. A second reason is that repetition is one of the most efficient forms of learning. We tend to know the words of countless songs in their entirety without having consciously memorised them, simply by a process of repetition. Finally, it becomes possible to gain new insights into the material as points which you overlooked in the past suddenly become obvious. Equally it is easy to add to your material by introducing new points on relearning as you become more familiar with the material.

Incidentally, detailed memory work may be aided by emphasis in repetition. This may involve, for example, reciting material out loud, perhaps whilst pacing about the room. Although guaranteed to drive your neighbours mad, this method ensures intense activity and aids concentration. Material continually recited tends to stick in the mind, whether it be nursery rhymes, prayers or police powers of arrest. A second method is to rewrite or reshape the notes continually. As they become more and more familiar, a line or an initial letter comes to suffice for a heading or a case and it becomes possible to slim down the notes to major headings and case law, in the knowledge that the gaps in between were fully covered and quite familiar.

However good you consider your memory to be, it is worth reiterating that understanding material is more important than remembering it. Make your primary task the clarification of uncertainty. Break the material down into small units. Set yourself a task of learning a unit in a particular time. Seek to reinforce material previously learnt. As you learn new material seek consciously to draw parallels between this information and earlier learning. Try to create a *structure* to your preparation of seminars, to your approach to course work, to your production and reproduction of notes, to your creation of (quality) study time, as well as to your revision timetable.

EXERCISE FOR THE EXAMINATION

Having made it this far, it is important not to rest on your laurels. There is room for improvement, remembering that the aim was to face the examinations knowing the questions and with answers prepared. By now, the student will have selected areas, and revised them thoroughly — but what about the answers? Practice at, and preparation for examination questions is all important. Gather together a range of questions on topics; tutorial sheets, essay titles and past examination papers are all useful sources. You will then be able to sit down and draft answers. There is no need to write the answers fully (although you can time yourself doing so, once or twice, if you wish). In general, it is sufficient to draw up a plan of what you would include if the question were set in an examination. Do this without notes, but check later to see that you managed to cover all of the points. One word of warning: do not be too disconcerted if there are questions with which you are unable to cope contained in past examination papers. The syllabus or the teaching may have changed considerably since that particular paper was set.

Beyond this, there are even greater refinements possible in preparing questions in advance of the examination. A planned introduction to each of the topics which you have learnt could prove useful. Even though the actual question on a particular topic could vary enormously, often a short, punchy introduction could form a common opening to a range of questions on a particular topic. Thus a question on delegated legislation will commonly fall into one of two broad forms, either a justification of delegated legislation ('"Delegated legislation is a necessary evil." Discuss.'), or a consideration of the controls over delegated power — procedural, parliamentary, judicial etc. It may even be a problem question. Whichever happens to be the case, a prepared, brief introduction may be appropriate — thus:

> Because the legislature in Britain is directly responsible to the electorate, ideally no less accountable body would be entrusted with law-making power. In practice, however, although only on the authority of the sovereign parliament, many subordinate bodies hold extensive legislative powers. The time is long past when the greater volume of legislation proceeded from Parliament rather than from the Executive. As the intrusion of the State into all activities continues, even under a Government disavowing such an approach, the trend towards delegated legislation rather than abating will continue to abound.

This gives you a springboard. If the question is on control, you can explain that control is, therefore, increasingly vital. If the question seeks justification, you are in an equally strong position to proceed.

Incidentally, what do you think of delegated legislation? Does it offend the notion of separation of powers within the constitutional framework? If you have not yet decided, you had better do so quickly. Make up your mind in advance on what your view is. Are rules regarding police interrogation of suspects too restrictive? Should Britain have a Bill of Rights? Should Members of Parliament be covered by absolute privilege during proceedings in the House? Should Government papers be openly available? These questions, and others like them, lie at the heart of many examination questions, but three hours is not long to begin, for the first time, to form your own evaluation of complex issues.

The advantages of a prepared view and a prepared introduction are twofold. They save time and they strike a harmonious note with the examiner. The opening words demand attention, and are followed up by a forthright delivery of an answer. You can take this pre-planning even further. Crucial definitions can be prepared, beginning with 'constitutional law'. These need not be your own, although they should be attributed. However, one curious feature of examinations is that it is not generally considered wrong to borrow arguments from learned writers, in situations in which you might be accused of plagiarism if you did so in course work.

Take as an example the Criminal Justice and Public Order Act 1994. This is a controversial piece of legislation, and while it is relatively recent it will prove a great favourite on examination papers. Yet lots of accounts of the Act, and views on it have appeared in the journals. You are free to use this material. You can assert with confidence these very same views if you are asked to express one. Pretend that they are yours if you like. Adopt them as your own. At the risk of showing his age, one of the authors, Bob Lee, studied company law shortly after entry to the EEC. His lecturer was publishing some material on the Common Market's impact on British company law. A few days before the examination a long article appeared in one of the leading papers (perhaps the *Financial Times*) detailing the future prospects for company law in its European setting. Lee's answer to the question, when inevitably it came, owed more to the erudition of some hard-working journalist than it did to the examinee. On any analysis, except that curiously adopted for examinations, this was cheating. (In defence, there was some skill attached, but probably only in foreseeing the question).

MOTIVATION

One final point needs a little discussion. If law examinations are so difficult, what drives students to do them? The motivating forces are many and varied. The stronger the motive, the harder the work. We would not run as quickly to the bus stop as to the air-raid shelter. The importance of the object to be attained governs the effort, if only unwittingly. It is no bad thing to explore your own motives; they may be quite attractive, such as interest in the subject, or less so, such as greed or ambition. Whatever they are, it is possible to harness this driving force to achieve the desired results. Continually set yourself targets, and if you reach them, then move them a little further away. Generally, study throughout the year is possible at a steady pace providing you develop a consistent work habit. The difficult days are during final revision when the sun shines outside, and studying the British constitution seems bottom of a list of a thousand plans you have for the summer weather. At that point you can only tell yourself that this is the one month from a whole summer in which you will not engage in all of the other nine hundred and ninety-nine. The advice stops there, as you grit your teeth and chain yourself to the desk. The rest is up to you.

CONCLUSION

By now you may have decided that cheating — even *in* the examinations — is distinctly preferable. Hopefully, however, you may have reached the conclusion that study and examination revision are little more than common sense. And so they are, but students can become so wrapped up in the process of taking examinations that they miss the obvious. They learn facts, but fail to understand them. They memorise topics, but never clarify to their own satisfaction a personal view of burning issues. They walk into examination rooms never having given a second thought to the content of the paper. Some arrive there in many cases more confused and less well prepared, both physically and mentally, than when they began their revision. Others already regret the wasted opportunity that their study of constitutional law represents, and in the certainty that they will fail as a result of lack of work or ill-organised study.

There is only one acceptable reason for failure, and that is a lack of intellectual capacity. Yet this is much rarer than one might imagine. In your own case, you have had the talent to reach your present stage. It may be possible that you have reached your ceiling, but to accept this is to accept that ceilings can never be heightened. If this were true, then at the end of the day you would have to accept the verdict of the examination. You could do this with an easy conscience provided you can eliminate shoddy work habits or lack of organisation from the reasons for your failure. Sadly, however, when students fail, these are the very reasons why.

3 COPING WITH EXAMINATIONS

BEFORE THE EXAMINATION

There is an obvious tendency to step up your effort as the evil day draws nigh. If you are desperately anxious, and convinced you have masses of material still to cover, then you are unlikely to be dissuaded from doing so. It is important to keep a sense of proportion. There is little point in having a detailed knowledge of your subject but under-performing in the examination because you are too fatigued to reflect your true abilities. It may help if you approach the examination as you would an important game of sport, or perhaps a marathon run. Of course you will wish to keep yourself fit, but you are aware not to overdo the exercise in order to build up reserves of energy for the big event. It seems hackneyed, but sleep, diet and exercise are important considerations. If you vary your sleeping habits, and especially if you take less sleep, and if you confine yourself to your room for days on end, and live on chocolate bars (especially if you normally eat heartily and do lots of walking) then you can only expect to feel less than 100 per cent by the time of the examination. Like any other event which puts you under strain, examinations need reserves of energy to help you cope.

It seems obvious that this is particularly true of the night before (or the morning of) the examination. It is impossible to say that working all through the night is counter-productive — some people claim it worked for them — but departures from your routine are difficult to advise. Moreover, at this stage you have to make an assessment between the competing values of a few extra facts and an uncluttered and alert mind. In our experience students weigh the former far too heavily in comparison with the latter. This is all the more true because of the danger of work revised immediately before the examination dominating your thinking, and making it difficult to recall other material. If you are ill, or suffer some personal upset in the immediate run-up to the examination, do inform your department, and obtain a medical note if you can. Once convinced of illness, all departments will react with sympathy, but they cannot make allowances if they are not informed of problems.

The best type of last-minute revision is to go for a gentle overview. If you work too hard at trying to recall facts and find that you are unable to do so, this will drive you to distraction. You must have confidence that in the context of specific questions, and under the pressure of the examination, the necessary information will be quickly and easily recalled. Students never allow for this, which is perhaps not surprising, but in the heat of the moment crucial facts, and even parts of the course long forgotten, are forced to the fore. One consequence of this is that you need not feel over-worried about examination nerves. To some extent all students suffer in this way, but being keyed up for an examination does have some advantages if you remain in control and harness the nervous energy to produce a concentrated period of high-level work.

EXAMINATION QUALITIES

A problem which seems to face some students is that they are unsure what is expected of them in the examination. In fact the qualities which any law examiner will seek in an examination script are relatively obvious ones, but it does no harm to dwell on them in advance of the examination and seek to introduce them into your work. It is likely that every law examiner would welcome a paper exhibiting the following 10 features:

(1)   A clear understanding of legal principle.

(2)   The ability to apply that principle to a factual situation if necessary.

(3)   The capacity to develop an argument logically and concisely.

(4)   The use of authority, in the form of case law, statute and learned writings, to support the argument.

(5)   The aptitude to recognise conflicting cases or dicta, and to suggest a resolution of that conflict.

(6)   The careful expression of ideas using legal concepts accurately and correctly.

(7)   The ability to think clearly and in particular to confine oneself to relevant issues.

(8)   A determination to answer directly the question set.

(9)   The proficiency to develop critical judgment and to present personal opinion in an informed and measured manner.

(10)   A consistency over the paper so that answers are of a uniformly high standard.

It is always helpful to bear in mind that your paper is likely to be one of many that the particular examiner will mark. Moreover, because examiners have to meet tight deadlines on marking, they are often forced to cram the operation into a series of long and tedious sessions. Is your paper going to be different from the rest? Examiners are only human, and if a paper contains carefully developed, relevant, and legible answers which prove interesting to read, then the pleasure (speaking in relative terms) of reading such a script will be reflected in the mark. On the other hand even carefully formulated arguments can be ruined by illegible handwriting. Few examiners would refuse to mark a script simply because it was difficult to read, but the problem is that by the time bad handwriting has been deciphered, the thread of the argument is lost. Finally remember that an examination is not a quiz. It is insufficient to spot all the relevant points in an answer if they are then presented in a totally confused and haphazard manner. Examiners mark answers to the question set, usually by evaluating the essay as a whole. This means that two students using the same body of information could gain widely differing marks, and that the onus is on you to present your information in its best light — a point which is developed below.

IN THE EXAMINATION ROOM

You should ensure well in advance that you have all that you need for the examination, including writing equipment and spares. If you are allowed to take statutes into the examination, as is increasingly common, check that you have these available and that they are unmarked and unannotated. It is a good idea to take a watch into the examination, although you will generally be seated in sight of a clock. Ascertain that the time on your watch synchronises with the invigilator's timepiece. Once in the examination room, it is no bad thing to ensure that you have all that you need, including sufficient paper. Before you open the question paper read carefully the instructions to candidates. Even if you have been informed of the structure of the paper, note carefully the time which is allowed, and the number of questions that you must answer in that time. Work out how much time this will give you for each question. In particular you ought to verify whether there are compulsory questions or compulsory sections. Finally, there may be rules as to presentation, for example, separate answer books for separate questions, and it is important to ensure that you comply with these.

Once you are allowed to do so, read through the paper. By all means skip quickly through the questions to reassure yourself. However, you must then read through the whole of the paper carefully. In an increasing number of law papers you are allowed some reading time — often 10 minutes — because of the length of problem questions. Unless you are told otherwise, you can use this time to outline the answer to your question by marking the major points on the question paper. The importance of reading through the whole of the paper cannot be stressed too strongly; no matter how sure you are on a quick reading that you know which questions you will answer, read the other questions thoroughly. A wrong choice of questions could prove disastrous. There are, however, a number of points which you might care to consider in making a choice.

CHOOSING QUESTIONS

To begin with, you must answer the number of questions demanded. It would be foolish to answer more, and it would be even more foolish to answer less. If you are asked to answer four questions, then answering only three may lose you 25 per cent of the marks outright. The consequence of this is that (for instance) three answers of a lower-second-class standard may be insufficient to gain you a pass mark. Knowing, therefore, that you must finish the paper, decide upon the questions which you will answer and the order in which you will attempt them. Always choose the questions which you feel that you are able to provide the best answer to. Do not therefore look for other criteria, such as those questions which appear the most difficult, simple, short or long.

Once you have decided which questions you will answer, decide upon the order in which you will answer them, and answer the questions which you favour first. The reasons for this are twofold. First, if the examination lasts for three hours, you may well tire during this period, so that the pattern of students gaining higher marks on earlier questions is common. Secondly, if you run out of time, at least you have the satisfaction of knowing that you have left your weakest question unfinished (or finished in a rush). It is dubious to argue that the best answer should be left until the end in order to finish strongly. Certain examiners choose to mark all of the answers to the first question, and then all of the answers to question two, etc., so that there is no guarantee that any particular order of questions will pay dividends in this way.

Do not be too disconcerted if you cannot answer every point in a problem question. Even good students rarely detect all of the relevant issues in a problem. Moreover the limited amount of time means that you may struggle to handle all points fully even if you are aware of them. Once you can cope with a majority of the topics included in the question, it becomes worth while considering an answer to it. The pity is that some students who are worried that they are not equal to a problem in a particular area turn to essay questions where their lack of knowledge is even more sadly exposed. For uncertain students, problems do have advantages since they direct the students towards specific issues, and they impose a structure on the answer. The essay question allows an opportunity to display a breadth of knowledge and to exercise critical faculties, but unless your knowledge is broad and your faculties critical, it may be safer to avoid the risk of producing poorly designed and ill-informed 'waffle'.

Finally, on the issue of choice, bear in mind that it is impossible to make a choice until you have done some work on the questions available to you. You may be able to discount certain questions immediately if you know little about a particular topic. Of the remainder, however, you can only exclude questions if you have worked your way through them. This is because questions which seem easy, and therefore attractive, can contain pitfalls on closer analysis. It is much safer to discover these at an early stage when an alternative choice may be open to you, rather than half-way through your answer. In many ways the first few minutes in the examination room are the most important. If you can keep calm and read quickly but carefully through the paper, and make wise and informed judgments, then you are well on the way to success. This can be difficult if you find to your horror that the paper seems much more troublesome than you imagined. By way of consolation you might remember that if you have worked consistently on your syllabus, then your fellow examinees will find the paper just as challenging. All that you can do is begin on your best question. By the time that you are half an hour into the examination, with your first answer proceeding satisfactorily, the picture will not seem nearly so gloomy.

PLANNING YOUR ANSWER

It is a good idea to outline your answer, perhaps in pencil to make it clear that it is not part of your answer. Your plan should be limited to save time and you will need to use abbreviations. Ensure that these are sufficient to enable you to recall the point. There is nothing more infuriating than to write into your plan '*A* v *A*', and then find that you are unable to bring to mind the case when you actually write the answer. If the case is *Agricultural Horticultural & Forestry Industry Training Board* v *Aylesbury Mushrooms Ltd* [1972] 1 WLR 190, another abbreviation may be more effective — 'Mush', for example. Prepare a plan for your whole answer, no matter how impatient you are to begin. The purpose of the plan is to enable you to structure your answer and not to check that you know the answer. If you leave points out of your plan you might omit them from your answer too. There is absolutely no point in undertaking a plan unless you intend to follow it, and although that sounds curious, it seems relatively common for answers to bear little relation to the original plan. However, examiners award marks for your answer alone. On the other hand, there is little point in following a plan if it is a poor one. It is insufficient to jot down points as they occur to you and decide that these jottings form a plan to follow. There is a middle stage of organising the points into a coherent pattern, and that is the purpose of the plan.

More specific advice is offered later in terms of both essay and problem questions, but the plan should enable you to link the issues together. Thus if you are dealing with a remedy open to one party, it will generally be wise to deal at the same time with other parties seeking the same remedy. Apart from improving the readability of your answer, this can save considerable amounts of time. At this stage you can take the opportunity of breaking your answer down into paragraphs. One common fault with examination answers is that students reject the rules of good writing that they have developed in their course work, and forget to paragraph their answers. This makes the examining of the paper much more difficult and new points fail to make an impact when introduced. New paragraphs introducing fresh topics give the impression of a well-prepared and logical student. Strong introductions have all of the obvious advantages mentioned in the previous chapter. A conclusion is helpful, but you should not allow this to make incursion into your time if you are running behind the clock. If the question is an involved problem, then a summary of the major legal remedies is advantageous. In an essay question, some direct reference to the question, indicating your own conclusion, is well-advised. You should consider your conclusion at the time of working on your essay plan.

ANSWERING ESSAY QUESTIONS

No matter how straightforward a question appears, take time and care to analyse the question. In general, essay questions will take one of two forms; either a direct question or instruction ('Critically assess the mechanisms designed to prevent the abuse of delegated legislative power') or a quotation followed by a question or an instruction ("The courts provide the only effective form of control over the abuse of delegated legislative power.' Discuss'.). The former type of question is generally wider ranging and may be easier to answer. It is important, however, to consider the specific instruction. In the question above, you are asked to assess the available controls. It is insufficient, therefore, simply to outline the controls since you are asked to make an assessment of the mechanisms in terms of the job which they are designed to do — namely preventing abuse of power — and you are invited to be critical. This does not simply mean that you are required to find fault, rather you are invited to play the role of critic, and form a value judgment on a particular issue.

One of the reasons why the question based on a quotation may prove more challenging is that it may leave a certain amount unsaid. Take the example of the question in the paragraph above. Although it refers to the role of the courts, since there are also non-judicial controls over delegated power, an answer which failed to deal with parliamentary control (for example) would not be complete. You have to consider carefully the question before answering that the courts are not the only means of control, and after outlining the others stating that judicial control in your view is the most effective check on abuse

— or whatever else it is that you wish to argue. Some examiners may acknowledge the source of the quotation on the examination paper, if the quotation is taken from a book or a judgment. In such cases you may gain an insight into the quotation by your knowledge of its author. To take an example, suppose the question was: "Someone has to be trusted. Let it be the judges." (Denning.) Consider the implications of this view for British constitutional law.' At first sight this seems highly confusing. However, it may be that you know that the former Master of the Rolls, Lord Denning, in his Dimbleby Lectures, was a proponent of a Bill of Rights. Indeed this question enquires whether judges ought to be the final arbiters of the constitutionality of executive action — as they would be under a Bill of Rights. This is somewhat easier because you may have revised the pros and cons of a Bill of Rights thoroughly. You may also know that other senior judges (such as Lords Hailsham of St Marylebone and Scarman) have made similar proposals. You can now begin to plan your answer, which may begin: 'In recent years there has been an increasing pressure, on the part of a certain element from within the judiciary, for a Bill of Rights'.

Another advantage of a quotation being accredited is that it may give you an indication of the authority of the view put forward. Thus if the quotation is from a standard constitutional law textbook, the chances are that it reflects mainstream thinking on a particular topic. On the other hand, beware of those quotations on the paper which are not attributed to a source where it is customary to cite the author. In such circumstances, the view expressed is probably that of the examiner, and it may have been concocted especially for the paper — perhaps because the examiner could not find so unconventional a view expressed elsewhere. Let us take examples of each type of question:

1   The whole ethos of our legislation on official secrets has been described by Munro as 'absurdly wide, over-severe, unacceptably obscure and inconsistently applied'. Discuss.

2   'The retention of primary legislation protecting official secrets continues to justly restrict only those activities clearly detrimental to the interests of the state.' Discuss.

In the first question, the statement is attributed, and you may be sure that Munro will not have written it without giving the matter some thought and probably offering evidence to support this view. This leaves you free to depart from the statement, nonetheless, and to argue along the line of argument contained in question 2. On the other hand you may decide that discretion is the better part of valour and that, since Munro, as a law profesor, will know more about the subject than you do, your answer will broadly follow his lead. Imagine, however, that you have not seen the first question.

In the second, the source is not acknowledged. You may know enough about official secrecy to know that the reform contained in the 1989 Act has been subject to strong criticism, and you may be puzzled by the statement because it does not coincide with what you have read in books (such as those by Munro!). It seems likely that this is a view expressed provocatively by the examiner and amounts to little more than a thinly disguised invitation to depart from the quotation by pointing out the shortcomings of the approach to official secrets legislation in the UK.

One difficulty which causes grave concern to all examinees — whatever the subject — is the fear that they will be unable to understand the question. Examiners are assiduous in avoiding ambiguity since their aim is not to confuse but to direct attention to the issues demanding discussion. However, unwittingly they may choose a quotation containing a word which is clear enough to them, but unknown to the student. More probably the student may miss some of the issues implied by a question. Let us take question 1 above. Taken alone, what the quotation says is quite simple, if we break it down bit by bit.

Most of the words are readily apparent in themselves. However it is possible that, wide though your vocabulary is, the word 'ethos' is entirely new to you. Of course you will go home and look it up, never to forget again after today, but that is little use in the present examination, and you begin to panic. One possible way ahead is to ask yourself if you can make a guided guess at the word by considering words which may be similar to the one proving problematic. In this case 'ethics', that is the study of the principles of human duty, or sometimes simply moral principles, would bring you close. 'Ethic' in the singular derives from a Greek word for 'character' and 'habit' or 'custom' — as in the phrase 'work ethic'. 'Ethnic' too bears a similar meaning and as an adjective refers to 'characteristic of a race'. This might lead you to conclude that 'ethos', in the context in which it is used above, means either 'moral tone' or 'custom' or 'character'. Of the three the latter is to be preferred, since 'ethos' means 'disposition' or 'spirit' or 'nature'. However, whichever you decide upon, you would not go far wrong. There may, however, be a simpler solution, provided by asking yourself how significant the word 'ethos' is. Suppose the question began with 'The whole of our legislation ...'. It would read just as well. Worrying too much may be unnecessary.

On the other hand it is important to consider each and every word of the quotation. The adjectives which Munro uses give you splendid leads on what to say by way of criticism. Why is the legislation 'absurd'? As Munro explains this is because of its width. Perhaps you could offer examples of minor and frivolous government information which might be considered officially secret. By working through the quotation in this way considering the severity of the legislation, its ambiguity (obscurity) and inconsistent application, you will find your essay plan is virtually written for you. You might also point out that the longstanding criticisms of the catch-all nature of the Official Secrets Act 1911 have only partly been assuaged by the 1989 Act: for example, there is no defence on the basis of disclosure in the public interest.

Questions will not always refer directly to the Official Secrets Acts. Often they will raise wider questions of open government. You can answer such a question by explaining some of the obvious shortcomings of the legislation, but should do so in the terms required by the question — that is, with examples of the lack of openness in government. Official secrecy has been a highly topical and controversial issue in recent years, so it is not surprising to find questions of this type on examination papers. You should look back over events and cases and you might, for example, mention *Secretary of State for Defence* v *Guardian Newspapers Ltd* [1985] AC 339. That case did not concern the official secrets legislation directly, but was concerned with a claim by the newspaper that the document leaked ought not to be handed over to the Secretary of State, since it might reveal the source of the leak (whose identity was then unknown). The *Guardian* argued that they had a right to protect their source, both under s. 10 of the Contempt of Court Act 1981 and at common law. The majority (3–2) held that the document should be delivered up, apparently on the basis that identification of the source might be necessary in the interests of protecting national security in the future.

Later strong disquiet was expressed both inside and outside Parliament at what was seen as the hounding down of the civil servant, but of course the documents had established her identity and she was duly imprisoned under the then s. 2 of the Official Secrets Act 1911 (cf. the Old Bailey trial of Clive Ponting in 1985).

In 1987 two newspapers attempted to publish details of the book, *Spycatcher*, written by Peter Wright, a former member of the Secret Service. An interlocutory injunction obtained by the Attorney-General restrained them. However, other newspapers not so restrained then published further material. The Court of Appeal held this to be an interference with the administration of justice and a contempt of court. In a separate appeal by the papers originally restrained, it was decided by the House of Lords that the injunctive relief would continue to trial notwithstanding the free access to the information outside the UK (see respectively *Attorney-General* v *Newspaper Publishing plc* [1988] Ch 333; *Attorney-General* v *Guardian Newspapers Ltd* [1987] 1 WLR 1248).

As is stated above, this material relates to contempt of court rather than official secrets legislation. However, much depends on how we categorise topics. Munro's question (above) refers to material beyond the Official Secrets Acts when he mentions their inconsistent application. In cases such as *Spycatcher* [1988] 3 All ER 545, and *Attorney-General* v *Jonathan Cape* [1976]

QB 752, the law of confidence was employed in seeking to restrain the publication of information rather than the Official Secrets Act. Yet although not Official Secrets Act cases as such, these are vital to an answer which properly addresses the statement by Munro. The ability to sort out the relevant from the irrelevant is an enormously important quality. It is useful to introduce a quick point of comparison with another area of law, but only if there is some direct relevance to your answer. In general, once a point has been made, dwelling on it is unlikely to gain extra marks and may even be disadvantageous. This is because amongst the necessary qualities for a good lawyer are precision and a conciseness of expression. In part these are being tested by the examination. A major cause of inadequate performance in examinations is the failure to answer the question. Thus, faced with a question concerning the importance of constitutional conventions as a source of constitutional law, it is not uncommon to find: (a) an answer detailing the student's knowledge of conventions, or (b) an answer detailing the student's knowledge of sources of law generally, or (c) an answer covering both topics but giving no assessment of the importance of the former to the latter.

In fact we shall review this type of question later, but from the very beginning it is necessary to establish the relationship between the two. To take another example, one common type of question directs you to compare A with B — for example: 'Compare and contrast the royal prerogative and parliamentary privilege'. This is straightforward and should present little difficulty. Unfortunately, however, many students will write about the two topics in turn, and any comparison that is made will take the form of a concluding paragraph. Only a slight improvement is the essay which alternates paragraphs on each, sometimes with no conclusion. Although this type of question appears easy in the sense that it is essentially descriptive, it may take some organisation and planning. However, the examiner will be delighted by the answer, which makes a clear attempt to amalgamate both issues from the outset. For example:

The most obvious similarity between the prerogative powers and the parliamentary privileges is that both form a recognised part of our constitutional law. This is so in spite of the fact that the courts have shown a traditional reluctance to challenge the exercise of prerogative powers or to question proceedings in the Houses of Parliament attracting privilege. However, the courts have shown that they are prepared to determine the ambit of each concept. This was made clear as long ago as 1610 in the *Case of Proclamations*, concerning royal prerogative. As to parliamentary privilege, the constitutional crisis surrounding the case of *Stockdale v Hansard* is instructive. This followed a claim by Stockdale that he had been defamed in a Hansard publication....

Later you may wish to qualify what you have said about the 'traditional reluctance' for, as we shall see in chapter 7, the judges have grown more assertive in relation to the review of the prerogative. But this can be brought out later, upon drawing contrasts. For now, you have said enough to locate accurately the similar constitutional status of the two concepts.

Another point which arises out of this is the use of case law. First of all you will notice that there are no references to reports of the *Case of Proclamations* ((1610) 12 Co Rep 74, or to *Stockdale* v *Hansard* ((1839) 9 A & E 1). You should certainly not try to remember case references, and it is not generally necessary to remember dates of cases. However, you will notice above that the date 1610 is given. It is sometimes useful to know of a date because it illustrates the long-standing nature of the rule (as above) or because a recent case has overturned earlier authority, or because the date is linked to some other event. Thus the case of *Stockdale* v *Hansard* in 1839 led to the passage of the Parliamentary Papers Act 1840. In general it is helpful to give dates of statutes because, for example, you may have to draw a distinction between the 1911 and 1989 Official Secrets Acts. The date of a statute will allow you a convenient abbreviation since once it is mentioned you can refer thereafter to the 1911 Act.

Once a full case name has been cited, then it is sensible to adopt an abbreviation as it re-occurs. This ought preferably to be the name of the first party, e.g., '*Stockdale*', which reads better than e.g., '*S* v *H*'. As to other abbreviations, it may be permissible to shorten the Parliamentary Commissioner for Administration to PCA by making it clear after the first full mention that you shall do so. Even here, however, the word 'ombudsman' can form a convenient shorthand and will be easier to read. On occasions it seems that students must spend as long devising their own shorthand as it would take to write the material out in full. Generally shorthand is not advised, as it can be infuriating to try to follow:

The main features of admin. law are jud. rev. of admin. actn and jud. con. of deleg. leg. thro' the doc. of u.v. As regards nat. j., since the case of *R* v *B*, the crts have . . .

In short, examination essays must be readable. They ought to be carefully structured in order to cover all of the points in a logical order and without repetition. Above all they must be relevant and answer the question set. Where possible they must follow any invitation to provide a critical and informed analysis of the topic. This can only be done by reference to case law, statutes and legal writings. An authoritative answer is all-important, and this will not be achieved by a series of half-baked and unrelated ideas thrown together without any support from substantive law.

ANSWERING PROBLEM QUESTIONS

Too many students treat problem questions as though they are a quiz. That is to say they believe that if they spot the correct answer, they will obtain full marks no matter how badly or even inaccurately expressed their answer is. This is certainly not the case. Let us suppose there is a problem in which a police officer stops a pedestrian (Arnold) who is walking home late at night in an area frequented by homosexuals. He searches Arnold on the street, forcing him to remove his footwear and he finds a pornographic magazine pushed down his socks. The officer confiscates the magazine, since Arnold admits he intended to sell it in a local club. Although not inaccurate, it would be totally inadequate to write:

> The police officer should not have done this. Arnold has the right to walk the street and the police are in the wrong here. They should not persecute gays.

Yet this is the type of answer given all too frequently. In fact the examiner is seeking something of this type:

> A general stop and search power, short of arrest, is available to the police officer under s. 1 of the Police and Criminal Evidence Act 1984. Other powers under s. 60 of the Criminal Justice and Public Order Act are not available as the police officer can have no anticipation of serious violence on the facts given. Moreover the s. 1 power is limited to a search for stolen or prohibited articles (as defined in s. 1(2)) so that the police officer ought to have had reasonable grounds for suspecting that these would be found. In addition, s. 2 of the Act makes no provision for removing footwear in public. It follows that the officer is acting outside the execution of his duty, and Arnold may have been within the law to have resisted the search — see *Collins* v *Wilcock* [1984] 1 WLR 1172.

The difference between the two answers is striking and we can only conclude that in the first example the student had no real conception of what was required in the answer. This ought not to be a problem, since questions are normally quite specific in their demands and generally end by saying, e.g., 'Advise Arnold'. The only way to answer the question is by offering Arnold the relevant advice. Imagine that you are a solicitor and that Arnold walks into your office, having undergone the indignity of the search. If you simply turn to him and say, 'Oh dear! They ought not to have done that' or 'That was very wrong of them', is your client going to leave quite satisfied? On the contrary, he is likely to become pretty angry and ask what you are going to do about it.

Equally, suppose you then advised Arnold that he has various common law remedies against the police, and also that he may make a complaint against the police, but you neglect to deal with the legality of the charges which might be brought against him, or the admissibility of the magazine as evidence of those charges. Arnold may leave your office quite pleased, assuming right is on his side. When, however, his next appointment is due, Arnold fails to appear, and further enquiries reveal that he was sentenced under the Obscene Publications Act to a short term of imprisonment by the Crown Court the week before, it is fair to assume that when you visit Arnold in the cells to advise him on his claim against the police, he will feel a little peeved. What was the use, he might argue, of advising that he could sue for trespass to person and goods implicit in an unlawful search and seizure, but not advising as to the admissibility of the goods seized as evidence. Yet this is not an uncommon fault in examination answers. If you are asked to advise Arnold, you must do so fully. Ask, quite simply, what does he want? It will vary from question o question. In our example it may be (a) advice on the likelihood of being convicted of the offences for which he is charged on the evidence available, and (b) the possibility of any remedies against the police. In other cases the parties may wish for other remedies — a fair hearing perhaps, damages in defamation against an MP, or compensation for property seized by the Government.

This method of asking yourself what would be the most appropriate and practical redress open to the party, and then searching for an available legal remedy, is the easiest way of ensuring your answer remains relevant. Do not spend too much time on unlikely or highly inventive actions. As with legal practice, it is the obvious solutions that are likely to prove the most effective. Relevance is no less vital in answering problem questions than in writing essays. It will be easier to achieve, however, if you stick strictly to the facts of the problem set. As is shown in later chapters (see, for example, chapter 10), most problem questions insert specific words to indicate particular legal issues, and additional detail is kept to a minimum. By far the best guide, therefore, is to direct your attention to the facts of the problem as set out. It may be possible to illustrate your knowledge quickly by varying the issue slightly but you must also deal with the question set. To take an example, let us suppose that, in a question on parliamentary privilege, an MP has written a letter to a newspaper containing defamatory remarks. It would be quite legitimate to answer:

> If the letter had been addressed to the Minister responsible for such matters, it seems likely that it would attract qualified privilege on the rather inconclusive evidence of the *Strauss* affair. Here, however, the letter is to a newspaper ...

On occasions it will be necessary to advise more than one party, or the parties may have competing claims and you are instructed to 'discuss' the problem. In such cases, deal with all parties. Even if you cover many of the issues relating to other parties in your discussion of the remedies open to X, try to recap the law as it applies to Y and then Z in turn. Similarly, if one issue is dependent on another, discuss both issues. In the above example suppose you conclude that the MP is not covered by qualified privilege in the letter to the newspaper. However, if the question goes on to say that the person defamed complains that the MP has acted maliciously as his remarks in an earlier parliamentary debate prove, you should deal with this point also. Technically if you are right and the letter is not protected even by qualified privilege, then the issue of malice is irrelevant. Nonetheless you should write:

> Although the issue of malice is redundant in the absence of qualified privilege, the case of *Church of Scientology of California* v *Johnson-Smith* makes it clear that matters arising in parliamentary proceedings cannot be relied upon to support legal action.

In this way you provide evidence of wider knowledge, and if you are wrong on the privilege issue (which seems unlikely), you are able to redeem yourself to a large extent. You will rarely be penalised for reaching a conclusion with which your examiner happens to disagree, if your argument is logical and supported by authority. Remember that few problems are likely to be directly in line with previous case law. Often they cover 'grey' areas of law, where black or white (right or wrong) answers may not be available. Bearing this in mind you should cover both sides of an argument if possible, but be brave enough to reach your own conclusion. In general, however, it is unwise to begin with your conclusion, although many students make this mistake. Thus if you begin by writing, 'in this case X can sue the MP for defamation of character' the danger is that you will change your mind during the course of the next half-hour in which you consider the question.

The most important point of all in answering problem questions is to cite authority for your propositions. Time and time again examiners see answers which do not refer to even a single case or statute as authority for the proposition stated. Some students happily write that 'the MP is not covered by privilege' as though the fact that they have said it is sufficient in itself. Your answer is only as good as the authority which it cites. Answers which fail to refer to the authorities are poor answers and are destined to failure. It seems incredible that students struggle to remember case names during revision and then neglect to refer to this precious information in the examination. You should imagine that you are going to debate with an examiner who will not readily be persuaded. Bombard him or her with case law in the way that you might say in an argument 'But look what Browne J said in *Johnson-Smith!'*

Even if you have forgotten case names, you must use the authority by referring to the facts which you can remember. *'Duncan* v *Jones'* is just as recognisable as 'the case of the lady standing on a soap-box making a speech outside a training centre for the unemployed'.

Statutes may prove less troublesome to cite as authority since many institutions allow these to be taken into the examination room. If so, however, the statutes should be a point of reference only. You can only make use of statutory material in answering problems if you are fully familiar with the legislation in advance of the examination and know where to look and what to look for. If you are not allowed the facility of statutes in the examination room, it is unnecessary to memorise statutes or even sections, but you will need a close working knowledge of them in order to answer problems. You will not be permitted to annotate your statute book, but you will probably be allowed to use markers pointing to the relevant statutes. You can also be assisted by thinking what you may wish to use for a particular question — e.g., sections 2 and 3 of the European Communities Act 1972 might prove useful for a question on parliamentary sovereignty. If you are allowed to take a statute book into the examinations, buy it at the beginning of the year. Take it to lectures and tutorials, and mark or highlight the relevant sections of statutes as you use them. Modesty forbids mention of the best available collection (but see Wallington and Lee, *Blackstone's Statutes on Public Law*).

Reference to statutory or case authority should be concise and give only as much detail as is necessary to support your argument. One approach adopted by some students is to present a detailed account of the facts of a particular case, followed by a consideration of the judgments spread over a couple of paragraphs. Whether or not the content is good, this approach allows for discussion of perhaps three cases at most, and often the point of the question is lost in the detailed review of the case. It is by no means always necessary to recount the facts of cases. Sometimes it is helpful to do so because the facts bear a close relationship to the issue in a problem question. At other times, however, the only point of a case is that it proves the accuracy or veracity of what you have just written. In such cases the name of the case may be sufficient. Knowing how much detail to present to the examiner is a sign of your ability to deal selectively with a large body of legal material — an immensely important quality in practice. Let us take an example, again from parliamentary privilege, of how case law can be quickly and concisely introduced to support arguments. Suppose that a member of the public has written a letter to an MP containing information contravening the Official Secrets Act, you might write:

It is clear that a letter from a member of the public to an MP enjoys qualified privilege in the law of defamation, at least if (as in *R* v *Rule*) it is on a matter of public concern. The status of such a letter for the purposes of the Official

Secrets Act is more problematic. Although in 1938 Duncan Sandys was said by the Select Committee to be immune from prosecution for a breach of the Act, this was in connection with a parliamentary question and not the receipt of a letter.

One advantage of keeping discussion of cases brief is that it saves time. Shortage of time is a worry for many students, and if it cannot be avoided it may be necessary to revert to note form, for example:

Letter to MP — qual. priv. in defamation but question protection under OSA. Cf. *Sandys* — immunity for parl. question & later refusal to disclose sources.

However, there is no other reason to adopt note form. The qualities necessary for examination success, especially that of critical analysis, are difficult to exhibit in note form. Intricate points may become impossible to convey accurately. It may even be unwise to adopt side-headings or sections (e.g., (a), (b), (c) etc.) in your answer. They may leave the impression of a lazy student who cannot be bothered to introduce new topics in a refreshing way, and they may actually draw attention to points which you have overlooked. However, if time is short, notes are preferable to simply failing to complete an answer. An examiner can only award marks upon proof of a particular level of knowledge. Tailing off your answer abruptly and pretending that you ran out of time — a strategy invoked by desperate candidates — is therefore unlikely to bring either success or sympathy.

CONCLUSION

Whether your examination question is of the problem or essay type you are going to need to formulate an argument. The better structured and more logical this is, the higher the marks awarded. It will be easier for the examiner to follow if it is concise and unambiguous. If you can show that you have rejected irrelevant considerations and stuck to an accurate analysis of legal principle, this will doubtless impress the examiner. If you can go further and exercise a critical analysis of the particular area, citing authority to support your argument, and if you can do so in a measured and considered manner, you should obtain a high mark.

Pay attention to your written style. Aim for strong introductory and concluding remarks which make an impact or leave an impression on the examiner. It is unwise, however, to spend too long on this, and as was stated in chapter 2, preparation may assist you with this. Avoid slang and make a careful attempt to weed out legal inexactitudes in your writing — e.g., using 'prosecute' when you mean 'sue'. It is also a good idea to avoid wit or sarcasm. What seems enormously funny to you may not be so humorous to an ill-tempered examiner on the fortieth script at 2 a.m. Remarks such as 'I advise X to see a solicitor' are rarely original. It helps to remember that examiners are only human, and that marking is a dreadful chore. The only way in which to use this to your advantage is to produce the type of script that makes the examiner sit up and read attentively for the next 15 minutes. Half-baked ramblings or dull repetition of facts or legal rules are unlikely to do the trick, but legible, concise and carefully developed answers throughout the whole script might just make an impression on even the most hardened and cynical marker.

You may now be in a position to commence a thesis on assessment generally and examinations in particular; pitfalls and opportunities. But so much is theory, without what follows. Our selection of themes remains, we hope, a fairly representative illustration of topics often found on Constitutional and Administrative law courses. Where you are having to tackle other topics, give yourself a treat by applying the same manner of approaches introduced so far, and developed in the following ten chapters.

We start also by giving you some indication of general reading which you may find useful.

FURTHER READING

Allen, M. J., Thompson, B., and Walsh, B., (1994) *Cases and Materials on Constitutional and Administrative Law*, 3rd ed. (London: Blackstone Press).

Brazier, R., (1994) *Constitutional Practice*, 2nd ed. (Oxford: Clarendon).

Brazier, R., (1990) *Constitutional Texts*, 2nd ed. (Oxford: Clarendon).

de Smith, S., and Brazier, R., (1994) *Constitutional and Administrative Law*, 7th ed. (Harmondsworth: Penguin).

Ewing, K. D., and Bradley, A. W., (1993) *Constitutional and Administrative Law*, 11th ed. (Harlow: Longman).

Marston, J., and Ward, R., (1993) *Cases and Commentary on Constitutional and Administrative Law*, 2nd ed. (London: Pitman).

Thompson, B. (1993) *Textbook on Constitutional and Administrative Law* (London: Blackstone Press).

4 CONSTITUTIONAL CONVENTIONS

In 1963 Griffith argued that it would be wise to 'delete those pages in constitutional textbooks headed Conventions, with their unreal distinctions and their word puzzles' ([1963] PL 401, 402). This is a sentiment with which many law students would agree! In a sense so do the textbook writers, for separate chapters on conventions are rare. Nonetheless, the topic is frequently favoured by examiners. The reason for this is that the nebulous concept of a constitutional convention allows a good deal of debate, particularly on the relationship between conventions and legal rules. Conventions are generally distinguished from laws. This is because, as political practices, they are not enforced by the courts. That is not to say that the courts will ignore the existence of conventions or that conventions carry no binding force — simply that any redress for the breach of a convention will not be available directly from the courts. Remember also that in discussions of constitutional principle, the notion of the supremacy of Parliament (see the following chapters) can never be sidelined. Indeed, an (apparent) convention would succumb to the passage of conflicting legislation, at any rate whilst that remained good law (see *Madzimbamuto* v *Lardner-Burke* [1969] 1 AC 645).

THE NATURE OF CONVENTIONS

This immediately raises a host of problems. What is the distinction between conventions and law in precise terms? What role do conventions play? Why are conventions obeyed if they carry no legal sanction as such? And how does one identify a convention if the technical processes necessary to pass laws are not required to create a convention? Not surprisingly, these are the very questions posed in examinations. As we shall see they are not put quite so bluntly as this, and two or more such questions could be linked. Nonetheless, as a first step it is useful to seek answers to the problems raised above.

How Can We Distinguish Conventions from Legal Rules?

The distinction between conventions and strict legal rules is one of those 'unreal distinctions' referred to above. This is why it forms such a popular line of questioning in examinations. The student is confronted with the question 'What is law?' — usually at an early stage in legal education. It becomes necessary to recognise two types of constitutional rules: those enforced by the court, and those followed habitually by those in public life, notwithstanding the absence of a formal enforcement process. Both are recognised as part of our constitutional law if only because we should be left with a highly artificial view if we took cognisance only of the strict laws. As Jennings stated, conventions 'provide the flesh which clothes the dry bones of the law' (*The Law and the Constitution*, 1959) — a memorable metaphor for examination purposes!

In his book, Jennings is highly critical of the traditional distinction between strict law and constitutional conventions proposed by Dicey (*Introduction to the Study of the Law of the Constitution*, 1885, reprinted as 10th ed. 1959). Dicey saw constitutional law as consisting of two parts — laws proper and constitutional conventions. According to Dicey, the latter rules regulated the conduct of officials but were not enforced or recognised by the courts. Some writers, and especially Jennings, have argued that Dicey's distinction between laws and conventions which rest upon the grounds of judicial enforcement is rather artificial, but most lawyers are happy to accept it.

However, it is not true to say that the courts do not recognise conventions. Especially in the area of ministerial responsibility, the courts sometimes refuse to intervene to challenge executive action on the basis that particular conduct is regulated by the operation of a convention. The case of *Liversidge* v *Anderson* [1942] AC 206 is one example discussed below, but you might also read the judgment of Lord Denning MR in *R* v *Secretary of State for the Home Office, ex parte Hosenball* [1977] 1 WLR 766. See also *Attorney-General* v *Jonathan Cape Ltd* [1976] QB 752, which contained interesting dicta on this question. The case concerned an (unsuccessful) attempt to prevent the publication of ministerial diaries: and raised the question whether a duty of confidentiality may arise on grounds of public interest. The convention of collective responsibility could be more than read between the lines, for although Lord Widgery CJ considered that a convention was 'an obligation founded in conscience only', he also recognised that the confidential character of Cabinet papers was 'derived from the convention of joint Cabinet responsibility'.

Finally you may wish to look at the Canadian Supreme Court case in *Reference re Amendment of the Constitution of Canada* (1982) 125 DLR (3d) 1. This case concerned challenges by the provinces within Canada to the attempts of the Canadian Government to force constitutional amendment without their agreement. The Supreme Court's recognition of obligations arising from convention, though not from strict legal rules, led to the Government holding back. The Constitution of 1983 which emerged followed detailed negotiations with the provinces.

Consequently, a majority view would be that Dicey's distinction between conventions and legal rules is not without substance, whilst admitting that the distinction is nonetheless a hazy one. The whole debate on this topic was considered in detail in two articles by Munro which you will find at (1975) 91 LQR 218, and [1985] PL 637, but be warned that in their support for Dicey's view they are unrivalled. For further debate see the response to the latter article at p. 649 of the same volume of *Public Law*; ch. 3 of Munro's *Studies in Constitutional Law* (1987); McEldowney's essay on Dicey in McAuslan and McEldowney, *Law Legitimacy and the Constitution* (1985); and Maley (1985) 48 MLR 139. Broadly, the outcome of this body of literature, in particular on the basis of Munro's *Studies*, is to accept the variable nature of the obligations arising under conventions. Munro suggests a 'continuum'. This may be seen as a sliding scale upon which some conventions are so well-entrenched and respected that their breach would be unthinkable. At the other end of the scale, certain conventions are so vague in scope that genuine doubt may surround their very existence. Brazier expresses distinctions in terms of a hierarchy which in particular seeks to distinguish conventions from practices, a flexible arrangement whereby certain non-legal rules are regarded as of greater limiting effect than are others ((1992) 43 NILQ 262). See also the analysis offered by Heard (*Canadian Constitutional Conventions* (1991)). Recent contributions point to the notion of fundamental constitutional principles (Brazier, McAuslan and McEldowney — cited above), though problems of enforcement and informality remain. Marshall warns that conventions can only be stated in general terms since their applicability may stretch from being clear to being debatable (*Constitutional Conventions* (1984)).

What Role Do Conventions Play?

Certainly both types of rule form part of our constitutional law. Custom is a source of law generally, although many customs have solidified over the years in the form of common law doctrines. But what is exciting about the concept of a convention is that we see customary rules and political usages providing a living part of our constitution. This sets constitutional law apart from other areas of law. This is a phenomenon not limited to Britain, but true of constitutions in general. Even in countries adopting a new constitutional framework, conventions quickly emerge. This is only to be expected, since human foresight is limited, and a written constitution cannot provide for every eventuality. Conventions are vital in so far as they fill out the gaps in the constitution itself, help solve problems of interpretation, and allow for the future development of the constitutional framework.

Britain does not have a written constitution, however, in the sense that the rules are not embodied in any one document or in a series of documents, and the unwritten conventional rules have formed a significant basis of our constitution. Thus the office of Prime Minister, and the existence of the Cabinet, stem from convention alone. The assent of the Monarch to bills passing through Parliament is secured only by convention. Proud of our unwritten constitution, we like to boast that, in Britain, conventions have assumed an exceptional importance. Certainly it is true that since 1688 we have moved gradually from government by the Monarchy to a more democratic and accountable process of parliamentary government, and in no small part conventions have made this possible. However, this traditional wisdom has been challenged in the article by Munro (1975) 91 LQR 218. He claims that it is arguable that in countries with written constitutions, the difficulty of achieving constitutional change may mean that conventions assume a greater significance in so far as they allow the constitution to adapt to meet changing requirements.

Why Are Conventions Obeyed?

The truth is that, whatever the nature of the constitution, a great deal may be left unsaid in legal rules allowing enormous discretion to politicians and officials. Conventions regulate the exercise of that discretion. Why persons respond to the demands of conventions is a difficult question. The courts do not enforce conventions directly, although as we have seen they do sometimes recognise them. Thus in *Liversidge* v *Anderson* [1942] AC 206, the detention of the appellant by the Home Secretary under defence regulations was not impugned by the courts. Whilst recognising the vast powers placed in the hands of the executive by Parliament, the courts also took notice of the exercise of control over the Home Secretary by Parliament through the convention of individual ministerial responsibility. Such decisions doubtless signify the importance of conventions and some entrench their status, but they do not assist greatly in explaining why conventions are obeyed.

According to Dicey (*Law of the Constitution*), conventions are obeyed because, if breached, there would also follow some breach of a formal legal rule. The problem with this is that it is certainly possible to point to conventions which have not been followed but which led to no subsequent legal intervention. A common example is that of Lloyd George who, in 1918, advised the Monarch to dissolve Parliament without consulting his Cabinet, as convention would seem to have demanded. Since the Cabinet acquiesced, however, there was no question of a clash with any legal rule. It is probably more accurate, therefore, to say that if a convention is breached some change in the constitution, and perhaps in the formal legal rules, will result. This may take the form of a constitutional crisis. Thus if the Monarch began to thwart the wishes of Parliament by refusing to assent to Bills, it seems safe to assume this would provoke a major constitutional crisis and perhaps eventual constitutional change. However, conventional rules are not constant and not every departure from them would have so dramatic an effect. This is not surprising since one major purpose of conventions is to allow political power to shift and the constitutional framework to evolve accordingly.

However one lesson of the Thatcher years of Government may be that we have to consider not merely formal legal consequences of the breach of a convention, but the political possibility of breach. This is an issue well-covered by Brazier in his book *Constitutional Practice* (1994). The simple point is that in relation to many issues concerning conventions, much will depend upon the political context. Thus although there are rules of ministerial responsibility it is idle to believe that these rules will always apply equally to all ministers. Much might depend upon the particular political power of an individual minister — e.g., to resist calls for resignation. One of the interesting features of the 1993–4 Scott inquiry into the Matrix Churchill affair (at the time of writing, the report is awaited) is the status of ministerial responsibility. Briefly, the inquiry arose out of a prosecution of three businessmen, for allegedly unlawful sales of arms to Iraq, which failed when evidence was given (by a former minister) concerning a change in government policy. Nevertheless, a number of ministers apparently acting on advice by the government law officers, had signed public interest immunity certificates, seeking thereby a blanket denial of access to Crown papers in the action. The claim of immunity was subsequently overruled by the trial judge.

How May Conventions Be Identified?

One result of the differing consequences which may flow from a departure from previous political practice is that commentators have been tempted to categorise conventions. Jennings in particular (*The Law and the Constitution*, and see *Cabinet Government*, 3rd ed., 1959) tried to distinguish between normative (binding) precedents and simple (not binding) precedents. In the case of the former, the precedents must show that the politician or official felt obliged to follow the rule, and there must have been a good reason for the rule. The vagueness of the test (e.g., in relation to good reason) and the requirement to question motives has led to the unpopularity of this line of thinking. Nowhere is this better illustrated than in the Westland affair (for a succinct account see Marshall [1986] PL 184). Here Leon Brittan's resignation appears to enforce individual ministerial responsibility for inexpedient actions on the part of his department (which leaked a letter of the Solicitor-General). Similarly Michael Heseltine's resignation seems to uphold collective ministerial responsibility since he was in clear disagreement with the Cabinet view. However it would be an oversimplification to assert that both men resigned *because* of the convention and Heseltine specifically disavowed such a view (*The Observer*, 12 January 1986).

Another problem with the Jennings test is the use of the word 'precedent' in relation to non-legal rules. Indeed it may be easier to avoid any attempt to consider the precedents for conventions. We know, by observing the workings of the constitution, that the strict legal rules coexist with non-legal rules of political practice. Although recognisable, classifying these rules in accordance with their 'precedents' may not be particularly helpful. They exist to provide a balance between competing needs of stability and constitutional change. The ability of conventions to adapt to changing circumstances is the major reason why they are not replaced by the more rigid alternative of strict legal rules. Thus to examine rules which are not necessarily meant to be constant in terms of 'precedent' (with all the implications that the word carries for lawyers) may be contradictory. This emphasis on change is significant because government has tended to become more accountable throughout our constitutional history. Notwithstanding their non-enforcement by the courts, conventional rules have formed a useful barometer of the political acceptability of governmental actions.

One excellent example of this concerns the resignation of Governments. It used to be widely accepted that a Government defeated in the Commons on an issue of principle should resign. In 1974 Harold Wilson declared that the vote would need to be openly accepted as a vote of confidence before he would treat defeat as a resignation issue. This statement, which reflected changing views and suited the needs of his slim majority would now be widely accepted. Moreover it is not unwelcome; it gives backbenchers an opportunity to express disapproval without necessarily putting the entire life of the Government at risk. This works well especially where the issue is one of principle. The Government in the mid-eighties had to abandon attempts to liberalise Sunday trading when faced with backbench rebels, even facing a three-line whip. Often, such pressure can produce a climb-down, as for example, regarding the video nasties amendment successfully pursued by David Alton MP in proceedings in 1994 on the Criminal Justice and Public Order Bill. Dealings by John Major with the so-called Euro-rebels in 1994-95 certainly seemed to follow the Wilson line on votes of confidence.

REVISION

In addition to the questions above, it is obviously important to check through your lecture and seminar hand-outs and ensure that your notes cover fully the content of your course. However, the main issues probably are considered above, and this material may provide a guideline for your revision notes. Rather than try to learn a mass of lecture notes, reorganise your material so that it will address particular questions. If you split your notes into separate units covering the main areas of study, they will obviously be easier to remember. Avoid too many separate units of this kind, but four to six subheadings could prove useful. Thus you could revise the relationship between conventions and legal rules in one session and the role of conventions in the next — and so on. Aim all the time at a brief set of notes which will trigger off your ability to recall the material and make your notes as logical as possible.

To give an example, a part of your notes might read:

Relationship between conventions and strict laws
1   Lack of formality in development of conventions (cf. strict law).
2   Courts will not enforce conventions directly (and they do not give rise to legal rights).
3   But courts do recognise conventions (cf. Dicey) and may be influenced by their existence (see *Liversidge* v *Anderson*).
4   Although not enforced by the courts, conventions do bind those persons to whom they apply.
5   Conventions generally regulate the exercise of an action which would be authorised by strict law.

It may take some time before you feel sufficiently confident to reduce your notes to such a few major points, but at least they should prove possible to remember in this form, and these in turn will provide a guide to recalling the detail of your wider reading, seminar work, etc. if there is some type of symmetrical pattern (e.g., five headings with five points under each heading), although this is rather artificial, it does provide a great aid to memory. It is rather like being asked to name the members of a soccer team — you are assisted by the fact that you know that there are eleven players, and that the first is a goalkeeper followed by two full backs, followed by... . Naming the side becomes suddenly much easier!

In many instances, there is no absolute answer to a question set. If you are asked about, say, advantages of conventions, and you can remember that in your notes there are six of these, do not worry unduly if you can remember only five. Another list, which may better set out the relevant material, may contain only four anyway. Nor does the fact that you name five, but I name only four guarantee you a better mark. Revision is not like remembering what your mum asked you to buy from the shops. This is because the examiner will not just check the contents of the shopping list, but will taste the meal which you cook. Getting the right ingredients helps, but the fact that you missed out the parsley may not affect the dish very much.

A Definition

Even if your notes are good, however, they are not an examination answer in themselves. The next step is to practise answering specific questions — preferably from past papers. Once you begin doing this it becomes clear that it is quite a problem simply explaining what a convention is. Yet it is necessary to enter the examination room with a workable definition of a convention of the constitution. To begin with, the vast majority of questions involving conventions will take the form of essay questions, so that it may be necessary to outline your understanding of the question if it talks, for example, of non-legal rules. In addition a carefully constructed definition may prove an effective conclusion to the type of question in which you are asked to outline (by reference to examples) the workings and purpose of constitutional conventions in Britain. The definition need not be your own, assuming that you understand it and can provide support for what it says.

You may wish therefore to examine your constitutional textbooks in order to seek a clear definition which is readily comprehensible and which you feel you could commit to memory. One of the clearest and most concise expositions of the nature of constitutional conventions is undoubtedly that by Marshall and Moodie in their book *Some Problems of the Constitution* (5th ed., 1971). You are strongly recommended to read their essay on conventions in its entirety. In this essay they define conventions as:

> Certain rules of constitutional behaviour which are considered to be binding by and upon those who operate the constitution, but which are not enforced by the law courts (although the courts may recognise their existence), nor by the presiding officer in the House of Parliament.

The last part of the definition is an attempt to differentiate conventions from parliamentary procedural rules which are generally enforced by the Speaker. However, the separation of such rules from the many conventions relating to the handling of parliamentary business is by no means easy. The reference to the presiding officer could safely be omitted without attracting criticism. In addition, Marshall and Moodie admit that the definition makes no reference to the purpose of conventions which they see (following Dicey) as the regulation of discretionary power. An amended definition, to take account of this, might read:

> Conventions are rules of constitutional behaviour which, in seeking to define the use of constitutional discretion, are considered to be binding by and upon those who operate the constitution and which, although recognised by the courts, are not enforced by the courts directly.

This definition should be attributed to Marshall and Moodie, for although we have changed the wording a little, the concepts are undoubtedly theirs. There is no point in seeking to pass off a definition as your own. Apart from the fact that it is unlikely to work, the examiner will be at least as impressed that you appear to be familiar with some of the finer writings on constitutional issues.

Examples

Marshall and Moodie, although offering this definition, also admit that one useful way of answering the question 'What are conventions?' is to point to particular examples. In examinations it may be necessary to offer specific illustrations of the workings of conventions in order to prove your point. Indeed the question may demand that examples are given. Drawing up a full list of constitutional conventions would be an enormous task and there would be much dispute as to the accuracy of the eventual list. The following list is by no means intended to be exhaustive in terms of either examples or suggested categories, but the examples may prove useful in answering examination questions:

Exercise of the royal prerogative

(a) The Monarch shall assent to bills which have passed through both Houses of Parliament.

(b) The Monarch should act on the advice of the Ministers of the Crown and in particular shall dissolve Parliament on the advice of the Prime Minister.

(c) Following a general election the Monarch should approach the leader of the party with the majority of seats in the House of Commons to form a government.

The Cabinet

(d) A Minister is responsible for the running of his department to Parliament, which is able to call for his resignation if dissatisfied with the conduct of affairs within the department.

(e) A Minister shall abide by the decisions of his Cabinet colleagues or offer his resignation.

(f) Equally the Cabinet is expected to unite behind government policy (i.e., so that it cannot be seen as offering conflicting advice to the Monarch).

(g) The composition of the Cabinet is determined by the Prime Minister, who shall choose which Ministers are to be Cabinet members.

(h) Certain Ministers (e.g., the Chancellor of the Exchequer, the Home Secretary and the Foreign Secretary) are by convention members of the Cabinet.

(i)   All Ministers are appointed by the Monarch, who acts upon the advice of the Prime Minister.

(j)   The Prime Minister may seek the resignation of any Minister at any time.

(k)   A Minister should disclose and if necessary divest himself of financial interests inconsistent with his duties as Minister.

The Lords and the Commons

(l)   If the Government loses support in the House of Commons, and is defeated in a vote of confidence in the House, the Prime Minister shall advise the Monarch to dissolve Parliament.

(m)   The election of the Speaker is the first business of the House of Commons following an election.

(n)   The Speaker of the House of Commons shall behave impartially, although the Lord Chancellor presiding in the House of Lords may leave the woolsack and speak for the Government.

(o)   The House of Commons is the source of all measures which involve public expenditure.

(p)   Although it would ordinarily be contempt of Parliament to seek to influence voting in either House of Parliament, the party whips hold office and perform their duties by convention.

The judiciary

(q)   Lay peers ought not to seek to hear appeals before the judicial body of the House of Lords.

(r)   The Lords of Appeal in Ordinary ought to include at least two Scots lawyers.

(s)   The conduct of the judiciary ought not to be questioned in Parliament other than on a motion seeking dismissal of a member of the judiciary.

(t)   A judge must sever political links on appointment to the bench.

It should be stressed again that these are simply examples and the list is not intended to be exhaustive. Many other examples exist, and some of these appear in the textbooks (see de Smith and Brazier, *Constitutional and Administrative Law*, 7th ed. (1994), ch. 9; Wade and Bradley, *Constitutional and Administrative Law*, 11th ed. (1993), pp. 20-23). There are also many instances cited in the most comprehensive survey of this topic: Marshall, *Constitutional Conventions* (1984). Again, this is a book which all students are recommended to read, but it is not a book with which to begin to prepare your notes. It will serve an excellent purpose if, once you have fully prepared the topic, you can read through it and see how Marshall structures his argument and advances his authorities.

It is useful to examine conventions discussed in such books and elsewhere, since often there is some consideration of how the conventions have operated in the past and specific instances are referred to. As we shall see, the best way to illustrate a knowledge of conventions is to point to practical problems from constitutional history. Thus if we take the last example (t), a Scottish judge, Lord Avondale, agreed in 1968 to serve on a Conservative opposition committee, but quickly resigned when faced with public criticism and a statement by the Lord Advocate that conventional rules had been breached. A less clear example (in terms of its consequences) was the embarrassment caused by the disclosure in 1984 that the Master of the Rolls had advised the government in respect of its policy on trade unions.

THE EXAMINATION

As is shown below, it is possible to set a problem question centred around some future constitutional wrangle, and to ask for a discussion of the problem in the light of existing conventions and illustrations of how these have operated in the past. In the main, however, examining on the topic of conventions will take the form of the more standard essay question. The remainder of this chapter will consider three possible lines of questioning. Two examples of essay questions are included. One of these is a wide-ranging question on the sources of constitutional law in which the area of conventions is clearly significant, and the other is a more direct question upon the topic of conventions alone. Finally a problem question is included.

Conventions and Other Sources of Constitutional Law

Although you may concentrate in your revision upon the topic of conventions, it is a possibility that the question may not be restricted to that topic alone, but may seek a wider analysis of the sources and nature of constitutional law in general. To take an example of such a question (from a law degree paper in constitutional law):

> 'To a great extent the sources of constitutional law are the same as those of other branches of the law. The relative importance of particular sources does, however, differ.' (Mitchell.) Discuss.

Clearly this question requires some discussion of non-legal rules which form part of our constitutional law, but the question cannot be said to relate solely to conventions. It may be useful to examine how such a question might be answered.

This is a question likely to strike panic in the hearts of many examinees. It is not designed to do so, but it is calculated to make the student think. If the question were put to a first-year law student studying constitutional conventions as the first topic in a law degree course, then it would be highly unfair, but by the end of the first year, it is quite reasonable to expect the student to possess sufficient knowledge to answer the question. However, that knowledge will not stem from work on constitutional conventions alone, or even from constitutional law alone. You may have studied the sources of law as a discrete topic, perhaps in a legal systems course, or you may have to draw upon your studies within other first-year subjects. It is quite fair for an examiner to demand this, because it is necessary for the student to learn not to take a blinkered attitude and view all law subjects apart from each other. Moreover, providing an examinee is able to think out an answer, rather than relying upon the repetition of points from notes used for revision, the questions are often surprisingly easy.

In this case there is an obvious twofold process before the question may be answered, and this is to outline legal sources generally, and then those of constitutional law. Any law student knows that the most significant sources of law are statutes and case law. It should be noted, however, that our own domestic legal system has been dramatically affected by the UK's accession to the EC — a topic frequently mentioned in constitutional law courses. Finally there is no doubt that legal writings do influence the development of the law. But are not these sources the same in constitutional law? To begin with, we have not considered conventions, and in any case Mitchell asks us to consider the emphasis placed upon different sources inside and outside constitutional law. The essay would look very untidy if it dealt with the sources of law generally, and then the sources of constitutional law. Obviously this information needs to be amalgamated, and your essay plan should seek to do this by taking the relevant sources in turn. The following sections offer a brief guide to the material to be covered.

Statutes
It is important to remember that the question does not ask us what the sources of constitutional law are, but whether these sources are of particular consequence, in comparison to other areas of law. If we begin by looking at statutes, it is obvious that, in the absence of a written constitution, statutes are an important (perhaps the most important) source of constitutional law. Examples abound and cover a great deal of ground: some provide a basic constitutional framework, such as the Bill of Rights 1689, others regulate the operation of the organs of government (as do the Parliament Acts 1911 and 1949), and many of our civil liberties depend on, or are delineated in, Acts of Parliament — the Public Order Act 1986 and the Sex Discrimination Act 1975 provide two examples.

Nonetheless, statute law makes an enormous contribution to private law also. Our company law is increasingly statute based, to take but one instance.

The question challenges us to state whether there is any qualitative difference between the role of statutes in our constitutional law and elsewhere. Dicey argued vigorously that constitutional law forms part of the ordinary law of the land. To reinforce this point he wrote that 'Neither the Act of Union with Scotland, nor the Dentists Act 1878 has more claim than the other to be considered as supreme law'. This is a matter of parliamentary supremacy which is discussed in chapter 5, and the doctrine of implied repeal dictates that a later Act prevails over an earlier Act where the two are inconsistent. As we shall see, if this doctrine were rigorously applied, it would become impossible to entrench legislation or offer constitutional guarantees. It may be, therefore, that the courts would be prepared to state that certain legislation is imbued with particular constitutional significance so that the provisions ought not to be impliedly overridden (at least) by a later, inconsistent Act of Parliament. This argument is fully considered in the chapter on parliamentary supremacy, but one example of such constitutional legislation might be the European Communities Act 1972.

One other issue that may be significant here is the growth, over recent years of what Ganz has called quasi-legislation' (*Quasi-legislation: Recent Developments in Secondary Legislation* (1987)). This is something which will be considered in the chapter on delegated legislation below. It is a significant constitutional development in its own right that much of our new law is not contained in primary legislation. However, this also concerns certain rules which themselves have constitutional significance. An example might be the codes of practice made under the Police and Criminal Evidence Act 1984.

To recap, therefore, if we begin answering the question by discussing the contribution of statutes as a source of constitutional law, it is clear that in the absence of a written constitution, the importance of statutes is considerable. It is possible to give obvious examples of statutes of constitutional signifi-cance, and it may be possible to label certain statutes as constitutional statutes. Thus, whilst in theory Acts of Parliament are equal in terms of their status, it may be that the judiciary would prove reluctant to allow the constitutional principles in such legislation to be overridden by later inconsistent 'ordinary' legislation.

Case law
As regards case law, Bradley argues that because governmental power is largely derived from statute, judge-made law resulting from the interpreta-tion of statutes is of greater importance in public law than in the common law proper. Since the judiciary have no greater powers in relation to constitu-tional law, what Bradley appears to mean is that the consequences of judicial intervention are more significant. By interpretation of the ambit of statutory powers, the courts provide a check upon the exercise of discretion. Dicey described the constitution as 'judge-made' and also as the 'result of the

ordinary law of the land'. In particular Dicey saw the courts as the guardians of our individual liberties. However, this is an area in which statutes have supplemented the common law to a great extent: see for example the discussion below of Public Order and Police Powers. Moreover, looked at from a civil liberties viewpoint, judicial activism may have been lacking at times. Thus invasions of privacy in the form of telephone tapping have not been outlawed by the English courts which refuse to recognise a right of privacy as such, whilst stating that the whole area 'cried out for legislation'. (See *Malone* v *Metropolitan Police Commissioner* [1979] Ch 344 and *R* v *Secretary of State for the Home Department, ex parte Ruddock* [1987] 1 WLR 1482.) The European Court of Human Rights later ruled unanimously that telephone tapping in the UK was in breach of the European Convention — see *Malone* v *United Kingdom* (1984) 7 EHRR 14. It took another five years for the introduction of legislation which provides limited control upon the interception of communications — see the Interception of Communications Act 1985.

In other areas, however, and particularly that of administrative law, the courts have proved more vigilant in reviewing executive action. Various examples of this are given later (chapters 8, 9 and 10), but it is worth noting that there has been a re-awakening on the part of the courts in the area of administrative law. In addition since the *Case of Proclamations* (1610) 12 Co Rep 74 the judges have claimed the right to define the limits of those powers exercised under the royal prerogative, so that in this area (and that of parliamentary privilege — see chapter 7) the courts have a significant constitutional role. However, in certain areas their action may appear rather timid (see *Council of Civil Service Unions* v *Minister for the Civil Service* [1985] AC 374, discussed in chapter 8).

Consequently, you might choose to respond to the quotation from Mitchell in the above question by arguing as follows. In the absence of a written constitution, the courts can claim no particular powers to challenge the constitutionality of the actions of government. However, in so far as they interpret statutes of constitutional significance, exercise their long-established rights to define prerogative powers, and utilise the developing body of administrative law, the courts play a significant role. Even if the courts act with no greater authority in the area of public law than private law, because public law is that body of law which governs the government agencies, case law in this field is of obvious importance.

European Community law

At the time of the accession of the UK to what was (prior to the Treaty of European Union 1993) the European Economic Community, it was a well-established principle of Community law that no member state would legislate in a manner inconsistent with that law, since Community law must prevail over domestic law (see, e.g., *Costa* v *ENEL* [1964] ECR 585). In consequence, the implications for the British constitution, with its central concept of parliamentary supremacy, are immense. This is a matter considered in detail in chapter 6, along with an analysis of the major sources of EC law.

Given that you cannot realistically cover this material in detail, what ought you to say of Community law? Here you have an opportunity to impress the examiner by proving your ability to select the relevant issues from a mass of material. Two points are especially worthy of mention, and neither will be discussed fully here because they are considered fully in chapter 6. These are the direct applicability of certain EC laws and the binding force of the judgments of the European Court of Justice on matters of Community law. These principles illustrate the significance of EC law to our constitutional law, especially because of the implications for the doctrine of the supremacy of Parliament. Your answer should make this clear, pointing to the direct applicability of EC law and its enforcement within the courts of the United Kingdom, following, as necessary, the lead of the European Court.

Legal writings
Legal writings are not a major source of law in comparison with the other sources discussed. Unlike Europe and, in particular, the USA, the English courts have never regarded the views of academics highly, although they have at least relaxed the rule that the writer must be dead before being cited as an authority! Thus if you found yourself with limited time to answer the question, this would be the issue to omit. If you do discuss it, then it has to be admitted that this is a source of both public and private law, since barristers with little precedent in their favour may clutch at any straw — even academic opinion! Nonetheless, because constitutional law also involves questions of political practice, certain works can be useful to establish the constitutionality of conduct. Thus highly regarded writings such as Erskine May's book on *Parliamentary Practice* or Chitty on the *Prerogatives of the Crown* carry considerable authority — probably more so than standard law textbooks.

As an aside, it is worth noting that there exists another type of book influential within the field of constitutional law — though not elsewhere. These are the writings and memoirs of politicians. Books such as *The Crossman Diaries* (the subject of *Attorney-General* v *Jonathan Cape Ltd* [1976] QB 752) tell us a great deal about political practices. The view may be partial and also incomplete, but there can be no doubt that such works help establish known practices of government upon which constitutional conventions depend.

Conventions
This leaves the final issue of conventions and their unique position in constitutional law. Custom can be recognised as law by the courts in dealing with private law issues — as in *New Windsor Corporation* v *Mellor* [1975] Ch

380, which concerned customary rights to indulge in sports and other pastimes on land claimed to be a village green. However, such cases are rare, whilst conventional political practices, whether customary or more recently established, are of recurring importance. Once again, the problem in answering the examination question is largely concerned with selecting that material which will contribute most appropriately to your answer. It is not intended to repeat much of the substantive material on conventions written above, but it will perhaps prove obvious that your answer should cover the following points:

(a)   Given that the question concerns the relative significance of sources of law, and since custom plays little part in private law, the significance of conventions in constitutional law must be stressed — possibly by giving examples.

(b)   Mention must be made of the role that conventions fulfil. If their role is to regulate the discretionary use of power, then clearly this assists in establishing the importance of conventions.

(c)   Something ought to be said on the difficult issue of whether conventions ought to be considered as law. Certainly the binding nature of conventions must be stressed along with some analysis of why they are obeyed.

(d)   There ought to be some explanation of the need for the extra dimension allowed by constitutional conventions. It is necessary to establish the need within the constitution for the flexibility which conventions offer — a need which is not apparent outside constitutional law.

A summary
Mitchell's quotation, and the essay based upon it, covers a great deal of ground. In order to answer the question, it is necessary to delineate the areas which you will cover and then to select, from these areas, the significant issues. The major task in answering the question lies in confining its ambit and making this selection — that is to say in planning the essay. Much of the comment which is offered upon the sources of constitutional law is relatively obvious. Certainly in order to answer the question we draw heavily upon other topics — such as parliamentary supremacy. In addition if, outside the pressure of the examination room, we sat down and thought about the question of whether (for example) the nature of an Act of Parliament differed in the area of constitutional law, we might reach similar conclusions to those above. That is, although formally there is little difference, it may become necessary to recognise certain statutes of constitutional significance if we are to guarantee rights within the constitution.

Perhaps the lesson is that, in certain questions concerning the nature of constitutional law, a great deal of progress can be made by drawing on the body of knowledge which, by the end of the course, you ought to possess. In reality, even if you have not studied the topic in isolation, you ought to be able at the end of any law course to outline the sources of the relevant body of law. Some of the more general questions on constitutional law ought to prove straightforward, providing you are prepared to think them through carefully and not expect the answer to come from rote learning.

The Role of Conventions

A second type of question may be that confined specifically to the topic of conventions. There are a number of possibilities here, but broadly there are two likely lines of attack. The first is to concentrate upon the difficult problem of the distinction between conventions and strict legal rules. This challenging question might be quite simply put:

How might one distinguish constitutional conventions from strict legal rules?

Often, however, the subject will be approached in a more oblique manner:

Why not codify constitutional conventions in a strict legal form?

This question suggests that, since conventions are binding rules, they could be enacted as strict law. To ask why this is not done is to ask if there are features of constitutional conventions, distinct from strict law, which we wish to maintain. The shorter questions are not always the easiest! Alternatively the question may ask why conventions are observed or how they might be identified — both issues being closely related to the non-legal/legal rule problem. (For an interesting account of the Australian experiment in codification containing a host of questions concerning the effect of codification and with an appendix containing the statement of conventional practices, see Sampford and Wood [1987] PL 231: and see the discussion by Brazier, *Constitutional Reform: Reshaping the British Political System* (1991).)

The other line of attack is to pose a more wide-ranging question concerning the role or purpose of conventions. It may be useful to take an example from this area to illustrate how an answer should be carefully planned — though it is not intended to deal with all of the issues in detail, since many of these may be familiar to you by now. Let us take the question:

To what extent are constitutional conventions necessary for the provision of responsible government?

Suppose that this question appears in an examination, and you read it with horror because it is not as straightforward as you had hoped. In fact you may have never considered whether or not conventions ensure responsible government. Perhaps you are even unsure what is meant by the phrase 'responsible government'. Faced with such difficulties, many students write all they know about conventions or offer a potted version of their notes. In fact, however, there are a number of issues which are not especially relevant to the question. For example, the question does not require discussion of how constitutional conventions are established, or how they may be identified. Nor are you required to distinguish conventions from strict legal rules, although it is clearly of significance that conventions do carry some binding force. A more important consideration, however, is what to include in your answer.

An introduction

One starting-point, despite your panic, might be the definition given earlier in this chapter. Two points within this are of immediate significance. The first is the statement that the role of conventions is to regulate the exercise of discretion — presumably to guard against the irresponsible abuse of powers. The second element is that persons in a system of government consider themselves bound by conventions, so that they will be held accountable, or responsible, if found in breach of them. It is this latter sense of responsibility that is adopted within the phrase 'responsible government'. Therefore if you choose to begin with the definition, this will lead you some way towards an answer to the question. The core of the essay which follows will outline the ability of conventions to curb discretion by reference to examples, and explain the binding nature of conventions in order to establish the obedience of those working within the constitution to these non-legal rules.

At the time of planning your introduction, you should consider your conclusion, since the two should be linked and both should seek to answer the question set. Dwelling on a conclusion for an instant, it is hardly possible to conclude that conventions are totally unnecessary. The question, beginning as it does with 'To what extent?', implicitly accepts some degree of necessity. This is reinforced by the definition which tells us that the role of conventions is to restrict the arbitrary exercise of discretion — not an unimportant task. You may decide at this stage upon a conclusion, therefore, and because it is always better to make out a case strongly (where possible), you may decide to answer the question, 'To what extent are conventions necessary?' by stating that they are vital. You are now free to consider the two central themes arising from the definition.

Regulation of discretion

Opening with the definition and focusing upon the limitations upon discretionary powers is not sufficient in itself, however. As was stated in chapter 3, it is necessary to produce evidence or authority for the proposition which you put forward. It is necessary, then, to point to illustrations of the regulation of discretion by constitutional conventions. This is not as difficult as it might seem, since, if conventions exist to check discretion, they all provide a potential example. You could mentally examine the examples you have revised, therefore, and choose those most obviously fulfilling this role. On the other hand a hotchpotch of examples is not a good answer to the question — some classification or structure would help. It is at this point that wider reading may prove invaluable.

Constitutional lawyers have grappled to explain precisely how it is that conventions regulate discretion. It is important to realise that the discretionary power is the product of a legal rule which the convention then seeks to limit. Wheare (*Modern Constitutions*, 2nd ed., 1966) analyses the operation of conventions within different constitutional frameworks in order to assess the ways in which they interact with legal powers. Consequently, if you are familiar with his work, you will have a ready-made structure for your essay, and a number of examples from his text. What a curious form of assessment an examination is — by citing Wheare you will undoubtedly impress the examiner, but by burgling the contents of the book you are saved the inconvenience of thinking out your own answer to a challenging question!

Wheare suggests that a convention may operate to affect the law of the constitution in three ways. The first is that it 'paralyses the arm of the law'. By this Wheare does not mean that the law is amended or abolished, but that a legal power, which does exist, is simply not used. He cites the most obvious example of this — the fact that the Monarch may refuse to assent to a Bill, but by convention does not exercise such a power. The second limitation upon a legal power is effected by the transfer of that power from one person to another. There are a host of examples within the British constitution of a discretion which in theory is exercised by one party (often the Monarch) whereas in practice it is exercised by another (perhaps the Prime Minister). An example of this is the Monarch's formal power of appointment of Cabinet Ministers, unswervingly acting upon the advice of the Prime Minister. Finally, according to Wheare, conventions may supplement the law. One example of this (not given by Wheare) is that the Monarch shall appoint the Prime Minister but shall approach the person best able to command the support of the House of Commons. You can cite as an example here the instance of the election (as leader of the Conservative Party) and eventual appointment (as Prime Minister) of Major following Thatcher's resignation in 1990. There is no formal legal rule requiring this, and indeed, in the past, the convention may have given the Monarch a greater degree of choice.

From here it is important to press home the argument. Having shown that conventions limit discretion, stress how important this function is. Explain, as in the introduction to this chapter, that the legal rules cannot provide absolute answers to every constitutional issue. Illustrate the historical significance of conventions, explain their central role within the constitution and point to those advantages which are inherently theirs. These particularly relate to the flexibility of conventions and their ability to encapsulate changing political ideals. Finally, indicate the unique nature of non-legal rules within constitutional law in comparison with other areas of law. Explain the necessity for such rules and their role in restraining discretionary power within that body of law which regulates the organs of government.

Obedience to conventions
This leaves you free to deal with the second element of your essay, the binding nature of conventions. After all, even if their role is to check discretion, they can only be said to be necessary if they operate successfully. You can doubtless point to conventions which are invariably followed. It is probably fair to say that whilst writers argue as to why conventions are observed, few seriously suggest that they are regularly ignored. Nonetheless it is perfectly legitimate to seek to impress the examiner by considering the thorny question of why conventions are obeyed. Some of this material was covered at the beginning of this chapter. Dicey's view that a breach of a convention would led to a breach of a strict legal rule is not of general application and you will find it easier to cope with this issue if you have digested Maley's article and Brazier's work (op. cit.). The notion that a breach of a convention is likely to lead to constitutional change, perhaps arising out of constitutional difficulties or crises, is more accurate. This also helps establish the importance, if one wishes to maintain stability, of obedience to constitutional conventions.

Indeed, Marshall and Moodie argue that conventions reduce friction within the constitutional machinery. So successful are they in doing this that they are a universal feature of modern constitutions (if you have read Wheare, you may be able to offer examples from constitutions other than that in Britain). Moreover — you could explain — even if the British constitution were written afresh, and all existing conventions incorporated within it, gradual usage or future constitutional requirements would lead to the emergence of further non-legal rules in the shape of conventions. Thus on this analysis, conventions are vital — a necessary, even inevitable, part of any system of responsible government.

A summary
What can be learnt from the above answer? It is suggested that the questions raised concerning the nature of conventions at the beginning of this chapter are central to the topic and reoccur frequently in examinations. The material here is limited, and not too difficult to learn. The problem in examinations is to select what is relevant from the material and illustrate to the examiner that

you fully comprehend it by answering specifically the question set. Using questions from tutorial sheets and previous examination papers, set yourself a limited time to produce not an essay but a plan which could form the basis of an answer. When you have done this use your notes and textbook (or ask your tutor) to check what might have been included. Not only will this serve to test your knowledge of the area, but it will increase your confidence in advance of the examination.

A Problem Question

Almost invariably questions which relate to conventions will take the form of those above and require an essay on a particular aspect of the subject. This is not inevitably so, however, for there is no obvious reason why a problem question based on future constitutional difficulties could not be included in exactly the same way as is common for those topics which include rather more case law. The following question is one example:

How would you advise the Queen to act in each of the following hypothetical situations?

(a)   A few months after the return of a Labour Government with a substantial overall majority at a general election, the Prime Minister dies suddenly. The Labour Party electoral college meets to elect a new leader of the party. The winner has the votes of a substantial majority of the trade union and constituency party sections, but the majority of Labour MPs voted for another candidate, and several prominent Labour MPs have said they will not serve in the Cabinet under the successful candidate.

(b)   A political party is returned to power at a general election having pledged in its manifesto to abolish the House of Lords. The Queen has invited the leader of the party to form a Government, but he has declined to do so unless she promises, if need be, to create enough peers to secure the immediate passage of a Bill to abolish the House of Lords.

(c)   About three months after a general election at which the Conservative Party was returned by a small overall majority, there is a split in the party and a group of about 50 MPs defect to the Centre party, which becomes the largest party in the House of Commons. The Prime Minister asks the Queen to dissolve Parliament.

Note the plausibility of the three events. It would be possible under present arrangements for the election of a Labour Party leader to arrive at situation (a). Situation (b) could occur since certain Labour Party members have not merely long supported abolition of the House of Lords but have advocated the creation of Labour peers as the best practicable way of achieving this.

Finally the presence of the SDP/Liberal Alliance in recent years and the emergence of the Liberal Democrats renders situation (c) a possibility in the case of a rift within the parties on either side of it in the political spectrum. Thus the question at least illustrates the practical need for the conventional rules.

The major difficulty with this type of question is that it requires you to point to specific precedents, but that is true of all problem questions. This provides a stiff test of your knowledge of conventions. One consolation is that, because the situations are hypothetical, and the precedents somewhat vague, there is no right or wrong answer. What you must do is arrive at conclusions upon a careful consideration of past constitutional practices. Marks will be awarded on the quality and consistency of the arguments which you advance. An answer to the question is not contained here, if only because a problem will rarely appear on this issue. It is as well to know that it might happen, however, and you are urged to work through the above question seeking those precedents upon which the Queen might choose to act. The conventions operative here relate to the exercise of prerogative powers and are central to the operation of our constitution.

CONCLUSION

The constitutional convention is not necessarily an easy concept to understand. However the questions which will be set on this topic fall into a limited number of categories. The following may serve as a checklist. Ask yourself if you can explain to the satisfaction of the examiner (probably your lecturer or tutor) these points:

(a) What conventions are, providing adequate examples of different types of conventional rules.

(b) What the distinction between law and convention is, and what the similarities are also.

(c) How conventions arise and how they may be identified.

(d) Why conventions are obeyed and what happens if they are breached.

(e) What purpose conventions have and with what degree of success do they operate.

(f) Why conventions are retained rather than re-enacted as strict legal rules.

Above all, remember that you may expect good marks if you show an awareness of constitutional principles backed up by a wide knowledge of those instances which have helped form and develop particular conventions. Ensure when you study conventions that you find adequate examples of their operation, and throughout your year studying constitutional law search for current illustrations, particularly in fields such as ministerial responsibility, of conventions operating in practice.

The ground that you will need to cover to prepare yourself to answer a question on conventions is not wide, although familiarity with examples may demand wider reading. Moreover, although there is some dispute between the writers on particular points, the nature of the debate is generally straightforward and clear-cut. Here is an area therefore which, whilst covering political theory and practice in addition to law, most students can face with confidence. Because it does include political issues, it ought to prove of interest to a student sufficiently well-versed in current affairs — a quality which, in an ideal world, all law students would possess.

FURTHER READING

Brazier, R., (1994) *Constitutional Practice*, 2nd ed. (Oxford: Oxford University Press).

Brazier, R., 'It is a Constitutional Issue: Fitness for Ministerial Office in the 1990s' [1994] *Public Law* 431.

Dicey, A. V., 'Ministerial Responsibility' (Chapter 5) in Jowell, J. and Oliver, D. (eds), (1959) *Introduction to the Study of the Law of the Constitution*, 10th ed. (London: Macmillan).

Jennings, W. I., (1959) *The Law and the Constitution*, 5th ed. (London: University of London Press).

Marshall, G., (1984) *Constitutional Conventions: The Rules and Forms of Political Accountability* (Oxford: Clarendon Press).

Tompkins, A., 'Public Interest Immunity after Matrix Churchill' [1993] *Public Law* 650.

Turpin, C., (1994) *The Changing Constitution*, 3rd ed. (Oxford: Clarendon Press).

Zuckermann, A., 'Public Interest Immunity — A Matter of Prime Judicial Responsibility' (1994) 57 MLR 703.

5 PARLIAMENTARY SUPREMACY

The legislative supremacy of Parliament was described by Dicey as 'the very keystone of the law of the constitution'. In more recent times, however, there has been much argument as to the scope of the doctrine, and the traditional wisdom that the legislative supremacy of Parliament is fundamental to our constitution has been under attack. Students reading the work of different writers tend to be disconcerted at the divergent views expressed. They find it difficult to know who is right and who is wrong. The fact is that few opinions are obviously wrong any more than others are obviously right. The nature of the subject involves speculation as to future events, and all that any academic writer can do is suggest the way ahead hoping to convince others with the clarity of argument and authority of precedent employed. But there is another problem here. Cases involving a direct challenge to the legislative supremacy of Parliament are few, and even when they do arise, the judiciary act with caution and decide the particular case whilst avoiding general rules. This is not surprising since this central area of constitutional law has a direct bearing upon their own role and authority. Case law from other jurisdictions may assist but this is at best persuasive authority and may even be misleading when incorporated into our own constitutional climate.

However, simply because the case law does not provide an answer in itself does not mean that the student may dispense with the necessity to cite cases. On the contrary, in this rather hazy area, a line of authority becomes vital to lead towards a solution. Indeed from the lecturer's point of view, one reason why legislative supremacy makes a welcome appearance early in the course is that it demands a relatively sophisticated understanding of the workings of precedent. Another reason is undoubtedly than the student is confronted with the question 'what is law?' and forced to consider issues of legal theory. As we shall see later, the presence of theoretical material presents particular problems of revision.

To recap, then, there exists a rather grey area of law in which a variety of hypotheses are advanced. The student becomes confused. Yet once it is accepted that opinions do differ, the subject-matter possesses a number of inherent advantages — there are no black or white answers to problem questions; there is only a limited amount of case law; it is easy to impress by showing an ability to grasp academic argument and so on. Nor are these arguments necessarily difficult to grasp. Let us begin with the traditional view referred to at the opening of this chapter. Before doing so it is necessary to point out that those issues dealing specifically with the impact of EC law upon our doctrine of legislative supremacy are dealt with in the following chapter.

THE TRADITIONAL VIEW

De Smith offers a useful explanation of the doctrine of parliamentary supremacy (which de Smith prefers to refer to as the sovereignty of Parliament):

> The Queen in Parliament is competent, according to United Kingdom law, to make or unmake any law whatsoever on any matter whatsoever; and no United Kingdom court is competent to question the validity of an Act of Parliament.

Blackstone has said that Parliament can do everything that is not naturally impossible (*Commentaries*, b. 1). It follows from this that the doctrine has a positive and a negative aspect. That is to say that Parliament is competent to legislate on any matter whatsoever (the positive aspect) whilst no court or other body is competent to determine the validity of such legislation (the negative aspect). (See *Blackburn* v *Attorney-General* [1971] 1 WLR 1037; *Gibson* v *Lord Advocate* 1975 SLT 134.)

This doctrine is the product of our common law and it establishes the constitutional superiority of the Queen in Parliament. It follows logically from the doctrine that at each new parliamentary session, the then Parliament is considered supreme, and no law which it enacts can be declared invalid by reason of the fact that it may conflict with earlier law. Such a notion can be easily defended. Future generations ought to be free to legislate unhindered to suit their particular needs, and because both human reasoning and foresight is fallible, it might be unfortunate to allow one assembly to legislate for future years. On the other hand, the fact that there is no higher law than that of Parliament is not so easily defended. Thus any argument that an Act of Parliament withdrew basic human rights, sanctioned arbitrary or capricious action, or offended natural law, would be doomed to failure. In *R* v *Jordan* [1967] Crim LR 483, the courts refused to entertain arguments that the

Race Relations Act 1965 curtailed freedom of speech, and Lord Reid in *British Railways Board* v *Pickin* [1974] AC 765 at p. 782 asserted the dominance of statute over natural law — a view which Blackstone had at one time doubted.

The traditional view of the legislative supremacy of Parliament is reinforced by case law relating to two particular issues: inconsistency between a later and an earlier statute, and the ability of courts to challenge the validity of an Act of Parliament.

Implied Repeal

Since Parliament is competent to legislate on any subject, it can expressly repeal earlier law. In the absence of express repeal, and in the event of inconsistency between later legislation and earlier law (either statute or common law) it is the later statute that prevails. This rule, that an earlier Act of Parliament must give way to a later one if the two cannot be reconciled, is commonly referred to as the doctrine of implied repeal. It follows from the doctrine and the concept of legislative supremacy that guarantees given in an Act of Parliament apparently covering the future, or purporting to apply 'henceforth', cannot bind a future Parliament, and that such legislation can be overridden by the clear implication of later inconsistent legislation.

This view is reinforced by two frequently cited cases. The cases, *Vauxhall Estates Ltd* v *Liverpool Corporation* [1932] 1 KB 733 and *Ellen Street Estates* v *Minister of Health* [1934] 1 KB 590, concerned s. 7(1) of the Acquisition of Land (Assessment of Compensation) Act 1919 which stated:

> The provisions of the Act or order by which the land is authorised to be acquired, or of any Act incorporated therewith, shall, in relation to the matters dealt with in this Act, have effect subject to this Act, and so far as inconsistent with this Act those provisions shall cease to have or shall not have effect.

Section 46 of the Housing Act 1925 was apparently inconsistent with the provisions of the 1919 Act, and owners of property acquired under powers contained in the 1925 Act argued that compensation should be calculated in accordance with the earlier Act. The owners argued that in so far as the later Act was inconsistent, it ought not to have effect.

In both cases, this approach was rejected. In the *Vauxhall Estates* case, Avory J, in holding that the 1925 Act repealed the inconsistent provisions of the 1919 Act, stated categorically that an Act of Parliament could not protect itself against future conflicting Acts of Parliament. This view was affirmed in the *Ellen Street Estates* case by both Maugham and Scrutton LJJ who both agreed, in effect, that Parliament could alter any Act previously passed either by express or implied repeal. This body of case law is fundamental to the traditional view (see Wade, 'The Basis of Legal Sovereignity' [1955] CLJ 172) but it is possible to question the authority of the judicial utterances. The real problems in relation to legislative supremacy arise in a much more complex form than did the questions under the 1919 Act. As is shown below the issues might be whether supremacy has been surrendered, or whether legislation can be entrenched. Such issues did not face the courts in the above cases. Moreover it is arguable that the strongest statements in the *Vauxhall* and *Ellen Street Estates* cases are *obiter dicta*. It seems doubtful that the 1919 Act did seek to limit future legislative ability. (See Mitchell, *Constitutional Law*, 2nd ed. (1968), p. 75 et seq.; Wade [1955] CLJ 172; and for a particularly detailed review of the cases see Jaconelli, *Enacting a Bill of Rights* (1980), p. 162 et seq., and Elkind (1987) 50 MLR 158).

Nonetheless those who would wish to uphold the traditional view at its strongest would argue that any attempt to place restrictions upon the legislative ability of a future Parliament is doomed to failure. Moreover, even if Parliament flouted guarantees contained in earlier legislation, they would argue that the courts would not intervene in order to question the validity of an Act of Parliament overriding those guarantees.

The Role of the Courts

The role of the courts here is crucial. Suppose an Act was passed which could not be amended except by a two-thirds majority of the House of Commons, and further suppose that by a simple majority the Act was amended by a later Act. The traditional view of the role of the courts in relation to the supremacy of Parliament would suggest that the courts would find that:

(a) the later Act would repeal the earlier one so far as the two proved inconsistent, and

(b) they had no jurisdiction to question the procedural issues relating to the passage of the later Act.

In a series of cases the courts have laid down the 'enrolled Act' rule: 'All that a court of justice can do is to look to the Parliament roll: if from that it should appear that a Bill has passed both Houses and received the royal assent, no court of justice can inquire ...' (per Lord Campbell in *Edinburgh & Dalkeith Railway Co.* v *Wauchope* (1842) 8 Cl & F 710, 725; for an entertaining case in support of this view see *Martin* v *O'Sullivan* (1984) 57 TC 709). The most recent expression of this view was in 1974 in *British Railways Board* v *Pickin* [1974] AC 765 in which Mr Pickin alleged that the British Railways Board had fraudulently misled Parliament when promoting a private Act which effectively deprived Mr Pickin of a strip of disused railway land to which he would have been entitled had the Act not been passed. The House of Lords held that whether a public or a private Act of Parliament is involved, the courts lack the jurisdiction to examine parliamentary proceedings and declare the Act a nullity — even when fraud is alleged.

Thus if Parliament sought to offer constitutional guarantees by entrenching them against implied repeal by a later inconsistent Act of Parliament, a strict adherence to the traditional view would mean that not only would the later Act prevail, but the procedural requirements necessary for the entrenchment would not be enforced by the courts. This manifests a degree of logic and consistency, but can cause constitutional problems in a number of areas. Thus arguments have developed which seek to challenge the wisdom of the traditional view.

DEPARTURES FROM THE TRADITIONAL VIEW

If Britain wished to adopt a Bill of Rights, the problem would be how to protect the whole or any part of it against implied repeal. It has been suggested (by Auburn (1972) 35 MLR 129) that a sufficiently strong statement against implied repeal might be heeded by the courts. This view rests largely upon a Canadian case R v Drybones [1970] SCR 282 in which Joseph Drybones successfully argued that a charge of being intoxicated outside an Indian Reserve under a Federal Indian Act of 1952 was inconsistent with provisions of the later Bill of Rights (1960) guarding against discrimination. However, it seems that the Supreme Court of Canada took the view that they had equal power to render inoperative provisions of statutes which (unlike the Indian Act) followed the Bill of Rights.

Other writers have suggested that legislation could be entrenched by placing procedural limitations upon future Parliaments — see, for example, Jowell and Oliver, The Changing Constitution, 3rd ed. (1994), ch. 2. In general these writers look to case law involving legislatures outside the UK for support. Thus in Harris v Dönges [1952] 1 TLR 1245, an entrenching provision of the South African constitution demanding a two-thirds majority in the Parliament of South Africa, prior to the revocation of provisions within the constitution, was upheld. The court refused to recognise purported legislation which did not follow this procedure as a valid Act of Parliament. And in the difficult case of Attorney-General for New South Wales v Trethowan [1932] AC 526 the Privy Council upheld the requirements for a referendum prior to the abolition of the Upper House of the New South Wales legislature. The Trethowan case may be of limited application because it involved a non-sovereign legislature which was subject to procedural requirements laid down by the United Kingdom Parliament (see the comments of Evershed MR in Harper v Home Secretary [1955] Ch 238).

Nonetheless Trethowan neatly illustrates the point that there exists a class of legislation for which it may be appropriate to prescribe the manner and form of any subsequent amendment. Indeed it may be possible to envisage a similar argument arising in the UK. Section 1 of the Northern Ireland Constitution Act 1973 states that:

> ... it is hereby affirmed that in no event will Northern Ireland or any part of it cease to be part of Her Majesty's dominions and of the United Kingdom without the consent of the majority of the people of Northern Ireland voting in a poll held for the purposes of this section.

The question arises as to why, in view of the doctrine of legislative supremacy, Parliament should choose to enact what appears to be a guarantee as to its future conduct. Logically there are three possibilities. Perhaps the Parliament in 1973 misunderstood the doctrine and believed it could bind for the future (in which case the mistake is a long-standing one since the 1973 Act replaces constitutional guarantees offered in the Ireland Act 1949). Or it may be that the section is intended only as a political guarantee. Commenting on a similar provision, s. 4 of the Statute of Westminster 1931, Viscount Sankey LC said, '... indeed, the Imperial Parliament could, as a matter of abstract law, repeal or disregard s. 4 of the Statute. But that is theory and has no relation to realities' (*British Coal Corporation* v *R* [1935] AC 500, 520). Perhaps we could say that in reality any future government would have to meet the requirements of s. 1 of the 1973 Act, but this does not explain why it was necessary to offer a political guarantee in statutory form when the statute could be disregarded and even impliedly repealed by later enactments. This leaves the final possibility that Parliament in passing the 1973 Act both desired and correctly believed that future Parliaments would be bound by the provisions contained in s. 1. Let us therefore examine the possibility that (contrary to the traditional view) limitations may be placed upon the supremacy of Parliament. Moreover, the impact of European Community law must lead to a reconsideration of the doctrine of implied repeal. In *R* v *Secretary of State for Transport, ex parte Factortame Ltd* [1990] 2 AC 85 (discussed in chapter 6), the House of Lords appears to have held that where UK law is inconsistent with directly enforceable Community law, the latter must prevail.

POSSIBLE LIMITATIONS

Constitutional theorists are forced to accept that some limitations could be placed on the legislative supremacy of Parliament, if only to accommodate fundamental constitutional change. Such limitations might be substantive (affecting the substance — the subject-matter — of the legislation) or procedural (governing the procedures to be adopted in passing valid legislation). The most obvious example of a substantive limitation is the Act of Union with Scotland 1707. A single British Parliament was achieved by the Parliaments of Scotland and England legislating to surrender their supremacy in favour of a new legislature. Having done so, the limitation was binding since the individual Parliaments no longer existed and could hardly reassert their supremacy (for a contrary view see Munro, *Studies in Constitutional Law* (1987), ch. 4). Although less dramatic, more recent examples are available also. Thus s. 4 of the Statute of Westminster 1931 provided that:

> No Act of Parliament of the United Kingdom passed after the commencement of this Act shall extend, or be deemed to extend, to a Dominion as part of the law of that Dominion, unless it is expressly declared in that Act that that Dominion has requested, and consented to, the enactment thereof.

Thus by granting autonomy to the Dominions, Parliament could not in practice ignore s. 4, since an Act which attempted to apply to a Dominion against its wishes would be disregarded by the legal system operative in that Dominion. Hence the view of Lord Sankey in *British Coal Corporation* v *R* [1935] AC 500, 520, quoted above. In addition since 1931 many dependent territories have also gained legislative independence by a surrender of legislative supremacy on the part of the United Kingdom Parliament. Thus Viscount Radcliffe stated in *Ibralebbe* v *R* [1964] AC 900, 924: 'There is no power to legislate for Ceylon: to do so would be wholly inconsistent with the unqualified powers of legislation conceded.'

These issues arose more recently in the case of *Manuel* v *Attorney-General* [1983] Ch 77, a complex case in which Canadian Indian chiefs sought a declaration that the Canada Act 1982 was invalid since the United Kingdom Parliament had no power to amend the Canadian Constitution without the consent of the Indian people of Canada. Megarry V-C found no reasonable cause of action — a view upheld in the Court of Appeal. However Slade LJ was prepared to accept (without finally deciding the issue) the argument put by the plaintiffs that the Statute of Westminster 1931 regulated the power of Parliament to make law for the Dominions so that no Act after 1931 purporting to extend to a Dominion could be valid unless it complied with the Statute of Westminster. In fact the case turned upon the issue that the Canada Act contained a declaration that the relevant consents had been obtained, and, in line with *British Railways Board* v *Pickin* [1974] AC 765 the Courts refused to enquire further. This case represents a slight chink in the armour of parliamentary supremacy — albeit in the form of yet another *obiter dictum*.

However, some procedural restrictions may be more straightforward than the consent of an outside body or third party to the legislative process. One point of view is that Parliament is free to redefine itself as it did by both the Parliament Acts 1911 and 1949. Therefore entrenchment becomes possible by an ordinary Act of Parliament redefining the legislature for certain purposes by, e.g., demanding a two-thirds majority of both Houses of Parliament. This view has its critics (see Mirfield (1979) 95 LQR 36) as does a necessarily companion view that the courts are free to challenge Acts of Parliament not meeting the procedural requirements of the existing law. This is because under a more traditional view, in spite of a purported requirement of a two-thirds majority, the courts would simply recognise the later Act. For an insight into this debate see Heuston, *Essays in Constitutional Law*, 2nd ed. (1964), ch. 1, as opposed by Wade, *Constitutional Fundamentals* (1980), ch. 3.

Although by no means an insignificant debate in terms of its practical implications, one may question how fruitful such argument is. Both sides debate the likely reactions of the judiciary in a purely hypothetical situation. In practice what would matter in that situation is the allegiance of the judiciary to whatever legal order was the subject of the legislation protected by the attempted entrenchment. After all, as Wade [1955] CLJ 172 opined at p. 188, 'The rule of judicial obedience ... is the ultimate *political* fact upon which the whole system of legislation hangs'.

There is no doubt that the doctrine of the legislative supremacy of Parliament poses complex problems relating to the interchange of constitutional theory and practical politics. This together with the fundamental role of the doctrine and the furious academic debate as to possible limitations upon the legislative ability of Parliament, has led to the widespread popularity of this topic on examination papers in constitutional law. You cannot be expected to reconcile all of the opinions ventured by legal academics. You can, however, set yourself the much more limited task of grasping the leading arguments and seeking to understand the practical consequences of the various viewpoints for the constitution of the United Kingdom.

REVISION

Topics like parliamentary supremacy present a problem when it comes to revision. Although there is not a great body of case law to familiarise yourself with, a good deal of your time will be spent considering the contrasting views of various theorists. This type of material is not so susceptible to learning by heart as various other parts of the course, and probably you are better avoiding attempting this. Considerable difficulty is experienced by students attempting to learn material from books which they do not fully understand. This topic is by no means the only legal material that is heavily theoretical in nature, but it is studied by most students at an early stage in their law course. It is important to discover a method of studying and revising this type of material that can be utilised later in the course while learning such subjects as jurisprudence.

The key to success in this area lies in careful reading of the relevant literature. Some of the significant works are cited above and in the reading list for this chapter. Others will appear on your lecture hand-outs and tutorial sheets, and it is obviously wise to concentrate on those contributions to the debate which your own tutor views as significant. Concentrate on understanding what you read. Be patient and avoid temptation to pass on before fully appreciating a particular line of reasoning.

Initially, only a persistent and disciplined approach to complex issues will lead to your gaining the ability to grasp arguments quickly and to a true lightening of your load. Prepare your own reading list drawn from a critical appraisal of the material on your hand-outs. Aim in advance to cover a range of issues, and do not be frightened to discard material if you fear that you have an impossible amount of ground to cover. Thus, as a beginning, you might decide to isolate a part of a textbook or a journal article covering the following issues:

(a)   How parliamentary supremacy arose.
(b)   The scope of the doctrine.
(c)   The doctrine of implied repeal.
(d)   The role of the courts in challenging the validity of statutes.
(e)   Possible limitations upon legislative supremacy.
(f)   The problem of entrenching legislation.

In seeking a clear exposition of the above subject-matter, do not be afraid to switch from one book to another. No textbook is universally strong on all issues, and you may find that a particular work expresses a difficult point in a clear and concise manner. On the other hand you should avoid the type of book that offers a straightforward explanation only by oversimplification. When you are satisfied that you have found suitable coverage of an issue, re-read the piece and this time note the key arguments adopted by the writer. Look for one strong thread of argument and avoid comments by way of an aside. You may start with quite detailed notes if you prefer, but try to rewrite these by condensing the argument so that you put less and less down on paper, knowing that more and more is carried in your head. Thus you become able with the help of a few headings on the paper to fill in the gaps in the argument, more than adequately, from your own knowledge.

Cover each of your major topics in turn by looking at a single text, so that even if it takes you longer than you wished, you are left, nonetheless, with some coverage of all issues. Once this is done, however, you may use spare time to add to your existing knowledge by further reading. This time detailed notes may not be so necessary, but ask yourself whether the new reading elaborates upon the earlier reading. If so, jot down the new material, and when you have finished the reading, incorporate this material into your previous line of argument, so that gradually your coverage of the area becomes more refined. Remind yourself that each such refinement adds to the quality of your analysis and therefore heightens your eventual examination mark. However, you must never include material that you have read inadequately, or which confuses rather than enlightens you. Of course, some of the later reading may be contrary to an earlier view. There is no need to worry about this just yet, simply add to your existing notes a reference to the conflict of views thus: 'But see X who argues that Y fails to take account of the case of . . .'.

The time to attempt any reconciliation of conflicting opinions (if this is even possible) is when your reading is complete in that you have reached the target which you have set yourself or exhausted the time available. Moreover you must leave time to reflect upon the material you have covered. The easiest way to do this is to work through past examination questions (and some assistance with this is given below) or to turn your mind to the practical political questions which centre around the doctrine of the supremacy of Parliament. Perhaps if you had read law in the 1950s or early 60s the study of this doctrine would have seemed an interesting academic exercise with little wider significance. This is no longer the case. There are a host of important political considerations which follow from the doctrine today. These include the impact of EC law, which is considered in the following chapter, and issues such as the constitutional position of Northern Ireland, the abolition of the House of Lords, the adoption of a Bill of Rights and so on. Awareness of the political consequences of a particular view of legislative supremacy is a quality increasingly valued by examiners. In addition because legal writers may allow desired political ends to shape their arguments on constitutional issues, the full comprehension of a line of opinion may lay in its consequences. Ask yourself, for example, what the consequences of a written constitution or modern Bill of Rights would be in terms of the transfer of political power. Too few students, for all their learning of case law, stretch themselves this far.

All of this is important for another reason. The issues referred to above are part of a live (and lively) political debate. This means that, especially in areas such as EC law, issues of sovereignty are dynamic. The stance taken by the House of Lords in such cases as *R* v *Secretary of State for Transport, ex parte Factortame Ltd* [1990] 2 AC 85 and *(No. 2)* [1991] 1 AC 603 and *Litster* v *Forth and Dry Dock Engineering Co. Ltd* [1990] 1 AC 546 (considered in the following chapter) are significant. They make it less easy to speak of a unified approach to all issues of sovereignty. A number of writers seem happy to assert that particular problems of parliamentary sovereignty require particular answers (see Allan (1983) Oxford J.L.S. 22; Munro, *Studies in Constitutional Law*). If this is so, you may wish to consider working through, in your revision, some of the particular issues concerning sovereignty. In other words you may approach the subject on a topic by topic basis — EC, House of Lords etc. This approach is good preparation for problem questions.

So much for revision, but how can a student be expected to convert the knowledge gained from this careful preparation into examination success? The following sections consider typical examination questions. They seek to illustrate that, although apparently difficult, many involve a reasonably straightforward application of the traditional view in juxtaposition with less fundamental views upon the legislative supremacy of Parliament. Such questions may take the form of an essay but unlike the material in the previous chapter, it is relatively easy to frame questions in this area in the form of a problem.

THE EXAMINATION

In terms of a problem-type question upon the doctrine of parliamentary supremacy, a little thought will tell you that there are only a limited number of questions which can be set. Most of these will be variations upon a theme involving the doctrine of implied repeal and the ability of the courts to adjudge the validity of legislation. Most will encapsulate the political issues referred to above. Thus rather than ask whether s. 1 of the Northern Ireland Constitution Act 1973 succeeds in binding further Parliaments, the question could be put as follows:

At the British general election of 1999, the Papist-Liberal Alliance gain a large majority on the basis of a manifesto which includes plans for the unification of Ireland, although they have won only one seat (Belfast: Falls Road) in Northern Ireland. Without any poll under the Northern Ireland Constitution Act 1973 having been held, the new Government introduces the Northern Ireland Constitution (Repeal) Bill, which seeks to repeal s. 1 of the 1973 Act. In the Commons second reading the Secretary of State for Northern Ireland, Murphy, states that a Unification of Ireland Bill will follow the repeal.

Using their powers under the Parliament Acts 1911 and 1949, the House of Lords reject the Repeal Bill. Murphy announces to the Commons: 'We shall bide our time, but Ireland shall soon be united'. Parsley MP, a Northern Ireland Protestant politician, wishes to prevent the passage of both Bills.

Discuss the legal issues.

Incidentally do not be concerned that this scenario occurs in 1999. The setting for such questions is often some time in the future in order to avoid confusion and emphasise that the events are fictitious.

A Problem Question on Entrenchment

Similarly questions upon a Bill of Rights and whether it might be entrenched can be expressed in the form of a problem. Let us take an example:

> The Centre Forward Party of Great Britain is returned to power at a general election by a narrow majority following a promise to introduce a Bill of Rights. The new Government passes through Parliament the Citizens' Rights Act 1999, s. 1 of which states:
>
>> No amendment or repeal of this Act shall be valid without the consent of a three-quarters majority of both Houses of Parliament.
>
> Section 9 of the Act states (*inter alia*):
>
>> All citizens indicted on a criminal charge shall be entitled to trial by jury.
>
> In 2000 the Centre Forward Party is defeated in the House of Commons during a debate on the Government's handling of terrorist attacks by the Pink Brigade. It loses the subsequent election and the Outside Right Party is returned to power with a small majority in the Commons and massive support in the Lords. Parliament then passes the Terrorism Act 2001, s. 36 of which gives the Home Secretary power to dispense with jury trial in cases involving terrorist murders, since threats to jurors are feared. The 2001 Act has a majority of five in the Commons, and almost total support in the Lords.
>
> Fawkes is arrested and charged with murder following the bombing of a Westminster wine bar. He is convicted after a hearing before a single judge and is sentenced to life imprisonment. He appeals on the ground that the 2001 Act is void.
>
> Discuss.

You ought to be able to commence your answer to this question with some prepared introductory remarks. Since the possibility of a question on implied repeal is relatively strong, this is precisely the sort of area in which (as was suggested in chapter 2) you can organise a carefully worded introduction in advance. This might outline the nature of the doctrine of the legislative supremacy of Parliament, establish its traditional and fundamental role within the unwritten constitution (perhaps using a suitable quotation) whilst pointing to the difficulties which might arise, as in this case, if an attempt is made to entrench legislation against future repeal.

It is then important to ensure that the main issues in the question are straightforward. In fact the problem is relatively simple. An earlier Act of

Parliament seeks to lay down a special amending procedure. A later Act seeks to make an amendment without following that procedure. The dual questions are whether the later Act will prevail over the earlier Act and whether the courts will intervene on the basis of an apparent procedural irregularity. It is probably better to deal with these issues directly and state the consequences of a particular view for the appellant in the problem. Thus the view that Parliament could never fetter its successors, supported by *Ellen Street Estates Ltd* v *Minister of Health* [1934] 1 KB 590 and *Vauxhall Estates Ltd* v *Liverpool Corporation* [1932] 1 KB 733, would be a basis for upholding the conviction on appeal. It might be argued, using *British Railways Board* v *Pickin* [1974] AC 765 and the related line of cases, that in addition the courts would claim to lack jurisdiction to rule upon the validity of the later Act. On the other hand, it could be argued, on the authority of *R* v *Drybones* [1970] SCR 282, that even without the special amending procedure, the courts would be prepared to accept that the Citizens' Rights Act imposed an effective check upon a Parliament wishing to legislate contrary to the provisions of that Act. On this view, *Drybones* (and perhaps *Manuel* v *Attorney-General* [1983] Ch 77) illustrates the preparedness of the courts to accept that a statute of constitutional significance may demand a modification of traditional judicial notions of implied repeal.

However, the Citizens' Rights Act goes further than did the Canadian Bill of Rights 1960 (in the *Drybones* case) by attempting to guard against repeal except by a particular procedure. The possibility of such control over the manner and form of later legislation is recognised by a certain body of case law such as *Attorney-General for New South Wales* v *Trethowan* [1932] AC 526 and *Harris* v *Dönges* [1952] 1 TLR 1245 and you could present the argument (as outlined by Heuston perhaps) that these cases, though persuasive in authority, form the basis of a view of legislative supremacy which allows a binding redefinition of Parliament for certain purposes. Of course, the consequence of this view is that it would necessitate the courts having the jurisdiction to question the validity of an Act of Parliament — at least in those instances that Parliament has attempted procedural entrenchment. *Pickin*, and the cases which you may have referred to earlier, may not seem to allow for this possibility, but as Jaconelli has written (in *Enacting a Bill of Rights*), 'Judicial recognition of the unique nature of a Bill of Rights may lead in turn to the abandonment of old views of the nature of parliamentary sovereignty'.

You should not forget to follow through the consequences of these arguments in terms of their practical implications for Fawkes. In this question you are not actually asked to 'advise Fawkes' but you are asked to discuss the case. Clearly if the traditional view prevails and the 2001 Act is upheld, then Fawkes's appeal against conviction must fail. On the other hand if the courts are prepared to uphold the 1999 Act then presumably the appeal would meet with success, for the later Act would be rendered inoperative, at least in so far as the two are inconsistent. The absence of a jury at Fawkes's trial is clearly contrary to the fundamental provision of the earlier statute.

However, important though these conclusions are to Fawkes, it matters little which, if any, you choose to promote. What does matter is that you evaluate fully the more significant counter-arguments. Some views contrary to your main argument may receive only limited treatment, for, in the above answer, we have hardly dealt with Wade's criticism of Heuston's view on procedural entrenchment. But examination time is precious and you may be restricted to writing 'Heuston's argument (strongly criticised by Wade) is that …'. What is certain is that the presentation of one side of the coin (say the traditional view) is insufficient. Flip the coin over and show both sides before allowing yourself, if you wish, to state your own considered opinion, or play safe, and state that the answer depends ultimately upon the allegiance of judicial opinion towards the Citizens' Rights Act.

Note that the above question deals with one form of entrenchment — procedural — and not with the wider-ranging possibility of substantive entrenchment. However, the latter is considered below in relation to the specific issue of EC law.

An Essay Question

As is illustrated, it is quite straightforward to present a question upon the supremacy of Parliament in the form of a problem if the examiner so wishes. Equally it is easy simply to ask the question outright. This is all the more true since very obvious questions are not likely to give obvious answers. Thus if the question was: 'To what extent can Parliament bind itself as to the subject-matter and the manner and form of later legislation?', then the question would be barely capable of being answered in 45 minutes. Essay questions may be widely based, therefore, and this is true even if they choose to concentrate upon particular problems arising out of the doctrine of parliamentary supremacy. The following is a good example:

To what extent is Parliament able to change its composition so as to produce statutes which will validly bind later Parliaments?

It is very important to consider all of the issues which might be encompassed within a question of this kind. On one reading, it might be said to express the problem question upon the Citizens' Rights Act in a different way. Can Parliament be redefined to produce the procedural entrenchment of particular legislation? But it is something more than this. Ought we not to discuss provisions such as s. 1 of the Northern Ireland Constitution Act 1973, and s. 4 of the Statute of Westminster 1931 which we omitted in our previous discussion? And what of the Parliament Acts 1911 and 1949, do they carry any binding force? Moreover the latter question could, if we wished, take us on to the question of the abolition of the House of Lords.

It is this type of question that best illustrates the need for careful planning. Even a well-prepared student could end up presenting a random set of ideas rather than a carefully argued essay. This is hardly surprising when two writers are able to devote 30 pages of the *Law Quarterly Review* in a closely reasoned, if somewhat provocative, debate: see 'Can the House of Lords Lawfully be Abolished?' (Mirfield (1979) 95 LQR 36) and 'Is the House of Lords Immortal' (Winterton (1979) 95 LQR 386). Faced therefore with a potentially huge question, the student should act as follows. Be positive and quickly list the range of issues which might arise under this head. Decide if there are any of these issues which might be omitted. However, it is wiser to cover a number of issues succinctly than to devote the whole of the time to a single limited line of argument. Let us take one example of how a bright and well-read student could fail to achieve a mark commensurate with ability by covering too little ground.

When considering the question of whether Parliament may change its composition, the Parliament Acts 1911 and 1949 are clearly important. So let us suppose our bright student begins here initially intending to argue that if Parliament has been able to redefine itself for the purposes of the above Acts, it would be able to do so for other purposes. This is a notion which our bright student has taken from a favourite textbook (de Smith) but because he or she is well-read a possible flaw is apparent to our student. Some writers argue that measures passed by the Parliament Act procedures are examples of delegated rather than primary legislation (delegated legislation is considered later in chapter 9). Wade has persistently taken this view, and Hood Phillips goes even further in concluding that the 1949 Act is of doubtful validity. His underlying arguments is that the body (Queen and Commons) receiving delegated power under the 1911 Act later proceeded to widen the scope of their delegated authority — a course which Hood Phillips views as illegal and illogical. However, in addition to de Smith, Marshall (*Parliamentary Sovereignty and the Commonwealth*, p. 42 et seq.) argues strongly in favour of the primary legislative force of measures passed under the Parliament Act procedures. This view arguably receives some authority in the use of the Parliament Act procedures to pass the War Crimes Act 1991 (see Ganz, 'The War Crimes Act 1991 — why no constitutional crisis?' (1992) 55 MLR 87). Note, however, that this whole argument is subject to criticism by Munro (*Studies in Constitutional Law*) as misconceived. In his view that Acts provide not limitations, but *additional* permissive powers. The considerations here are complex and involve questions as to the nature of delegated legislation and concerning the interpretation of the Parliament Acts themselves. Whilst our student is embroiled in such difficulties three-quarters of an hour slips quietly by, and there is still no answer to the question of the validity and status of the

1911 and 1949 Acts and the procedures thereunder — let alone an answer to the question actually set.

A happier scenario would include the student who decided on two important issues at the outset, namely to give a wide coverage of the issues involved and to argue along a particular line (for example, that Parliament can redefine itself in order to either facilitate or restrict the legislative process). This student might begin with the traditional view, and note that on any analysis some limitations must be possible in that they involve the surrender or delegation of sovereignty. The Parliament Acts could be considered although long discussions could be avoided by writing the examination answer thus:

Clearly Parliament has proved capable of redefining itself as with the Parliament Acts, and whilst measures passed under the procedures introduced by the Acts have been regarded as delegated legislation (Wade) and the 1949 Act is thought to be of doubtful validity (Hood Phillips), such a change in the composition of Parliament is widely accepted as valid. Certainly writers such as Marshall and de Smith would so regard it.

Acceptance of the redefinition of Parliament under these Acts would necessitate allowing the possibility of abolition of the upper chamber and a more permanent change in the composition of the legislature. Equally, therefore, changes which added additional stages to the legislative process could prove valid. The Northern Ireland Constitution Act, and its require-ment for a poll approving a legislative measure, could be mentioned here before moving on to the question of entrenchment (citing the case law from other jurisdictions and admitting its limited authority). You would have to argue, of course, that in the case of any redefinition of Parliament, much would depend on how the courts perceived their role in their new and rather precarious position. Note here the decision of the Court of Session in *MacCormick* v *Lord Advocate* 1953 SC 396. Even assuming that the Act of Union 1707 created 'fundamental law', this is a far cry from asserting that the courts have jurisdiction to rule that there was primacy over later legislation (here, the Royal Titles Act 1953).

Such an answer involves a race through some of the most significant issues of the supremacy of Parliament. But the question is a wide one and involves a broad answer. By being sensitive to the need to point to authority at the right time, it is possible to convince an examiner that you know the area well without becoming entangled in detail. It is equally possible and quite permissible to follow one line of argument providing that the range of authorities, and the debate thereon, is considered. At the end of the examination it is better to leave having proven your competence to answer challenging questions fully and directly, rather than having illustrated your brilliance in a single area of a much, much larger question.

CONCLUSION

No one can say that the legislative supremacy of Parliament is an easy topic to understand, if only because the doctrine is bedevilled by diametrically opposed arguments. But one can say that many students make the subject more difficult than it is. The subject becomes easier if the following points are borne in mind. It is not necessary to be able to resolve the various arguments — many are incapable of resolution involving, as they do, speculation as to events which may (or may not) occur in the future. What you can do, however, is to split the arguments up into two main camps. Those who support the traditional view that limitations upon the legislative supremacy of a future Parliament are generally impossible, and those who argue that such limitations as to either legislative substance or procedure could be achieved. You ought to be familiar with at least some proponents of each view, and certainly with the authorities which they cite in their favour.

Above all, be patient in your revision. The material on this topic cannot be mastered, literally, overnight. Be prepared if necessary to break from this topic and revise another area which involves a less theoretical input, and which contains more substantive law (police powers, for example). Often there is not the time to take too long a break in a hectic revision schedule, but, in this context, a change is the next best thing to a rest. By careful reinforcement in a series of shorter sessions you may become sufficiently familiar with the material to provide yourself with a basic armoury with which to attack even the most difficult of examination questions.

From there, examination preparation consists of following through the consequences of such learning in terms of both legal theory and practical political problems. Too much learning and too little thought can produce some obvious faults in students studying this topic. Finally, perhaps more than with most topics, practice in working through questions on previous examination papers may pay dividends. Avoid the temptation to learn, by heart, notes which you do not fully understand. Favour methods which will force you to rehearse, again and again, the complex material which comprises the legislative supremacy of Parliament.

FURTHER READING

Blackburn, R., (ed), (1993) *Written Constitution for the United Kingdom* (London: Mansell).

Bradley, A. W., 'The Sovereignty of Parliament — in Perpetuity?' (Chapter 4) in Jowell, J., and Oliver D., (eds), (1994) *The Changing Constitution*, 3rd ed. (Oxford: Clarendon Press).

Dicey, A. V., (1959) *An Introduction to the Study of the Law of the Constitution*, 10th ed. (London: Macmillan).

Griffth, J., (1991) *The Politics of the Judiciary*, 4th ed. (London: Fontana).

Harlow, C., (1986) *Public Law and Politics* (see Chapter 10 — 'Refurbishing the Judicial Service') Harlow, C., (ed) (London: Sweet and Maxwell).

Hewart, G., (1929) *The New Despotism* (London: Benn).

Institute for Public Policy Research, (1993) *A Written Constitution for the United Kingdom*, Blackburn (ed) (London: Mansell).

Jennings, W. I. (1959) *The Law and the Constitution*, 5th ed. (London: University of London Press).

Klug, F. and Wadham, J., 'The "Democratic" Entrenchment of a Bill of Rights: Liberty's Proposals' [1993] *Public Law* 579.

Wade, H. W. R. (1980) *Constitutional Fundamentals* (London: Stevens).

6 EUROPEAN COMMUNITY LAW

On 1 January 1973, following the passage of the European Communities Act 1972, Britain became a member of the European Economic Community. As a result of the Treaty on European Union, negotiated at Maastricht, which finally came into force in 1993, we now have the European Community ('EC') and European Union (a wider concept, including the various treaties of the Member States, plus other policy agreements, formulated with regard to such matters as home and foreign affairs and defence). In June 1975 a referendum was held upon the issue of Britain's continuing membership of the Community. A wide-ranging debate ensued as leading figures in Government argued passionately for or against membership while notions of collective ministerial responsibility were abandoned. The result was a two-to-one majority in favour of remaining within the Community. From then on, there has been no doubting the considerable and growing impact of accession to the Community upon British constitutional law. Moreover as the Community expands across Europe, and Community law develops, we move ever nearer to a federal system. In the words of Lord Denning in *H. P. Bulmer Ltd* v *J. Bollinger SA* [1974] Ch 401, 418: '... the Treaty [of Rome] is like an incoming tide. It flows into the estuaries and up the rivers. It cannot be held back.'

Law schools, despite the arrival of separate options in EC law within the degree structure, are likely to include the legal implications of EC membership within the constitutional law course. This is because, notwithstanding the passage of time since British accession, many constitutional problems remain. In large part these problems are simply an extension of those raised in the previous chapter. Does the traditional view of parliamentary supremacy hold good, or has EC law achieved what many claimed (even feared) that it would, and dealt a body blow to such theories of legislative supremacy?

If this is so, however, why deal with the issue in a separate chapter? There are two significant points to bear in mind when directing your mind towards problems of legislative supremacy in the context of EC membership. The first is that although you will have to consider the status of the European Communities Act 1972 as fundamental or entrenched legislation, the question is one which might be described as substantive entrenchment. This is to say that the restrictions arguably placed upon the supremacy of the British Parliament relate to the subject-matter of legislation (as opposed to the imposition of procedural restrictions). Secondly, it seems clear that the Community purports to be a new legal order, raising the question of whether there exists the one new legal order to which Britain subscribes, or whether Britain takes what might be described as a 'dualist' approach assuming there to be two separate legal systems operating alongside each other. In fact, Britain clearly takes the latter view whilst the Community institutions clearly take the former — hence the constitutional problems. This difference of view is illustrated by political arguments concerning a 'federal' Europe, which Britain opposes. However, the Community possesses some powerful weapons in its legal armoury, including an assumption of the primacy of Community law over domestic law and certain laws having direct application or direct effect in Member States.

So these are good reasons to devote a separate chapter to the material. Indeed, so much ground is there to cover that it is less easy here to give a comprehensive analysis of the material before examining how best to revise it and prepare for examination questions upon it. Consequently some detailed legal issues are left until late into the chapter. This material is largely concerned with questions of parliamentary supremacy, and both chapters 5 and 6 must be considered as a package.

One reason why there is a wide expanse to be covered is the necessity to be familiar with the European institutions and sources of EC law. You may be faced with a problem question which refers (for example) to a Council Directive. What is the Council? What are Directives? You are hardly in a position to offer an effective answer to the question unless you know. However, since whole books are devoted to the EC institutions, you cannot be expected to know the material in extensive detail. Clearly you must be guided by your own course, and the level of the coverage therein, but as a general guideline the material may be divided into two parts. First there is the role of the European institutions and sources of EC law, and then the questions relating to the impact of British accession upon our constitutional and legal systems. Broadly you will require a working knowledge or understanding of the former, and a more detailed appreciation of the latter. More is said about this later, in the section on revision; let us examine the above topics in detail before considering this.

AN OUTLINE OF THE EUROPEAN INSTITUTIONS

There exists not one Community, but three: the European Coal and Steel Community (ECSC, 1952), the European Community (EC, as founded under the Treaty on European Union 1993, amending the Treaty of Rome 1958) and the European Atomic Energy Community (Euratom, 1958). Although after 1958 these communities had a common parliamentary and court structure, they originally had separate commissions and councils. However, in 1967 there was an important step towards merger when a single Commission, and Council, were instituted to deal with matters arising out of all three treaties. Thus there are four main institutions, Commission, Council, Parliament and Court, vested with the responsibility of furthering the aims of the treaties. We shall examine these in turn.

The Commission

Each Member State, with the agreement of other Members, must appoint Commissioners. Britain, along with other larger Members, appoints two Commissioners. Such appointments last for four years and are renewable. Member States cannot dismiss their Commissioners although, as Margaret Thatcher showed in 1984, it is possible to show your disapproval of a Commissioner by failing to renew the appointment — as was done with Ivor Richard who was the Labour nominee. There is a rapidly developing convention in Britain that the two Commissioners (currently Leon Brittan and Neil Kinnock) will be chosen from each of the two major parties. Commissioners are supposed to remain independent of the Governments of Member States and the Council.

The Commission may be seen, therefore, as protecting the Community interest as a whole, by seeing that the treaties are upheld, and by initiating Community policies. If it seems that a treaty provision is infringed, then the Commission will be the relevant body to investigate and rule upon the infringement (subject to review by the Court of Justice). In the case of a breach of the EC Treaty it would seek explanation from the State involved, but if these explanations are not accepted and the breach continues, it will issue a reasoned *opinion*. If the Member State refuses to take note of the *opinion*, the Commission will refer the matter to the Court of Justice, whose judgment is binding.

This policing role is not the only or even the most significant function of the Commission, however, since it also occupies an executive position. There is no obvious parallel to this in Britain. Unlike the Cabinet, the Commission is not so obviously responsible to the Parliament. Moreover its decision-making is subject to the agreement of the Council (see below) prior to implementation. On the other hand, the decision-making takes the form of the preparation of detailed laws which will seek to implement Treaty articles and Community policies. This is not to suggest that the Commission itself has no responsibility for policy initiatives. The Commission is given extensive powers to promote the efficient working of the treaty provisions in their respective fields.

The EC Treaty outlines the broad areas of economic activity to be pursued, leaving the institutions of the EC to decide upon the detailed plan. Not only does this allow the Commission to innovate, but it passes to the European institutions a considerable body of law-making power, for as we shall see, much of this law is directly applicable and enforceable in all Member States, and may radically revise the existing domestic law of those States.

The Council of Ministers

The Council is a body of representatives of the Governments of the Member States. The representatives are generally Government Ministers, but the same Minister will not generally attend all meetings of the Council. This is because it may be more appropriate (for example) to send the Minister of Agriculture to a particular meeting than to send the Foreign Secretary. Having said this, the Foreign Secretary of the Member State will generally be regarded as that country's representative on the Council. Each State will provide a President of the Council in turn, since the position rotates each six months amongst the Member States.

The votes within the Council are allocated in accordance with the size, and political and economic influence of the Member States. The voting procedures under the Treaty are complex since a simple majority vote may be necessary for certain issues, whilst a qualified majority (of weighted votes) or unanimity may be necessary elsewhere. The proposed accession of Austria, Finland, Norway and Sweden led to protracted negotiations over whether the majority required should be increased — or not; and a compromise solution was reached such that two larger Member States may be able to combine in order to block legislation. In practice, however, following a French boycott of Community institutions in 1966 in dissatisfaction at a majority decision against their interest, there is a convention of unanimity being required where significant interests of a Member State are at issue. Attempts are made to avoid embarrassing rifts by reaching unanimous decisions. In consequence, decision-making has traditionally been the result of protracted negotiation and compromise over long periods of time. In order to overcome such delays, the passage of legislation has been considerably speeded up of late. Under the Single European Act of 1986, measures necessary for the completion of the single market (see below) may be passed under a revised legislative procedure requiring only qualified majority. This particularly affects such issues as free movement of goods, services and capital, and the abolition of tariff barriers. The range of policies where a qualified majority will suffice has been extended in the 1993 Treaty.

In order to overcome these difficulties, since 1974 the various heads of Government have met to discuss the possibilities of political cooperation between Member States and to discuss at the highest level the more contentious issues of Community policy. Somewhat confusingly, the meetings have been given the label of the 'European Council'. A good example of the type of issue dealt with in such meetings would be the renegotiation of the provisions of UK membership in the early 1980s. The presence of the European Council provides a useful illustration of how the EC institutions have evolved to meet problems arising under the treaties. The European Council has no formal status under the treaties but its presence is vital to the smooth running of the Council of Ministers.

The Council of Ministers receives proposals from the Commission, and the Ministers are assisted in their consideration of such proposals by a body known as the Permanent Representatives Committee. As the name suggests, this Committee comprises of representatives of the various Member States who carry ambassador status and who are attached on a permanent basis to the Council. Such assistance is necessary because of the major role of the Council in the decision-making and legislative process.

The European Parliament

Since 1979 Members of the European Parliament (MEPs) have been directly elected. Prior to this, there were simply nominated representatives from the legislatures of the Member States. The UK returns 81 MEPs, the same number as France, Germany and Italy. Other Member States have been apportioned fewer seats. There are no national groupings within the Parliament, but a series of broad political groups have developed. The Parliament's role cannot be compared to that of the UK legislature, since it is not a legislative body. It does, however, have increasing consultative powers, even in some areas extending to a veto, and acts as a barometer of opinion available to the Council in its consideration of proposals emanating from the Commission. On the other hand certain functions of the European Parliament are easily recognisable to the UK observer. The committee work of MEPs in reviewing the activities of the Commission might be compared with the Commons' select committees. Written and oral questions are also an obvious method (as in the UK) for both discovering and influencing the current work of both Commission and Council.

Although the Parliament is not so powerful a body as one might expect, therefore, in three respects it can wield considerable power. Firstly, the Commission is answerable formally to the Parliament. Parliament may dismiss the Commission in its entirety providing it does so by a two-thirds vote of the whole assembly. The Parliament has never exercised this power — as one might expect — but it does focus the attention of the Parliament upon the activities of the Commission. The second major power concerns budget. Apart from powers of allocation of the budget for institutional, administrative and social expenditure, the Parliament does have the right to reject the budget as a whole. In December 1979, the Parliament exercised its authority in this area by rejecting the budget proposed by the Commission for 1980. It took similar action in 1984 and 1985 — for the background see *R v HM Treasury, ex parte Smedley* [1985] QB 657. When it took further action in 1986, the European Court ruled void a declaration of the President of the Parliament that the 1986 budget had been adopted. Finally, the Parliament may bring enforcement proceedings in the Court if either the Commission or the Council fails to meet an obligation to take action — see, for example, *European Parliament v Council of the European Communities* (case 13/83) [1985] ECR 1513. The trend seems to be, therefore, that the influence and authority of the directly elected Parliament is growing over time.

This is a process which has been assisted by the Single European Act, which introduced new powers (in Article 149) for the Parliament to amend or reject the decisions of Council under the cooperation procedure. A rejection by Parliament will require unanimity on re-consideration by Council. An amendment will force the Commission to review the Parliament's suggestion within a month. In the light of these powers, the Committees of the Parliament have assumed significant influence in the single market programme. These powers have been extended in key policy areas, to enable an effective veto, under the co-decision procedure, instituted by the 1993 Treaty.

The Court of Justice

The European Court is given the title of the Court of Justice which differentiates it from another 'court', namely the Court of Auditors — the body charged with the auditing of the Community budget. More recently, also, a Court of First Instance has been introduced, by the Single European Act, to relieve the case load of the Court of Justice by hearing some of the less weighty cases. The judges of the Court of Justice are appointed by agreement between the Member States and they then elect a President from amongst their number. The legal process within the Court is akin to the Continental rather than the UK system. Written arguments are usual, the procedure is inquisitorial and the judges are assisted in their deliberations by an advocate-general. An advocate-general will prepare an opinion in a case prior to the decision of the Court. The advocate-general's opinion is not dissimilar to the judgment in an English court, but the judgment of the Court of Justice is much more typical of European courts — generally a rather brief statement of the relevant legal principles. It will be a unanimous judgment divided succinctly into two parts — the reasons and the ruling.

Initially many of the issues arising before the Court concerned the alleged infringement of the Treaties by Member States in actions brought by the Commission. More recently actions by the States against the Commission's decisions have been brought in addition to individual applications. Article 177 of the Treaty of Rome allows national courts to refer matters involving questions of Community law. These referrals take the form of a request to the Court of Justice to rule upon a question of interpretation (or occasionally applicability) of Community law. A distinction must be drawn between primary Community law (e.g., a Treaty Article) and secondary Community law (i.e., the acts of Community institutions). In the case of the former a request can be for interpretation only, but in the case of the latter, the Court of Justice is permitted to rule on the validity of the law. A national court cannot hold an act of a Community institution invalid (see *Foto-Frost* v *Hauptzollamt Lübeck-ost* (case 314/85) [1987] ECR 4199). Article 177 offers individuals significant, if indirect, opportunities to challenge Community acts and throughout the Community such referrals have increased. This has had two effects. Firstly, Community law has become inseparable from the domestic law of Member States in certain areas. Secondly, a consistent body of case law has arisen from the rulings of the Court of Justice, and this in turn has allowed courts in Member States to apply Community law. As Lord Denning MR said of the ECJ in *Application des Gaz SA* v *Falks Veritas Ltd* [1974] Ch 381, 'That Court is moulding the law of Europe into a single whole which every country of [the Community] must obey'.

We must be careful, however, not to talk of precedent. As with continental courts, the Court of Justice does not consider itself bound by its previous decisions. These may be influential, of course, but so too will be the comments of jurists in the analysis of those provisions. In a similar way approaches to statutory interpretation will vary. A literal and a mischief approach may be used, but the Court will also seek to ensure that any interpretations reached will fit easily into the domestic law of Member States. This is no easy task for it involves more than finding an outcome satisfactory to a majority of States — rather it ought to be appropriate to all. In addition, because the Court looks to further the application of the Treaty, it will generally pay regard to the social and economic consequences of a particular interpretation in a manner which would seem odd in a UK court. However, this point should not be overemphasised, for the ECJ is modelled in part on the Conseil d'Etat in whose tradition past decisions tend to be more significant than in civil law systems generally. If you have a chance to attend the ECJ during your course (and increasingly opportunities to visit the European institutions are offered to law students), then go. You will find it different but not totally foreign to the English approach.

Let us examine the case of *Macarthys Ltd v Smith* (referenced below) which illustrates the workings of the European Court of Justice and its relationship with the United Kingdom courts. This was a case which concerned equal pay for men and women under the Equal Pay Act 1970. Under the Act, a woman was entitled to equal pay if employed upon 'like work' to that of a man in the same employment. In the case the woman applicant was appointed as a stockroom manageress. She was paid £10 per week less than the man whom she replaced, and brought a claim for equal pay which both the industrial tribunal and the Employment Appeal Tribunal upheld ([1978] ICR 500). The Court of Appeal had some doubt, however, as to whether the applicant fell within the 1970 Act for arguably she was not employed on like work to a man in the same employment — the man having left the employment before she commenced the work. However, the Court of Appeal had to consider an *article* of the EC Treaty, art. 119, which states that:

Each Member State shall ... ensure and subsequently maintain the application of the principle that men and women should receive equal pay for equal work.

Unlike the UK statute, the Treaty *article* and its principle of 'equal pay for equal work' made no obvious requirement of contemporaneous employment between the man and the woman. Moreover this view was reinforced by a Council *Directive* of 1975 which read:

The principle of equal pay for men and women outlined in article 119 of the Treaty ... means, for the same work or for work to which equal value is attributed, the elimination of all discrimination on grounds of sex.

Lord Denning MR felt that art. 119 was clear and ought to apply on the facts of *Macarthy's* case notwithstanding the fact that the woman succeeded the man. He was prepared to construe the UK statute in conformity with the Treaty in order to reach such a result. The other two judges could not agree with this. They felt that a grammatical interpretation of the Equal Pay Act demanded contemporaneous employment between the woman and the man. This produced a conflict between the European view expressed in both the *article* and the *Directive*, and the UK statute, and a preliminary ruling from the European Court of Justice was therefore requested under art. 177 of the Treaty (see [1979] ICR 785).

In effect the ruling, when it came, supported the interpretation of Lord Denning. The Court of Justice were not prepared to go so far as to state that a woman could introduce a hypothetical man and claim that if he happened to be in employment he would receive higher pay, but where comparison was possible with a predecessor, this should be allowed. On reference back to the Court of Appeal, this ruling was accepted (see [1981] QB 180). Article 119 took priority over any inconsistent provision within the 1970 Act, and Mrs Smith's claim was therefore allowed.

Later, in *Commission of the European Communities* v *United Kingdom* (case 165/82) [1983] ECR 3431 the European Court ruled that the Equal Pay Act failed to comply with art. 119. This led to the passage of the Equal Pay (Amendment) Regulations 1983, amending the Equal Pay Act 1970. However, doubt remained as to how far these amendments met the requirements of EC law. In *Hayward* v *Cammell Laird Shipbuilders Ltd* [1988] AC 894 the employer argued that although the employee got less money, this was redressed by other more favourable employment terms. Had this argument succeeded, it would have effectively rendered the 1983 amendments a nullity. However, in the House of Lords, Lord Mackay of Clashfern LC, giving the leading judgment reviewed the whole history of the legislation before construing the Equal Pay Act to allow a woman on work of equal value with a chosen male in the same employment to claim the same basic wage and overtime rates as that male. In the later case of *Pickstone* v *Freemans plc* [1989] AC 66 the House of Lords were faced with another equal value claim which the Act did not apparently cover. Yet they took a purposive approach to s. 1(2)(c) of the Act using *Hansard* to help construe the regulations (a precursor to the radical review contained in the House of Lords' ruling in *Pepper* v *Hart* [1993] AC 593) so as to interpret the subsection in accordance with EC law. In so doing they evaded some of the wider issues of the relationship between the two legal systems. (See the remarks of Lord Oliver on the role of industrial tribunals in handling EC law and cf. *Duke* v *GEC Reliance Ltd* [1988] AC 618).

SOURCES OF EC LAW

It may be clear from what is written above the there are a number of sources of Community law, and a short note is necessary in order to clarify the workings of a complexity of legal provisions. The Treaties are the starting-point of any examination of Community law; in the words of Donaldson MR, they are 'designed to express principles' (see *R* v *HM Treasury, ex parte Smedley* [1985] QB 657 at p. 669). The *Treaty articles* provide the principal source of EC law, and these may have direct application within the territory of a Member State. An illustration is provided by the case of *Van Gend en Loos* v *Nederlandse Administratie der Belastingen* (case 26/62) [1963] ECR 1 which involved a reference to the ECJ, by a Dutch court, asking whether art. 12 of the EC Treaty applied directly so as to allow individuals to claim rights which the courts must protect. The European Court expressed the view that:

Independently of the legislation of Member States, Community law therefore not only imposes obligations on individuals but is also intended to confer upon them rights.... These rights arise not only where they are expressly granted by the Treaty, but also by reason of obligations which the Treaty imposes in a clearly defined way.

This principle of direct effect has been extended to cover not merely the primary *Treaty articles* but also secondary sources of law. By this we mean legislation emanating from the Community institutions. Thus, for example, there may be *Regulations* of the Council or the Commission. These are directly applicable and binding in their entirety upon all Member States and may be directly effective. They may be compared with *Directives* which require each Member State to achieve a particular result, but allow some freedom as to the method adopted to reach the required end. Notwithstanding this freedom given to Member States, there may be a possibility of a Directive creating enforceable individual rights in the national courts. Thus in *Van Duyn* v *Home Office* (case 41/74) [1974] ECR 1337 (but cf. *R* v *Secretary of State for the Home Department, ex parte Santillo* [1981] QB 778) which concerned a *Directive* upon the free movement of workers, it was said that a provision of Community law could produce a direct effect upon the State or a body which is an emanation of the State if:

(a)   there was a clear and precise obligation upon a Member State;
(b)   which was not subject to condition or limitation;
(c)   and which left the Member State with no real discretion as to whether to apply the Community rule.

See further *Marshall* v *Southampton and South West Hampshire Area Health Authority* (case 152/84) [1988] QB 401 and *Foster* v *British Gas plc* (case 188/89) [1991] 1 QB 405.

Indeed, it now appears that a person who suffers loss because of a Member State's failure to implement a Directive may sue the State for damages: see *Francovich* v *Italy* (cases 6 & 9/90) [1992] IRLR 84.

Finally a *Decision* made by the Council or the Commission may be addressed to a single State or an individual (or individual company) within a State, and it will bind in its entirety those to whom it is addressed. You will notice that there is a distinction between law which is directly applicable (requiring no transformation to incorporate the rule into the national legal system) and that which has direct effect (allowing an individual to rely in the national courts on a particular Community right). (See further *Amministrazione delle Finanze dello Stato* v *Simmenthal SpA* (case 106/77) [1978] ECR 629.)

THE INCORPORATION OF EC LAW INTO THE UK

The conclusion of a treaty is an exercise of the royal prerogative. As such, a treaty will need to be given legislative effect before it will be enforced by the courts of the UK. Thus, to take an example which is often a source of confusion for students, the European Convention on Human Rights is a treaty, signed by the UK in 1950. Therefore, if this country is in breach of the provisions of the Convention, although a citizen of this country could take a case before the European Court of Human Rights, there may be no legal redress before our own courts. Thus in *Malone* v *Metropolitan Police Commissioner* [1979] Ch 344, it was held that the tapping of Malone's telephone was not contrary to English law but in *Malone* v *UK* (1981) 4 EHRR 330 it was found to be a breach of art. 8 of the Convention.

In the case of the EC Treaty, however, this was originally given legislative effect by the European Communities Act 1972. This was necessary if only because of the direct applicability of certain Community laws (discussed above). Section 2(1) of the Act provided a mechanism whereby Community law was transported into the British legal system by stating that:

All such rights, powers, liabilities, obligations and restrictions from time to time created or arising by or under the Treaties, and all such remedies and procedures from time to time provided for by or under the Treaties, as in accordance with the Treaties are without further enactment to be given legal effect or used in the United Kingdom shall be recognised and available in law, and be enforced, allowed and followed accordingly.

Note that the words 'from time to time provided for' allow future directly applicable Community laws to be incorporated without further enactment. In the case of conflict with UK law, EC law would prevail if only because such a requirement is already one of the 'obligations ... arising ... under the Treaties' and such a resolution of the problem would be in 'accordance with the Treaties'. This view is reinforced by s. 3(1) which states that questions as to the validity, meaning or effect of Community law shall be determined in the courts of the UK in accordance with the principles laid down by the European Court. The significance of this is that the European Court of Justice long ago held that in the event of a conflict between domestic law and Community law the latter should prevail (*Costa* v *ENEL* (case 6/64) [1964] ECR 585). Section 3(1) is curiously British in flavour, giving binding force to the judgments of a court which (as we have seen) does not operate within a formal system of precedent.

The final piece in this jigsaw of incorporation is s. 2(4) which reads (in part):

... any enactment passed or to be passed ... shall be construed and have effect subject to the foregoing provisions of this section.

This provision is open to a number of interpretations, and the judiciary have often shunned opportunities to explore its intricacies (see, for example, *Garland* v *British Rail Engineering Ltd* [1983] 2 AC 751 at 771 but see also *R* v *Secretary of State for Transport, ex parte Factortame Ltd* [1990] 2 AC 85 and *Litster* v *Forth Dry Dock and Engineering Co. Ltd* [1990] 1 AC 546 discussed below). However, the phrase 'foregoing provisions of this section' obviously includes s. 2(1) and the principles of direct applicability thereby allowed. One possible interpretation of this section therefore (and, it is submitted, the most likely one) is that in the event of a conflict between UK and EC legislation the latter will prevail. This is not necessarily to include the situation in which there is express repeal of the 1972 Act, but would include all possibilities of implied repeal or amendment so as to entrench the statute against such possibilities.

The consequences of the passage of the 1972 Act are striking and we begin to understand why EC membership commands the attention of constitutional lawyers. The sovereign power of Parliament has been restricted by imposing limits upon the subject-matter of UK legislation. EC law may apply directly in this country, and the courts are asked to enforce it. Thus to take an example, when a female worker was dismissed at age 62 as having passed the normal retirement age (60 for women and 65 for men) art. 5(1) of Directive 76/207 prohibiting discrimination in working conditions was said to apply to dismissal and to be sufficiently precise in its terms to apply against a State authority acting as employer. This ruling led to legislation allowing harmonisation of retirement ages for men and women (see *Marshall* v *Southampton and South West Hampshire Area Health Authority* (case 152/84) [1986] QB 401 and the Sex Discrimination Act 1986). Indeed, State restrictions on the level of award in respect of the discrimination (without reference to the level of loss) were in breach for not providing an effective remedy: see *Marshall* v *Southampton etc. (No. 2)* (case C 271/91) [1994] QB 126. In another case, *Barber* v *Guardian Royal Exchange Assurance Group* [1991] 1 QB 344, the Court of Justice declared that payments under Guardian Royal's pension plan constituted pay so that differential age qualifications for eligibility to the pension breached principles of equal pay under art. 119. As UK pension schemes have traditionally worked differently for men and women you can imagine that this decision is likely to prove costly for the pension industry, although the effective date of the change has been limited by both the European Court and the terms of the Treaty of European Union (see also *Coloroll Pension Trustees Ltd* v *Russell* (1994) *The Times*, 30 November 1994).

If a UK statute conflicts with a Community law then the 1972 Act suggests that the Community law must be applied by our own courts in preference to the conflicting statute and this is true even if the statute is passed long after

1972. This is a line of argument which runs contrary to the whole of the traditional view of the legislative supremacy of Parliament. But is the argument a valid one?

Of late, the judiciary in the UK courts have been forced to consider the issues of potential conflict between EC and UK law more directly than before — although, as we shall see, they have not shown a great deal of relish for the task until the *Factortame* case, which concerned new criteria for registering fishing vessels under the Merchant Shipping Act 1988. This legislation would have disallowed the registration, as British, of some 95 fishing vessels, largely owned by Spanish nationals, which had traditionally operated out of Britain. The owners of these vessels challenged the legislation on the grounds that it violated a number of Treaty articles (which broadly gave rights to establish and run businesses anywhere within the Community). The UK argued that since there were fishing quotas for each Member State (to preserve fish stocks), legislation was necessary to determine who could take advantage of a national quota. The Divisional Court made an art. 177 reference to the Court of Justice, but, in view of the time that it would take for this to be heard, granted an interim injunction in favour of the shipowners restraining the impact of the 1988 Act. Neither the Court of Appeal nor the House of Lords upheld this injunction. However, the House of Lords (*R v Secretary of State for Transport, ex parte Factortame Ltd* [1990] 2 AC 85) referred the point to the Court of Justice, and although refusing an interim injunction against the Crown, conceded a number of points on sovereignty.

Lord Bridge stated that if the fishing vessel owners 'succeed before the European Court in obtaining a ruling in [their] support ... those rights will prevail over the restrictions imposed by ... the 1988 Act and the Divisional Court will ... be obliged to ... give effect to those rights'. Indeed, this was the eventual outcome, the ruling of the ECJ being accepted, to the effect that the local and national residence requirements were discriminatory and contrary to EC law and ineffective in relation to other Member States of the EC (see *R v Secretary of State for Transport, ex parte Factortame Ltd (No. 3)* (case C 221/89) [1992] QB 680, and see now *R v Secretary of State for Employment, ex parte Equal Opportunities Commission* [1995] 1 AC 1 discussed below. So it seems that directly effective Community legislation prevails over legislation in the member state. The precise consequences of this decision for the doctrine of implied repeal, or for the significance of entrenched legislation or, indeed, for the precise relationship between UK and EC law remain to be elaborated.

In the meantime, a separate action was taken by the European Commission against the UK seeking the suspension of the 1988 Act on the basis of its breach of a number of articles in the Treaty of Rome. The Court of Justice held both that the Act breached Treaty articles concerning discrimination on grounds of nationality, and that, in view of the fact that the fishing vessel owners' livelihoods were at stake, an interim order should suspend the operation of the Act (*Commission of the European Communities* v *United Kingdom* (case 246/89 R) [1989] ECR 3125). This was implemented by the Merchant Shipping Act 1988 (Amendment) Order 1989 (SI 1989/2006).

On an art. 177 reference by the House of Lords themselves, concerning whether interim relief could be available against the Crown, despite established principles in the UK to the contrary, the ECJ ruled that a national court was required (not simply permitted) to set aside national law if that would have prevented the grant of interim relief giving effect to Community law. The Court of Justice said that effective enforcement of EC law demanded this.

In view of this judgment, the House of Lords granted the relief that the vessel owners sought, saying that the balance of convenience demanded that they stay in business (*R* v *Secretary of State for Transport, ex parte Factortame Ltd (No. 2)* (case C 213/89) [1991] 1 AC 603). They made it clear that they would only do so where they were satisfied that a challenge to what seemed, otherwise, valid law was so obviously valid on the face of it that the exceptional course of intervening would be justified. Clearly, however, a good prima facie argument that EC law had been breached was one ground of this highly exceptional course of action (see Oliver, 'Fishing on the Incoming Tide' (1991) 54 MLR 442). Compare *R* v *Secretary of State for the Environment, ex parte RSPB* (1995) *The Times*, 10 February 1995 where interim relief was held to be inappropriate.

This case tells us much about how the English courts would deal with a conflict between directly effective EC law and an inconsistent, later UK statute. There appears to be a recognised duty on the part of the UK court to override any rule of national law in conflict with a directly enforceable rule of EC law. This is on progression from previous pointers in this direction, for instance, the case of *Litster* v *Forth Dry Dock and Engineering Co. Ltd* [1990] 1 AC 546. That case involved the Transfer of Undertakings (Protection of Employment) Regulations 1981 which were said to implement inadequately Directive 77/187 which sought to protect the employment rights of workers whose employer was changed by a business transfer. In an earlier ECJ case, *P. Bork International A/S* v *Foreningen af Arbejdsledere i Danmark* (case 101/87) [1988] ECR 3057, it had been said that employees dismissed for reasons connected with the transfer ought to be protected by the Directive. The UK Regulations demanded employment 'immediately before the transfer'. In *Litster* there was a gap between the dismissal of the employees and the business transfer. Therefore, although the employees were dismissed for reasons connected with the transfer, they were not employed immediately before the transfer. Citing *Pickstone* v *Freemans plc* [1989] AC 66, the House of Lords claimed to adopt a purposive construction of the UK Regulations. In fact it actually changed the wording of the UK Regulations to achieve harmony with the EC Directive. Again, a number of issues remain. Would the court have done so if the Regulations had not been designed to implement directly effective EC law (cf. *Duke v GEC Reliance Ltd* [1988] AC 618)? Would the court have changed the wording of primary legislation? Suppose the UK Regulations had been specifically worded to reject the EC provision? Nonetheless *Litster* is important. It shows that the UK courts will give effect not only to EC law but also to the ECJ interpretation of it. Note also the important ECJ ruling in *Marleasing SA v La Comercial Internacional de Alimentación SA* (case C 106/89) [1990] ECR I-4135, which suggest that national courts are required to construe domestic law in accordance with the terms and objectives of a relevant Directive, whenever that law came into force.

We shall return to these cases when examining the handling of examination questions. Before that, let us consider some issues relating to revision.

REVISION

At the beginning of this chapter, we spoke of acquiring a background knowledge of EC institutions, before considering the impact of EC law upon UK law. It is impossible to generalise but you are unlikely to be questioned simply upon the role of the EC institutions in your constitutional law course. Instead, the examination is more likely to concentrate upon those issues which are seen as being of prime concern to constitutional lawyers. Such issues relate to the impact of UK accession upon traditional notions of the legislative supremacy of Parliament. There are two significant consequences for your revision strategy which would seem to follow from this.

The first is that you must be sufficiently familiar with EC law to answer a question concerning its impact within the UK. Although direct questions upon the EC institutions may not appear, you might need to know, therefore, what force an EC Regulation carries. You may be asked directly about the working of art. 177 of the Treaty, or you may be expected to possess knowledge of the direct applicability of EC laws, because of the major consequences of such material for the independence of the UK courts and for the doctrine of parliamentary supremacy. On the other hand you will not ordinarily be expected to know the details of treaty articles or the substance of EC law in general. You might choose to divide up the subject for revision purposes, therefore, so that you have a broad working knowledge of (say) the functions of the European Parliament, gained through a thorough reading of a sufficiently good text upon the institutional framework of the EC. You may, then, divert your efforts to a more detailed learning of issues having a direct bearing upon legislative supremacy.

The second consequence tied to the concentration upon issues of supremacy of Parliament is that the EC material should be grouped together with the material in chapter 5. In other words it would be idiotic to revise the general area of parliamentary supremacy without considering the specific instance of the effect of EC law. For revision purposes, therefore, especially if revising a selection of topics only, it is wiser to treat the whole area as one topic rather than two. This may mean that the topic is a vast one, and it is not impossible that two questions will appear upon the paper, but you should not count on this and if it happens then that is a bonus.

Handling Statutes

One point which may be clear from the substance of this chapter, thus far, is the significant nature of the European Communities Act 1972. Clearly it is vital to familarise yourself with this statute in general and ss. 2 and 3 in particular. You may be permitted to take *Blackstone's Statutes on Public Law* or some other collection of statutes with you into the examination room or you may be provided with them. If so, this will save you the trouble of detailed learning, but it is imperative that you are fully aware of the workings of the Act in advance of the examination. You will not have time to begin to construe the statute in the middle of an examination. The only advantage of the provision of the Act is to jog your memory if you find yourself stuck, or to make available the precise wording if your argument rests upon an exact construction of a particular section. Consequently, it is not so great a disadvantage if no such facility is available. In this case, it may be necessary to learn small portions of the Act in order to illustrate a particular point, but for the most part a careful paraphrasing will suffice. For example, you might state that s. 2(1) provides that: all Treaty obligations 'from time to time arising ... are without further enactment to be given legal effect'. This is quite manageable and gives the sense of the section. Do not try to be clever by learning the full section. It is difficult to do, wastes valuable revision time, and may even waste valuable examination time where you could offer a quicker rendition of the sense of the statutory provision.

As with any other area of law, the use of case law and the citation of authorities are essential ingredients in a good answer. In this instance, much of the case law will stem from the European Court of Justice, and may concern a wide range of issues arising in cases from a number of different countries. Because of the incorporation of the principles emanating from the European Court into our own legal system by virtue of s. 3(1), these cases are a significant part of a good answer. Potentially, the case law here is vast, but there are examples available from both textbooks and case books. Few cases have been mentioned thus far, but the following section on examination technique shows how European cases may be introduced into an answer.

We shall also see in that section that, at least in terms of problem questions, the examiner is likely to try to manufacture a conflict between the EC and domestic law. Once again therefore, you are able to deduce a number of variants which might appear as an examination question. More is said on this theme later, but one obvious form of preparation is to devise a number of situations which might produce a conflict and decide in your own mind what the likely consequences will be. To date major and direct conflicts between EC law and a UK statute have been rare, so that what might happen is a matter for speculation. There is, however, a wealth of helpful material which you might use to devise your answers. This is now considered in the context of the type of questions which might be asked.

THE EXAMINATION

The type of problem discussed in relation to the supremacy of Parliament in the previous chapter may well appear in relation to EC law. That is to say that a question on implied repeal might include the scenario in which an Act of Parliament comes into conflict with an EC law, raising the question of whether the attempted entrenchment of the European Communities Act 1972 successfully limits Parliament in the future, and protects itself from implied repeal. This is an issue discussed below, but it is the type of issue that may be raised as an essay question. In such a case the question may be slightly wider in its scope than the more particular points raised in the problem. An example of this would be the following question which utilises a memorable metaphor from de Smith's *Constitutional and Administrative Law*:

> The United Kingdom Government has seated Parliament on two horses, one straining towards the preservation of parliamentary sovereignty, the other galloping in the general direction of Community law supremacy.
>   Discuss.

There is a vast range of material which might be included in an answer to this question. One immediate point to sort out is when and how has Parliament been seated upon these horses? The answer is that in theory they seated themselves upon the horses for the executive decision to enter the Community gave rise to the passage through Parliament of a statute in 1972 seeking to make provision for the UK entry. The question primarily relates to the 1972 Act therefore and essentially it demands to know the constitutional and other legal implications of that Act.

Many students faced with the type of question which seems to split into two or more parts are immediately tempted to devote an equal amount of space or effort to each part in turn. This is not always wise. An essay which begins 'Let us examine the first horse' is likely to spend a good deal of time explaining in fairly basic terms the notion of parliamentary supremacy, and runs the risk that there will be no time left to discuss the subject of Community law. And it is Community law to which the question primarily relates. The good student will recognise this to be at the heart of the matter, and realising the limitations upon time may well choose to concentrate efforts in that direction.

This is a strategy which students find hard to grasp and equally hard to accept. The point is that you do not always need to work upon your answer by beginning at basement level. It is quite legitimate to assume that your examiner has ample knowledge of the subject-matter, so that it may not be necessary to deal with the nuts and bolts, leaving you more time and opportunity to illustrate your grasp of more challenging material. Moreover, the particular essay question may dictate to you upon what level you do begin and it is helpful to recognise this. Thus a question which simply asks whether parliamentary supremacy is indeed the keystone of our constitution (as Dicey described it) may require an exposition of the basic foundation of the traditional view of parliamentary supremacy. In the above question, however, especially in view of the time factor, it ought to be perfectly legitimate simply to refer to the traditional view without offering a detailed analysis. If this material is bypassed in order to allow the introduction of case law which relates specifically to the relationship between EC and UK law, the examiner is likely to appreciate this.

This will, of course, require careful planning, but in the question referred to above, the logical way to proceed is to explain the way in which the 1972 Act seeks to incorporate EC law, and since the question refers to Community law supremacy, explain the concept of the primacy of EC law. Then working towards a conclusion, it is possible to consider the inherent conflict between these notions and those of the legislative supremacy of the UK Parliament. If time allows, some attempt at a possible resolution of this conflict would be an ideal ending.

The incorporation of EC law into the legal system of the UK by the 1972 Act is discussed above, and it is not intended to repeat the arguments here. Suffice it to say that a complete answer might explain how EC law is given effect by virtue of the 1972 Act before explaining the nature of the Community law given direct application and effect. The significant point is the underlying assumption within Community law that, in so far as domestic law is incompatible with it, the former must prevail. Some authority for this proposition should be cited. If you are able to locate a short passage from a judgment which seems especially pertinent, then this will obviously impress. Thus in *Van Gend en Loos* v *Nederlandse Administratie der Belastingen* (case 26/62) [1963] ECR 1 it was said that:

> ... the Community constitutes a new legal order ... for the benefit of which the States have limited their sovereign rights, albeit within limited fields.

This is apt and accords with *Costa* v *ENEL* (case 6/64) [1964] ECR 585 (see above), in which the European Court ruled that the whole notion of the direct applicability of EC law would be meaningless 'if a State could unilaterally nullify its effects'. Thus the rule within EC law would be that directly applicable Community law would render existing or even new domestic legal provisions inoperative (see *Amministrazione delle Finanze dello Stato* v *Simmenthal SpA* (case 106/77) [1978] ECR 629 and *Internationale Handelsgesellschaft GmbH* (case 11/70) [1970] ECR 1125).

What the question asks us is whether Britain has accepted the concept of a new legal order as mentioned in *Van Gend en Loos* or whether our primary allegiance is to the principle of the continuing legislative supremacy of Parliament. This is a question faced by other Member States which have shown themselves willing to apply Community law even though there exists conflicting domestic law which is later in time. The latter has been disregarded (see the Belgian example of *Minister for Economic Affairs* v *SA Fromagerie Franco-Suisse 'Le Ski'* [1972] CMLR 330). From here you ought to link up once more to your consideration of ss. 2 and 3 of the 1972 Act and explain that they would seem to allow the possibility of the *'Le Ski'* approach in the UK, but explain, also, how such an approach would run absolutely contrary to traditional notions of sovereignty.

Thus you have explained successfully how it is that Parliament is seated upon two horses, and technically this answers the question. However, since it is so obvious that they are straining in quite different directions it is helpful to conclude with some assessment of which horse is the stronger of the two. To abandon the metaphor, has Parliament surrendered its legislative supremacy or not? In the final analysis, few commentators would seriously suggest that if Parliament wished as a matter of political judgment to leave the Community they would be unable to do so because the 1972 Act is entrenched against express repeal. The UK courts do not seem to subscribe to such a view (see *Macarthys Ltd* v *Smith* [1979] ICR 785 and *Garland* v *British Rail Engineering Ltd* [1983] 2 AC 751). To that extent Parliament remains supreme. However, to a lesser extent it does appear to have placed a limitation upon itself so as to prevent the implied repeal of the 1972 Act by a later inconsistent Act of Parliament.

It can indeed be argued that *Factortame* takes this a stage further. Now, in *R* v *Secretary of State for Employment, ex parte Equal Opportunities Commission* [1995] 1 AC 1, the House of Lords has granted declarations to the effect that certain differences in the protection of full-time and part-time workers under the Employment Protection (Consolidation) Act 1978 were incompatible with art. 119 of the EC Treaty (and related Directives 75/117 and 76/207). In this, the EOC's concern, according to Lord Keith of Kinkel was 'simply to obtain a ruling which reflects the primacy of Community law enshrined in s. 2 of the 1972 Act'.

This view can be supported by dicta from a growing body of case law. This is considered below in relation to the problem question in the next section. It may be summarised by saying that there has been a gradual realisation on the part of the judiciary of the necessity of giving effect, and even primacy, to EC law. At the same time this is done in the context and under the permit of the 1972 Act rather than through any allegiance to the 'new legal order'. The lesson for the student is twofold. First, in one sense it is wiser to put your money upon the Community horse the longer the race continues to run. The position changes rapidly and we are more attuned to Community law in a European structure. In time even express repeal may seem inconceivable. A good student should remain aware of the growing influence of the Community upon our legal system. Secondly, therefore, it is important to keep abreast of political and legal developments in this area. This is one sphere of our constitution in which change is rapid. An awareness of current developments is vital. The question which follows, for example, was drafted at a time of dispute with the blockade upon imports of British lamb into France, a set piece which appears to be re-enacted from time to time! Perhaps recent demonstrations against the export of live animals from the UK could lead to similar scenarios.

A Problem Question

Article 30 of the EC Treaty provides that 'Quantitative restrictions on imports and all measures having equivalent effect shall ... be prohibited between Member States'.

In order to protect the ailing fan-belt industry from competition from cheap French fan belts, Parliament enacts the Fan Belts Act 1999, which prohibits the importation of fan belts without a licence, and specifies that licences will not be granted in respect of more than a half-million fan belts a year (about a quarter of the number imported in 1998). Claude, an importer, seeks a High Court declaration that the Act is invalid by reason of its contravention of the Treaty, or alternatively that it only applies to imports from outside the EC. The Attorney-General concedes the breach of the Treaty but contends that the court has no power to declare an Act invalid or alter its plain meaning.

Discuss.

This question is really rather straightforward. To begin with it involves a relatively obvious type of conflict between UK and EC law — a direct conflict between a Treaty article and a post-accession UK statute. It could have been even more straightforward if the Fan Belts Act predated accession to the EC. In such a case since the 1972 Act would be the later statute the earlier Act would be modified in accordance with Community law on the authority of the 1972 Act. This would be rather too straightforward, however, since it would leave little scope for discussion. Consequently you can assume that in this type of problem question you may presume that there will be a conflict between post-accession UK legislation and Community law. Then there are a number of variables which you might need to consider. For example, the UK legislation may be primary or delegated legislation while the Community law may not be a Treaty article but a Directive or some other form of secondary legislation. Then again, the timing of the EC law in relation to both UK accession and the date of the UK statute may be significant. The obvious course of action is to sit down in advance of the examination and to work through the possibilities. If you can isolate the different types of question which may be put in advance of the examination, and decide how you might present the answer, the advantage is obvious.

A second reason why the above question is straightforward is that it outlines a number of possible answers in the body of the question itself. Three suggestions are made:

(a)   That the court uphold the 1999 Act.
(b)   That the 1999 Act be declared invalid.
(c)   That the 1999 Act be held to apply only to non-EC imports.

By following these points, it is not difficult to provide a comprehensive answer. Point (a) represents the traditional stance which has been fully explored in the previous chapter. A coverage of the relevant case law and academic argument, including a consideration of the ability of courts to challenge the validity of an Act of Parliament (see, for example, *British Railways Board* v *Pickin* [1974] AC 765) would lead to the following conclusion. Since it is in obvious conflict with a Treaty article, the 1999 Act must be taken to have restricted the reception of Community law as allowed by the 1972 Act in so far as the 1999 Act and the Treaty article are inconsistent.

Then it is possible to deal with points (b) and (c) and consider to what extent the UK courts would be prepared to accept the 1972 Act as entrenched with the consequence either that the whole of the 1999 Act be declared invalid, or that the 1999 Act be given effect only to the extent that it does not conflict with art. 30 (i.e., it is to be applied to non-EC imports only). Note that in fact point (c) is capable of two meanings. The one assigned to it above follows (for example) *R* v *Drybones* [1970] SCR 282 in suggesting that rather than declaring the whole of an Act invalid, the courts would seek to give effect to it in so far as it is possible and consistent to do so. However Claude's argument in the High Court that the court apply the Act only to non-EC imports may be a rather different argument. It could be argued that the combined effects of ss. 2(4) (especially the words 'shall be construed') and 3(1) of the 1972 Act allow as a matter of construction the judges of the UK courts to interpret Acts of Parliament so as to avoid the question of conflict with EC law wherever it would be possible to do so. Such an argument would support the liberal construction of the Equal Pay Act by Lord Denning MR in *Macarthys Ltd* v *Smith* [1979] ICR 785, or perhaps the more deliberate re-interpretation of UK law adopted by the House of Lords in *Litster*. The latter case did not involve primary legislation, however, and you might wish to point this out. Courts are used to challenges on secondary legislation but much more wary of confrontation with Parliament in relation to statutes.

Returning to the likelihood of the 1972 Act being found by the courts to be entrenched against repeal, the courts have on occasions considered this issue. The problem is that it is not always easy to find a consistent stream of dicta from an increasing number of cases. One way ahead might be to refer in your material to the lack of clear authority and say that:

> There was certainly an initial reluctance to depart from notions of the primacy of UK law as evidenced by the dicta of Lord Denning MR in *Felixstowe Dock & Railway Co.* v *British Transport Docks Board* [1976] 2 CMLR 655. However, in the equal pay case of *Shields* v *E. Coomes (Holdings) Ltd* [1978] 1 WLR 1408 the same judge seemed to accept the approach of the European Court in *Amministrazione delle Finanze dello Stato* v *Simmenthal SpA* (case 106/77) [1978] ECR 629 so as to allow directly applicable Community law to prevail even over a post-accession UK statute. This view presumably rests, however, upon an assumption that any such conflict was purely accidental for in another equal pay case *Macarthys Ltd* v *Smith* [1979] ICR 785 Lord Denning expressed the now renowned view that:
>
>> If the time should come when our Parliament deliberately passes an Act — with the intention of repudiating the Treaty or any provision in it — or intentionally of acting inconsistently with it — and say so in express terms — then I should have thought that it would be the duty of our courts to follow the statute of our Parliament.
>
> In the first *Factortame* case Lord Bridge's seeming acceptance of the supremacy of Community law seems to rest solely upon the powers given to the courts in the 1972 Act. This clearly raises the problem of how the courts might decide whether an Act of Parliament evinces an intention to repeal one or more of the provisions in the Treaty, but in so far as it suggests that the 1972 Act is entrenched against implied but not express repeal, it seems broadly to accord with judicial utterances upon this question, and a logical interpretation of ss. 2 and 3 of the 1972 Act.

Note the strategy that is adopted here to cope with the multiplicity of views in differing cases which have arisen. By confining discussion in the earlier part of the answer to cases involving Lord Denning, it is possible to convey the nature of the problem in a self-contained series of cases which ought to be easy to remember. No one can pretend that the remarks made by Lord Denning represent the last word on the subject, but they do fit neatly into the essay and produce a self-contained package which should appear attractive to examiners. A good examinee ought to consider in advance whether authority is quickly and easily available to answer points which it is possible to foresee might arise.

Dealing with the three points in this way does not entirely dispose of the question. So far what we have said is that if convinced of an intention to legislate in a manner directly contrary to EC law, the courts might demonstrate their allegiance to the legislative supremacy of the UK Parliament by refusing to declare the 1999 Act invalid. If not so convinced, however, the courts are increasingly likely to assert the primacy of EC law. It is in this area that some loose ends need to be tied in order to deal with the arguments of the Attorney-General, in the question, that the courts have no power to declare an Act invalid. Firstly, although *Pickin* is a House of Lords authority it does concern a private Act of Parliament and we saw in the previous chapter that there is some judicial recognition (albeit obiter) that the courts would recognise certain legislation as sufficiently fundamental to be considered entrenched (see *Manuel* v *Attorney-General* [1983] Ch 77). Secondly the UK courts have been increasingly prepared to make a reference to the European Court in accordance with art. 177 of the Treaty, and decide the case accordingly. The earlier discussion of *Macarthys Ltd* v *Smith* provides an example of this, as does *Factortame* (see also Ellis (1980) 96 LQR 511). Rather than directly rule on the validity of a UK statute in a situation of possible implied repeal, therefore, it seems likely that a reference would be made under art. 177.

CONCLUSION

Although the above discussion has concentrated on how best to approach examinations, this is not to say that the sole purpose underlying the study of a particular topic should be examination success. Thus one important reason for achieving a clear grasp of public law principles is that these will provide a foundation for your later law courses which may draw heavily upon these principles. This is true of course of the material relating to membership of the EC. In later courses as diverse as labour law, commercial law and social security law, you will be faced with relevant substantive provisions of EC law which exist alongside the UK law. Your understanding of the legal and constitutional implications of this dual system will be assumed. Hence it is wise to take the opportunity to become fully conversant with the material while you are able to do so.

In a sense this is not difficult to do. A careful reading of the case law will make you familiar with such issues as the workings of art. 177 and the principles of the direct applicability and effect of EC law. It ought also to increase your understanding as to the nature of secondary legislation within the Community, for example. On the whole you ought to be able to develop a sufficient grasp of the mechanics of the Community, leaving yourself free to grapple with the more complex constitutional questions arising out of the reception of EC law into the UK.

FURTHER READING

Bogdanor, V., *Britain and the European Community*, Chapter 4, in Jowell, J., and Oliver, D., (eds) (1994) *The Changing Constitution*, 3rd ed. (Oxford: Clarendon Press).

Lewis, C., and Moore, S., 'Duties, Directives and Damages in European Community Law' [1993] *Public Law* 151.

Walsh, B., 'The Appeal of an Article 177 EEC Referral' (1993) 56 MLR 581.

7 PARLIAMENTARY PRIVILEGE

Constitutional law students commonly regard the subject of parliamentary privilege as amongst the easier subjects within the syllabus. There is no doubt that this view stems in part from an underestimate of the complex nature of parliamentary privilege. Not only is the extent of the privilege obscure (especially in relation to freedom of speech) but there is an obvious conflict between the jurisdiction of the courts and Commons in this area, and this arises from the indistinct nature of the boundaries between the law and custom of Parliament, and the general law of the land. Moreover, it is difficult to come to terms with authority which stems from previous parliamentary practices and to reconcile this, or weigh it against, decisions in decided cases. Indeed there is a great temptation not to make this distinction and talk of, e.g., the *Strauss* case (1958) in one sentence and *Rivlin* v *Bilainkin* [1953] 1 QB 485 in the next as though both are decisions of the courts carrying equal authority. Moreover, if one deals with previous practices of the Commons alone, because Parliament does not seek to reach its conclusions in the way that a court might, and lay down guidelines for the future, the decision of the House in a particular instance may be inextricably bound up with the facts of that case, making it difficult to abstract any wider principle.

In addition the subject-matter is quite wide-ranging since the concept of privilege applies to both Houses of Parliament, although the nature of the privilege may vary between the two chambers. In fact this chapter deals only with the privileges of the Commons, since most examination questions will relate to these. The reason for this is that there is relatively little that is significant within the privileges of the Lords which does not apply equally to the Commons. In addition the history between the Lords and the courts or the Lords and the Monarch is relatively trouble-free, hence the more troublesome and problematic issues relating to the Commons are usually chosen for examination purposes. A second reason for the width of the subject-matter is the variety of privileges claimed by the Commons alone. Learning the list of privileges is very much a first step. Some students stop there, however, and are disconcerted to find that the examination question does not require a list of the various privileges, but detailed discussion of one of them alone.

It is common to divide the privileges of the Commons into two groups — those claimed by the Speaker at the opening of a new Parliament, and those others which are not specifically claimed. In fact the distinction between the two groups is purely formal and of no practical importance. However, in line with the principle that one long list is easier to recall in the form of two shorter lists, it may be worth while to retain the distinction. Thus the privileges of the Commons are:

(a) Those claimed by the Speaker:

(i) Freedom of speech.

(ii) Freedom from civil arrest.

(iii) Freedom of access to the Crown.

(iv) That the Crown will place the most favourable construction upon the proceedings of the Commons.

(b) Other privileges:

(i) The right of the Commons to regulate its own composition.

(ii) The right of the Commons to regulate its own proceedings (sometimes expressed as the right to take exclusive cognisance of its own affairs).

(iii) The right to punish both members and strangers for breach of privilege and contempt.

(iv) The right to control finance and initiate financial legislation.

To the latter list we could add a fifth privilege — the right of impeachment. However, this ancient judicial proceeding is now obsolete, and since two lists of four have an appealing symmetry, it may be conveniently omitted.

Although these lists may seem daunting at first glance, in fact the significant material is not so broad. If we look down the lists, freedom from arrest does not apply to arrest upon criminal charges and is therefore of little practical significance. Freedom of access to the Crown is not an individual right, but rather a collective one, the importance of which is purely historical. The requirement for the best construction to be placed upon proceedings is again of historical significance only, since it dates back to times of conflict between Crown and Commons. The privileges claimed in list (b) are of some continuing importance, although (b)(iv) relates to the claims of the Commons to exercise the primary role in the control of national finance (rather than the Lords) and is a matter of parliamentary procedure in the main.

Thus it is possible to reduce the significant material here to two major privileges — (a)(i) and (b)(i) — and the matters under (b)(ii) and (iii) which relate primarily to the relationship between the courts and the Commons in the adjudication and enforcement of matters of privilege. It is to these issues that we should turn in a brief outline of parliamentary privilege.

FREEDOM OF SPEECH

Article 9 of the Bill of Rights 1688 states that: 'Freedom of speech and debates or proceedings in Parliament ought not to be impeached or questioned in any court or place out of Parliament'. In addition to providing a statutory declaration of the privilege of free speech, this provision establishes the exclusive jurisdiction of Parliament in relation to the exercise of privilege (considered more fully below). This privilege ensures that no member may be liable in either a civil or criminal action in respect of words spoken during proceedings in Parliament. Its major importance, in practice, is in relation to the law of defamation, for the privilege seeks to ensure free speech in debate by shielding the members of the House from civil proceedings on this account. Of course, those defamed and denied redress might question the necessity for such wide immunity. Less commonly, the protection has been invoked in relation to criminal proceedings. A good example relates to the MP Duncan Sandys, who was threatened in 1938 with prosecution under the Official Secrets Act when he refused to divulge the source of information included in a parliamentary question concerning the shortage of anti-aircraft equipment. The Select Committee ruled that a member ought not to be threatened with prosecution in such circumstances, and seemed to imply that to so threaten could amount to a breach of the privileges of the House (extracts from the Select Committee Report appear in Wilson, *Cases and Materials on Constitutional and Administrative Law*, 2nd ed., p. 451). Another example of the width of the privilege is the case of *Church of Scientology* v *Johnson-Smith* [1972] 1 QB 522. In this case the plaintiff was not allowed by the court to substantiate allegations of malice (in a defamation action) by reference to speeches made by the defendant in the House — a decision supported in *R* v *Secretary of State for Trade, ex parte Anderson Strathclyde plc* [1983] 2 All ER 233.

One question which immediately arises is what is meant by 'proceedings in Parliament'. It seems clear that the phrase is wider than simply 'debates in Parliament' and would cover questions in the House, remarks in committee, and statements during any parliamentary business in the House. We shall see later that the effect of the Parliamentary Papers Act 1840 is to ensure that privilege attaches to papers published by order of either House. However we are in danger here of simply substituting 'proceedings in Parliament' by a phrase which is no more helpful — 'parliamentary business'. Clearly parliamentary proceedings may take place outside the House (see *Attorney-General of Ceylon* v *Livera* [1963] AC 103). Equally clearly, simply because a statement is made within the confines of the House, it ought not to be protected if it has no connection with parliamentary proceedings. This is well illustrated by the case of *Rivlin* v *Bilainkin* [1953] 1 QB 485, in which B defamed his former wife in one letter delivered by hand to an MP and four others posted and delivered in the House of Commons to another four members. The court held that no question of privilege arose because the publication was not connected in any way with proceedings in the House. On the other hand, a Member of Parliament may have a legitimate interest in a communication alleged to be defamatory — but is this sufficient to attract privilege?

The case of *G.R. Strauss* (1958) is instructive, though hardly conclusive. George Strauss was an MP, and he wrote a letter to the Paymaster-General in which he made allegations concerning the behaviour of the London Electricity Board in inviting tenders for the purchase of scrap metal. The Paymaster-General was representing the then Minister of Power in the Commons since the Minister sat in the Lords. In spite of the apparent responsibility of the Paymaster-General in the matter, he refused to act upon Strauss's letter and because he claimed that it concerned merely the internal administration of the Board, he passed the letter on to the Electricity Board. George Strauss was then informed that the Board intended to sue him in defamation, and on hearing this he claimed that such a threat amounted to a breach of privilege. Although this claim was upheld by the Committee of Privileges, on the basis that Strauss's action in writing to a Minister amounted to proceedings in Parliament, the House of Commons voted to reject the Committee's conclusion. In fact the action for libel was dropped, even though a later report found no substance in Strauss's allegations. (See also the related opinion of the Privy Council in *Re Parliamentary Privilege Act 1770* [1958] AC 331.)

One unsatisfactory consequence of the *Strauss* case is that if an MP asks a question in the House of a Minister which contains a defamatory remark, then that will be covered by privilege; whereas an attempt to deal with the matter less formally may expose the MP to legal action. Of course if a letter on a particular matter by an MP to a Minister followed immediately upon a parliamentary debate on the same subject, then it could be classed as part of ongoing proceedings and attract privilege. Otherwise it seems likely that the only protection available to the MP would be the defence of qualified privilege in defamation. That is to say the MP would only be protected if he or she acted honestly and without malice. It is open to the plaintiff to displace such privilege by proving malice (whereas absolute privilege allows complete freedom of speech). One reason why we may assume that a letter between an MP and a Minister attracts qualified privilege is that the courts have considered parallel cases. Thus in *R v Rule* [1937] 2 KB 375, a letter by a constituent to an MP complaining of the conduct of public officers (a police officer and a magistrate) was held to enjoy qualified privilege. One final point on the *Strauss* case is that in 1967 the *Report from the Select Committee on Parliamentary Privilege* (HC 34; 1967-8) recommended that legislation should reverse the decision of the House on the *Strauss* affair. Such legislation has never been introduced.

FREEDOM OF SPEECH AND OUTSIDE INTERFERENCE

One issue which ought to be considered along with freedom of speech is the possibility of improper influence over the conduct of MPs by bribes or perhaps threats. This must be set apart from the influence of the political party via the party whips since they are, by convention, an allowable part of parliamentary procedure (as we saw in chapter 4). Until shortly before the First World War, MPs received no salary, and in consequence outside employment, consultancies and sponsorships became quite acceptable. This remains the case in spite of the salaries and expenses available today. The problem is obvious. Organisations value the presence of an MP to represent their views in Parliament, but what happens if they feel they are not gaining value for their money? Broadly this situation arose in 1947 in a case involving W.J. Brown, an MP who held office as Parliamentary General Secretary of the Civil Service Clerical Association. Unfortunately the MP and the Association grew apart in their political perspectives. This led to a recommendation by the Executive Committee that Brown's appointment be terminated. Brown viewed this as a threat calculated to influence his actions in the House, and the Committee on Privileges allowed that financial pressures upon an MP designed to restrict the member's independence could amount to a breach of privilege. However, in *Brown's* case the Committee decided (though not unanimously) that no breach of privilege had occurred since it had to be possible for the Association to terminate the contract legitimately. Brown must have contemplated this possibility at the outset, and he ought to have done so in the resolve that such an eventuality would not influence him in the conduct of his parliamentary duties.

Clearly problems may still arise in this area (see, for example, the actions of the Yorkshire Area of the National Union of Mineworkers in 1975 — reported in de Smith). However, since the *Brown* case a Select Committee on Member's Interests (1969) has sanctioned the payment of financial assistance on a regular basis, while questioning financial inducements to assist in specific matters. The most recent example of this is the so-called 'cash for questions' episode of 1994-95 which led to MPs being disciplined for having accepted financial inducements to pose certain parliamentary questions. In addition, since 1975 a register of member's interests has been established by resolution of the House of Commons (see also *Rost* v *Edwards* [1990] 2 QB 460, below). This supplements a longstanding convention of the House that members declare any interest when speaking in debate or in standing committees. This rule itself was extended, again by resolution, to cover communications between MPs and Ministers in 1974.

FREEDOM OF SPEECH AND PARLIAMENTARY PAPERS

In 1829, a constitutional crisis occurred which related to a libel contained in a report published by Hansard upon the order of the House of Commons (*Stockdale* v *Hansard* (1839) 9 A & E 1). Hansard were sued by the defamed party, Stockdale, and their defence was (upon instructions from the Commons) that the report was covered by parliamentary privilege, since it was published by order of the House. The court refused to recognise such a privilege, deciding that papers available to the general public fell outside the ambit of protection. The House of Commons allowed the damages to be paid in this action but also passed a resolution stressing the essential nature of freedom of speech in reports, claiming to be the sole judge of the extent of its own privilege, and threatening that further action would be treated as a contempt. Stockdale then brought a second action against Hansard, and they, acting again on instructions from the House, failed to enter a plea. Judgment was given therefore in Stockdale's favour, and in order to recover the damages, the Sheriff of Middlesex levied execution upon the property of Hansard. The Commons held him in contempt and in breach of privilege and ordered his imprisonment. He applied for a writ of habeas corpus (*Sheriff of Middlesex's Case* (1840) 11 A & E 273) but his application was refused by the court. The warrant of the Speaker by which the Sheriff was imprisoned simply stated that the reason was for contempt, and the court refused to challenge the authority of the House on this matter by making further enquiry.

This was a rather convenient solution since it brought to an end the wrangling between the Commons and the courts, whilst allowing the courts to indicate their preparedness to intervene in situations in which the reasons for imprisonment for breach of privilege are given by the House. Happily, the unfortunate Sheriff was released after only a short time, since the parliamentary session was almost at an end. Thereafter, Parliament passed the Parliamentary Papers Act 1840, which ensured that parliamentary papers attracted absolute privilege. Whether this was an acceptance on the part of Parliament that privilege could not be extended by a simple resolution of the House is unclear. In effect there was a climb-down by both parties in order to avoid an even greater constitutional wrangle. The courts clearly yielded ground in the *Sheriff of Middlesex's Case*, while the passage of the 1840 Act may be seen as some form of apology on the part of the Commons. The outcome was satisfactory upon one level, therefore, but highly unsatisfactory in terms of establishing for the future a clear division of responsibility between the Commons and the courts in the matter of privilege.

The dispute between courts and legislature had a forerunner in the early 18th century, which also resulted in two famous cases. The first, *Ashby* v *White* (1703-4) 2 Ld Raym 938; 3 Ld Raym 320; 14 St Tr 695, concerned an award of damages by the House of Lords to an Aylesbury constituent prevented from voting. The Commons objected to this on the basis that it was a violation of their privilege to determine disputed elections, and imprisoned Aylesbury constituents with similar outstanding actions. Their application for a writ of habeas corpus was refused in the Court of Queen's Bench (*Paty's Case* (1704) 2 Ld Raym 1105; 14 St Tr 849). When counsel for the would-be voters began to prepare an appeal against the refusal of the writ, he too was imprisoned. At this point the Monarch (Queen Anne) intervened by proroguing Parliament. Note that rather than a simple dispute between the courts and Parliament, because the House of Lords was involved in its role as an appellate court, this issue may well have been viewed at the time as an altercation between the two Houses of Parliament.

THE RIGHT OF THE COMMONS TO REGULATE ITS COMPOSITION

In fact this privilege covers a bundle of rights relating to the composition of Parliament. One of the major rights, to determine disputed election returns, has effectively been relinquished. In practice the House is happy to leave the matter to an election court and act upon its finding. Similarly although the House retains the jurisdiction to determine whether or not an elected member suffers from a legal disqualification, it has shown itself willing to seek the advice of the Privy Council on such difficult matters (see, e.g., *Re MacManaway and Re The House of Commons (Clergy Disqualification) Act 1801* [1951] AC 161). In two areas, however, this right remains important. The first concerns the issue of a writ for a by-election to fill a vacancy. The Speaker may authorise such an issue by warrant. However, the Speaker acts only upon the order of the House, and by custom the motion to fill the vacancy is moved by the chief whip of the party among whose ranks the vacancy has occurred. Since there is no time-limit imposed, this has led to certain occasions when a party in Government, suspecting that it faces by-election defeat, has delayed in acting to fill the vacancy.

The other significant area relates to expulsion from the House. Here the right is a broad one which would allow expulsion simply on the basis that it believes a member to be unfit. The only remedy available to that member would be to stand for re-election, but, in the 18th century, so successful was *John Wilkes* at doing this that Parliament has long been deterred from exercising such powers frivolously. Indeed in recent times expulsions have been considered and at times effected, but only for serious criminal offences or contempts. Thus expulsion was considered in 1975 in the case of an MP *John Stonehouse* (who finally resigned when convicted of criminal offences) and effected in 1947 in the case of the MP *Garry Allighan*, who was held in contempt for making unsubstantiated allegations concerning other members and misleading the Committee of Privileges.

THE RIGHT OF THE COMMONS TO REGULATE ITS OWN PROCEEDINGS

You may already be aware from your reading of *British Railways Board* v *Pickin* [1974] AC 765 that the courts decline jurisdiction to enquire into proceedings in the House in part on the basis of privilege. Even though the exact scope of this privilege is difficult to determine, the broad principle is well-established, as in the case of *Bradlaugh* v *Gossett* (1884) 12 QBD 271. The facts are a little complex, but essentially they are as follows. Bradlaugh, an atheist, was elected as a Member of Parliament. Instead of taking the oath he was allowed by the House to affirm. He was then sued by Clarke (a common informer) on the basis that he was not entitled to affirm and could therefore not sit or vote. This was in accordance with the Parliamentary Oaths Act 1866, which allowed that persons affirming when unauthorised could be sued for penalties. Bradlaugh then stood, successfully, for re-election and this time sought to take the oath. Although there seemed nothing in the 1866 Act requiring a person taking an oath to believe in God, the House refused to allow him to do so. He was excluded from the House, and he brought an action seeking to restrain Gossett, the Sergeant at Arms, from excluding him. The courts refused to interfere on the basis that they lacked jurisdiction. In spite of their ability to interpret the provisions of the Act in an action to recover a penalty, on all other matters regarding rights exercised within the House, including sitting or voting in the House, the House alone had the jurisdiction to interpret the Act.

Once again, however, the privilege will by its nature only apply to proceedings within the House. It seems unlikely that the Commons would seek to assert its authority over a criminal act unconnected with proceedings but committed within the confines of the House. On the other hand, the courts act with some timidity in this area, as illustrated by the famous case of *R* v *Graham-Campbell, ex parte Herbert* [1935] 1 KB 594, in which an application for summonses for breaches of the licensing laws within the Members' Bar was refused by a magistrate on the basis of a lack of jurisdiction in view of parliamentary privilege. The Divisional Court upheld the decision.

Early in 1987 an interim injunction was sought by the Attorney-General to restrain the showing of a film concerning a defence project (the *Zircon* affair).

The injunction named a number of MPs, including Robin Cook, who had intended to show the film in a Commons Committee Room. The application was rejected on the grounds that it was for Parliament to regulate its own proceedings. However, the Speaker then imposed a ban on the showing of the film in an action which was criticised and referred to the Committee of Privileges. The Committee split on the constitutionality of the Speaker's action, but the majority took the view that the Speaker had exercised legitimate control in the Palace of Westminster and in the interests of national security. No breach of the members' freedom of speech was involved as the private showing of a film was not a proceeding in Parliament (see further [1987] PL 488).

One aspect of the right of the House to control its own proceedings is the right to punish breaches of privileges and contempts. Students often treat breaches of privileges and contempts of the House as though the two are one and the same concept. Contempt is the much wider concept, however. Although it includes all breaches of privilege it encompasses also all obstructions of proceedings and of members or officers as well as any conduct which produces such results that the House decides it must treat the matter as contempt. The difference is quite significant, then, since the House may rule upon and extend the concept of contempt, whereas attempts to so extend privilege may be disputed by the courts (see *Stockdale* v *Hansard* (1839) 9 A & E 1). In relation to contempt, the House is called upon to rule on a variety of conduct in situations in which there is no obvious precedent. Thus in 1956 an opposition MP was forced to disconnect his telephone following an article in the *Sunday Graphic* publishing the MP's telephone number and urging readers to make their views known to him on the subject on which he had tabled a parliamentary question. This was held to be a breach of privilege (since the newspaper sought to influence his conduct in the House by 'improper interference') and a contempt of the House. In 1969 a question arose concerning disruption of parliamentary business away from the House. It was held that attempts to obstruct a meeting of a subcommittee of the Select Committee on Education and Science, taking place at Essex University, amounted to a contempt.

Finally, the House has the right to punish those found in contempt. The penalty will vary according to the status of the offender. Thus members may be expelled (as was *Garry Allighan* in 1947) or suspended for a period of time. The Select Committee on Procedure (1988-9) expressed alarm at the number of times that the Speaker was having to 'name' and often suspend members as a disciplinary measure. Outsiders may be called to the bar of the House in order to face a reprimand from the Speaker and to apologise, and the press face the loss of reporting facilities. Publications found to be in contempt may be withdrawn from distribution upon the order of the House — as happened in 1981 to a pressure group publication relating to the Wildlife and

Countryside Bill. The most severe penalty is that adopted in the case of the *Sheriff of Middlesex* (1840) 11 A & E 273, namely imprisonment, but as in that case this can only last until the end of the parliamentary session. The one rather grey area in terms of penalties seems to be the fine. Historically, fines have been imposed — but not for centuries. The recommendation of the Select Committee in 1967 that a statute permitting fines be passed, tends to suggest their belief that, at present, the imposition of a fine is not an available penalty open to the House in the case of contempt.

REVISION

As a first step in the process of revision, it is wise to delineate the topics from within the subject of parliamentary privilege which you will choose to revise. This decision will be based upon the content of your own course. In spite of what is said above, if your own course has covered the privileges of the Lords in detail, then you should revise these. Nor should you necessarily ignore a point simply because it relates to the proceedings of the Lords if it is equally applicable to the Commons. To take an example, *Cook* v *Alexander* [1974] QB 279 concerned a fair and accurate, though unauthorised, report of a debate in the Lords. The Court of Appeal held that such a report attracted qualified privilege in the law of defamation. There is no doubt that this principle would apply equally to a report of a debate in the Commons.

Moreover, aspects of privilege which you do not revise in detail ought not to be ignored completely. Thus, in asking a question in which an MP is threatened with prosecution in relation to a matter which might form part of proceedings in the House (i.e., similar to the *Sandys* case) it would be easy to include a point concerning the arrest of the MP. Since as is stated above, the privilege of freedom from arrest relates largely to civil arrest, the point is hardly likely to prove substantial. However, it would help if you could state with confidence that a member is not protected from arrest upon criminal charges or from detention in relation to acts prejudicial to the safety of the realm (as is clear from a wartime example concerning a *Captain Ramsey* (1940)). One question to look out for is whether the offending action was committed in the House. This is because in only one case (*R* v *Eliot, Hollis and Valentine* (1629) 3 St Tr 294) have the courts heard a charge relating to a criminal act committed within Parliament. Such time has elapsed since then that it seems possible that, unless Parliament waived privilege, the courts might be happier to see the matter dealt with by the House itself (along the lines of *R* v *Graham-Campbell, ex parte Herbert* [1935] 1 KB 594) as part of the privilege to regulate its own internal affairs.

This seems to provide two lessons. One is a point previously made in chapters 1 and 2 — whatever you select to revise, you cannot afford to go into the examination without a broad knowledge of the subject. Students tend to place too much emphasis on learning by heart so that they come to believe that what they have not committed to memory they do not know. This is an obvious fallacy. Many lecturers have made no deliberate attempt to learn the material which they cover in a class, yet they know it well enough. So read through the whole of the material on parliamentary privilege at an early stage in your revision and have the confidence that, when forced to consider an issue which is not part of your revision proper, some of the material will be retained. The second point is that you cannot afford to divide any law subject into artificial compartments. Thus in the example in the previous paragraph, if you directed your mind towards the privileges relating to freedom of speech, it would be easy to omit the issues relating to both freedom from arrest and the regulation of Commons procedures. No matter how obvious the question appears, a safe strategy would be to ask which privileges might apply, and mentally run through them all one by one.

This advice is relevant upon a wider scale. It is easy, and indeed tempting, for an examiner to include material from the area of parliamentary privilege on the end of a question relating primarily to another area. Thus a question on the official secrets legislation could include an element of privilege centred upon the *Sandys* case. In fact most problem questions on the examination paper could include a privilege point by introducing a comment by an MP which may or may not be privileged. A natural justice question involving a trade union might end with the comment:

Windbag MP has written to the Secretary of State for Employment suggesting that Scarface, the union leader, is a Communist agitator paid by the Russians.
Discuss.

The moral is: be prepared for your material on privilege to arise in other guises. In any question which relates to the conduct of MPs or to proceedings of either House, be on the look-out for issues of privilege. These do arise quite regularly. In 1986, Geoffrey Dickens MP began to name in Parliament individuals whom he believed guilty of child abuse. He succeeded in naming a doctor and was not permitted by the Speaker to name a vicar. His actions were supported by certain newspapers and the whole episode gave rise to much criticism. However, Mr Dickens' point, which was the failure to prosecute, was made when, as a result of the outcry, both the vicar and the doctor were prosecuted. What is your view: abuse of privilege or useful action in the public interest? (See also *Attorney-General* v *News Group Newspapers plc* [1989] QB 110.)

Be aware also of the procedural aspects of privilege, for your problem question might be 'Advise X'. We have spoken little of parliamentary procedure so far, but if X is an MP facing a threat, for example, what would you advise? No matter how much you know about the content of privilege, you will need to give X some practical advice if you are to answer the question. In fact X should raise the matter in writing with the Speaker, who will, if he feels the allegation raises a serious matter of privilege, inform the House accordingly. The House will generally vote to refer the matter to the Committee of Privileges, if the Speaker so recommends. The Committee will investigate and make recommendations which will generally, though not invariably, be adopted by the House. Consequently you ought to be able to guide X with some degree of certainty towards a remedy, and perhaps to consider the penalties or punishments generally available to the House.

Within the area of punishment for contempt, as with many aspects of privilege, the best guide to future conduct is probably the previous proceedings of the House. Rather like the area of conventions (chapter 4), examples from parliamentary practice are extremely useful, and you should be sure to familiarise yourself with some of these. Make sure, however, that you fully understand the outcome of previous issues of privilege, and the status that the decision may hold for the future. Thus in *Strauss's* case, the vote of the House was contrary to the recommendation of the Committee of Privileges. However, the 1967 Select Committee on Parliamentary Privilege strongly suggested legislation to reverse the decision of the House. This tends to suggest that, if the events of *Strauss* were to recur, the House may choose not to follow its own earlier lead. We are not dealing with legal precedent here then, although elsewhere, where the courts have ruled on matters of privilege, the principles of *stare decisis* will apply.

The presence of the 1967 Report, referred to above, is quite valuable from a student's point of view. In an essay question, you might choose, or you might be specifically required, to give your views upon the reform of parliamentary privilege. The rules are open to a good deal of general criticism in so far as they give the Commons a good deal of autonomy, deny redress to individual citizens, and are misused by MPs on occasions. You ought to be able to suggest more particular reforms, however. With privilege, as with other subjects, it is most useful to be able to offer an opinion which you have thought out clearly in advance of the examination. The Select Committee Report of 1967 is a useful starting-point in this process, for although you may not agree with what is said there, it is useful information to know and upon which to build.

Similarly it is useful revision for you to consider problem questions by way of practice. These can include various situations which might confront you in an examination setting. They may be taken from previous examination or seminar questions, but it may even be an idea to devise your own situations and consider possible answers. Thus you might ask yourself what would happen if an MP repeated a defamatory remark, originally made in debate, on a television chat show later the same night? Ask yourself what precedents you would use to construct an answer. One advantage of your devising problem situations on your own is that it is quite cheering. Even in an area like freedom of speech, there are relatively few possible variants upon rather well-worn and hackneyed themes! With this heartening thought in mind, let us examine some (well-worn) examination questions.

THE EXAMINATION

If we consider the essay questions that might be asked in an examination, it is possible that a single topic, perhaps freedom of speech, or financial interests and pressures, could be chosen. However it is more likely that the examiner will take the opportunity to ask a question which cuts across the different categories of privilege. This might be a wide-ranging question concerning the pros and cons of the rules of parliamentary privilege, but a more specific question would seek out particular areas of controversy and choose a related question. The following is an excellent example:

'[Within the area of parliamentary privilege] only 20th-century restraint prevents an irreconcilable deadlock between legislature and judiciary' (Marshall and Moodie). Discuss.

Do not be confused by the early part of the sentence appearing in brackets. This is a device used at times to include words which did not appear in the original quotation. Thus the words outside of the brackets probably appear alone in the middle of a chapter on parliamentary privilege. Once taken out of the context, the extra words become necessary. Not all examiners would bother to put them in brackets for fear the students might find this disconcerting, but it is a practice which you might meet.

As was stated in chapter 3, the source of the quotation may lead you towards a particular answer. Marshall and Moodie are respected writers upon constitutional matters. They may be wrong when they speak of 'an irreconcilable deadlock' but it would take a brave and probably foolhardy student to argue that line. It is probably safer to consider what they say with great care — that only restraint has prevented a constitutional wrangle this century. Implicitly, this points to difficulties between the courts and Parliament prior to the 20th century. Two pairs of cases, *Ashby* v *White* and *Paty's Case*, and later *Stockdale* v *Hansard* and the *Sheriff of Middlesex's Case*, were considered earlier in this chapter. These are of obvious relevance, but the onus is on you to show not merely a knowledge of these cases by reciting the events surrounding them, but that you understand their significance. Too many students see this type of question, realise that they have revised a relevant body of case law, and give a review of that case law without doing anything more. The vital ingredient in a strong examination paper is a direct answer to the questions set.

Thus, in this answer, it becomes necessary to explain why the early case law seems to indicate that irreconcilable deadlock between the courts and the legislature could occur. To say that it might because it did in the past in *Paty's Case* is not an answer in itself. The point is, of course, that neither *Paty's Case* nor the *Sheriff of Middlesex's Case* led to a resolution of the jurisdictional wrangles between the Commons and the courts. The question of whether the courts or Parliament shall be the final arbiter of the existence of privilege remains. Moreover both cases show that if a dispute did occur, then the Commons might well use their powers in relation to contempt (e.g., by imprisoning a party to a legal action) to attempt to ensure an outcome satisfactory to the House. Hence the need for restraint.

It is necessary to consider the extent to which restraint has been exercised. One example of an area in which the Commons have begun to waive a privilege in favour of determinations by the courts concerns the right of the House to determine its own composition — especially in relation to disputed election returns and possible disqualification of elected candidates. This would fit in well with the discussion of the older case law since *Ashby* v *White* and *Paty's Case* revolved around such issues. Similarly, one could point to the passage of the Parliamentary Papers Act 1840 as an attempt to avoid a recurrence of the *Stockdale* v *Hansard* dispute and point out that this resolution has lasted well into the present century.

One can see the potential for conflict in a matter such as the *Strauss* affair. Had the House followed the line taken by the Committee of Privileges, that is that Strauss's action did attract privilege, then the Electricity Board and their solicitors would have been in breach of such privilege. It is not certain in this situation that they would have dropped their action for libel, nor is it certain that the courts would have conceded a lack of jurisdiction to examine the existence of privilege. On the other hand, there are cases, of which *Church of Scientology of California* v *Johnson-Smith* [1972] 1 QB 522 might be one, in which the courts have steered well clear of any decision which might be read as a narrowing of, or indeed a review of, the ambit of privilege.

It seems clear that in areas in which Parliament has traditionally supervised as 'proceedings in Parliament', the courts will not seek to intervene. Thus at the time of the *Zircon* affair (above) the Attorney-General's application for an injunction to restrain the showing of the film in the House of Commons was dismissed by the courts who were happy to leave the matter to the House. On the other hand, where a 'grey area' of privilege is involved the courts will be astute to prevent their jurisdiction being ousted. This was the view taken in *Rost* v *Edwards* [1990] 2 QB 460. In that case, the question arose in a libel action whether the plaintiff could lead evidence, which the defendant sought to challenge, in relation to the Register of Members' Interests. The Solicitor-General had sought to argue that the Register formed part of the business transactions of the House so as to amount to proceedings in Parliament. On that basis, he argued, the courts ought not to adjudicate on the matter. This view was not accepted. Interestingly the court stated that the courts' jurisdiction should be ousted only in the clearest terms. If Parliament wished to assert exclusive jurisdiction over a matter, they could always do so by legislation.

Thus, to summarise the answer so far, this is a question in which you need to give a reasonably detailed review of earlier conflicts between the courts and the legislature partly because these are complex, but partly because they illustrate precisely the nature of the problem. These earlier conflicts link in well with current examples of restraint which allow you to reach broad agreement with the quotation cited in the question. Essentially that is sufficient, but there is no reason why you could not go a little further. Your essay might appear a little stale if you simply conclude (along with half of your class), 'I should agree therefore with Marshall and Moodie'. What might make the examiner sit up and take notice? Perhaps you could point out that members of the House have not always used their privileges in a wise manner, and that this brings into question whether the House should be the sole judge of their own privilege. This is all the more true given the wide powers of the House to deal with breaches of privilege. In theory defamed persons seeking legal redress against a member might find themselves committed to prison by the House for contempt. In this situation, you might argue, the courts do well not to concede jurisdiction to the House alone. On the other hand, to have dual jurisdiction is an obvious nonsense, notwithstanding the restraint exercised by both parties. Such restraint, whilst desirable, is no real alternative to reform.

A Problem of Parliamentary Privilege

An examination question on parliamentary privilege is by no means certain to take the form of an essay question. It is not difficult for the examiner to devise a problem question, and a relatively short question might raise a host of difficult issues — for example:

> Prude MP in the course of a House of Commons debate on pornography reads out a letter which he has received from a constituent, Chaste, alleging that Smut MP is paid a retainer by the National Association of Sex Traders and Industrialists (NASTI) to safeguard their interests in Parliament. The letter also alleges that Smut has been instructed to vote against the compulsory licensing of sex shops in return for an agreement that none will be opened in his constituency.
>
> The following day NASTI issue a writ against Prude and Chaste, and Smut gives notice that he wishes to raise a question of breach of privilege by Prude. The *Daily Stir* publishes an editorial on the debate, which refers

to a forthcoming prosecution of the Exotic Aids Sex Shop for selling obscene literature, and adds the comment that 'MPs who are financially involved with criminals like this, who deprave the minds of honest citizens, should be thrown out of Parliament'.

Discuss.

There are a number of characters in this problem and it is important to ensure that you do not confuse them. A key at the side of the question or in your rough notes on your examination paper may help, e.g., Chaste — constituent; Smut — retained by NASTI, etc. You are not asked to advise all or any of the parties, simply to discuss the issues arising. On the other hand most examiners try to limit the number of characters in a problem, otherwise questions become confusing. You may assume, therefore, that there will not be superfluous characters and that the predicament of all parties requires discussion. You need not begin by dealing with characters in the order in which they appear and exhaust all the points relating to them before moving on to the next character. This can cause a great deal of repetition of the facts, and very often will produce a less than logical order for the consideration of the issues.

It is not uncommon in problem questions for certain facts to be omitted or certain issues to be deliberately left open. Thus in the question above we are not told whether the allegations made concerning Smut are true. In consequence it becomes necessary to consider the position if the allegations are true and if they are false. Examiners will readily adopt such practices which keep the question reasonably short and demand that the examinee uses a degree of initiative in answering the question. In fact Smut provides a useful starting-point for an answer to this question, since, as we shall see, many of the issues revolve round him and his intended courses of action.

Let us suppose that the allegations made about Smut are true. Although we are told that he wishes to raise an issue of breach of privilege by Prude, it seems extremely unlikely that the Committee of Privileges would find such a breach of privilege even if the Speaker chose to refer the matter to the Committee. Rather in view of the agreement between Smut and NASTI, the Committee might well recommend that Smut's own conduct is improper and amounts to a contempt of the House. This seems to follow from the *W.J. Brown* affair and mention should be made of this. This case, or certain other instances which you might have included in your revision, suggest that whilst remuneration of MPs for specialist advice rendered to organisations may be permissible, a retainer paid specifically to argue a cause in Parliament is improper. This is certainly clear from the 'cash for questions' scandal in 1994. Whatever the financial arrangements in this case, there can be no doubt that the agreement relating to the siting of the sex shop will amount to a breach of privilege on the part of NASTI, and a contempt of the House on the part of

Smut. (See further the *Report from the Select Committee on Members' Interests (Declaration)*, HC 57, 1969-70.) Although the point does not arise directly, you might care to quickly add that Smut ought to have admitted to his connection with NASTI by declaring it in the Register of Members' Interests, and if necessary by declaring an interest before speaking in the debate.

If, on the other hand, the allegations against Smut are false, and in particular if Prude knew the letter to be scurrilous, the situation would change somewhat. Smut could have no action against Prude in defamation, since, according to art. 9 of the Bill of Rights, freedom of speech in debate ought not to be questioned in any court or place outside Parliament. However, Prude might be subject to disciplinary action by the House of Commons if the House chose to regard the misuse of the Parliamentary platform as a contempt. In relation to NASTI, however, Prude would seem to be protected by parliamentary privilege against any action in defamation since there can be no doubt that the remarks formed part of parliamentary proceedings (cf. *Rost* v *Edwards* [1990] 2 QB 460). Indeed Prude may raise the question of NASTI's writ in the House on the basis that it might amount to a breach of privilege (as did Strauss in 1957 in relation to a threat of legal action following a letter he had written to a Minister).

We are told also that NASTI issues a writ against Chaste. This raises the status of Chaste's letter to Prude. Clearly a communication unconnected with parliamentary proceedings but posted to an MP will not attract any form of privilege (*Rivlin* v *Bilainkin* [1953] 1 QB 485). However, since the letter is clearly on a matter of public concern, we know from *R* v *Rule* [1937] 2 KB 375 that it will enjoy at least qualified privilege in the law of defamation. *Beach* v *Freeson* [1972] 1 QB 14 illustrates the width of this rule. There, a letter sent by a Member of Parliament to the Lord Chancellor containing allegations about a firm of solicitors attracted qualified privilege on the basis that the Lord Chancellor was responsible for the courts and all solicitors are officers of the court. Thus, if the letter is privileged, in the absence of malice on the part of Chaste, NASTI cannot succeed. Moreover, Chaste may be assisted by the rule in *Church of Scientology of California* v *Johnson-Smith* [1972] 1 QB 522 to the effect that the courts will refuse to examine statements made in Parliament which might support an action in defamation arising outside of Parliament.

The issues in relation to the *Daily Stir* cause one point of concern which all students should be aware of. We are told that in the editorial on the debate the newspaper refers to the forthcoming prosecution of a sex shop for selling obscene literature. This passage, almost casually added, may not seem especially relevant to the issues of parliamentary privilege — and indeed this is true. It does, however, raise another point relating to a topic covered on many constitutional law courses, namely contempt of court. You must be ready to seize upon such references and deal with them. This ability to think across areas of law is not necessarily easy, but, on the other hand, it is a vital skill in a lawyer. It may be easier for you, as an examinee, to spot the additional points if you ask yourself why should the examiner suddenly mention a prosecution of a sex shop not previously referred to. If you think hard about the answer, it ought to appear fairly readily.

Of course, this technique will only apply to areas which you have covered in your syllabus. If you have not been taught contempt of court, then you cannot be penalised for not commenting upon it in answering the question above. If you have been taught it, it is perfectly fair to ask a question on the topic, even though the remainder of the question relates to privilege. If you have not revised contempt of court as a topic, there is no need to worry unduly. Spotting the issue is half of the battle, since not everyone will do this much. Even if you only state that the action of the *Daily Stir* might amount to contempt of court, credit will be given for a perceptive answer. If, however, you possess a reasonable knowledge of the topic you should include a sufficient amount of information to answer the question, bearing in mind time constraints. In this case you would need to explain the operation of the strict liability rule in relation to criminal proceedings under the Contempt of Court Act 1981, which would apply if the proceedings against the sex shop were 'active'.

This leaves us with the critical comments in the *Daily Stir* editorial. If the House considered these to be an affront to the dignity of the House, either because they were grossly inaccurate or injudicious, then this matter might be treated as a contempt. If the Committee of Privileges was in the process of dealing with issues arising out of the problem, then the comments by the newspaper might be viewed as a breach of the privilege of the House to regulate its own proceedings. If you had time it might be worth adding that a mere report of parliamentary proceedings or an accurate, though selective, sketch of those proceedings would attract qualified privilege in the law of defamation (*Cook* v *Alexander* [1974] QB 279) but this issue does not arise directly and could easily be omitted since it is the outspoken nature of the editorial which is the potential cause of difficulties. You might also point to the wide jurisdiction of the Houses of Parliament to deal with contempts, though in the case of an editor, an apology at the bar of the House is more likely than imprisonment in the Clock Tower.

CONCLUSION

Parliamentary privilege is not so difficult a concept to grasp, and although in constitutional theory the topic is quite wide-ranging, the practical problems arising in this area are much narrower and many of the old-established privileges of both Houses are effectively redundant today. This reduces the material to be learnt for examinations, but it does not eliminate all sources of confusion for the student. For example, one common mistake is to fail to differentiate between parliamentary privilege and the defences of absolute and qualified privilege in the law of defamation. If the student has studied or is studying defamation in the tort syllabus, then it might be easier to eliminate this fault, but not all students have studied defamation. As always the key to avoiding such errors lies in careful reading of the literature.

The area is also one in which new developments, in the form of disputes concerning abuses of privilege, frequently occur. Each new parliamentary session sees references made to the Committee of Privileges. Not all of these are as dramatic or controversial as the examples contained in textbooks but they do have particular advantages for the student. They provide the opportunity for the student to show a recognition of the importance of the rules of parliamentary privilege to the workings of our legislature and to demonstrate that some positive interest has been shown in the course material. Careful reading of a good newspaper will provide a fund of relevant illustrations and this is a habit which any aspiring constitutional lawyer ought to acquire.

FURTHER READING

Hartley, T. C. and Griffith, J., (1981) *Government and Law* (Law in Context Series) (London: Weidenfeld & Nicholson). See Chapter 12.

Lock, G. F., 'Parliamentary Privilege and the Avoidance of Conflict' [1985] *Public Law* 64.

Marshall, G., 'Impugning Parliamentary Impugnity' [1994] *Public Law* 509.

Munro, C., (1987) *Studies in Constitutional Law* (London: Butterworths). See Chapter 7.

8   THE ROYAL PREROGATIVE

Prerogative: notice the spelling. There are two Rs in the word, but for some reason students have a habit of ignoring the first of these. It is worth making an effort to avoid misspelling central concepts such as this one. You have been studying the subject throughout the year, and ought to have read the word tens, if not hundreds, of times. Failure to spell it correctly throws doubt upon the thoroughness of your approach. In comparison with all of the other learning required of you, remembering how to spell the word prerogative is not so difficult. Indeed, we might make this point for spelling and written English generally. It is worth spending time in your first year eliminating spelling errors and improving your overall standard of written work. There is no doubt that the favourable impression created will gain you valuable marks in examinations and course work, not to mention enhancing your career prospects.

To return to the royal prerogative, it may be that the correct spelling is the simplest of the tasks facing a student. In many other respects it can prove a difficult subject to study. It is fragmented in nature, obscure in origin and uncertain in scope. (We could almost add 'discuss' there and create a typical examination question!) It is complex in some areas and downright confusing in others. The very label can mislead. There are prerogatives which are royal in the sense that they are personal to the monarch, but these tend to be less significant in practice than the political prerogatives — exercised by the Crown. It is also common to talk of prerogative powers, but this is over-simplistic. The notion that the sovereign can do no wrong is not best described as a power, and elsewhere in the course of the chapter we will see requirements upon the Crown which look suspiciously like duties.

It is perhaps necessary to pause here and clarify some of the terminology. We are speaking quite freely of the monarch, Sovereign, Crown, Executive, etc. Do you know what these terms mean? The Queen, of course, is the

Monarch or Sovereign. The Government is Her Majesty's Government (which we sometimes refer to as the Executive to distinguish between the legislative and judicial arms of the State). This being so, when we speak of the Crown, then in one sense we simply mean the Queen — as Head of Government (but see for a much fuller analysis *Town Investments Ltd* v *Department of the Environment* [1978] AC 359). However, it will become important to distinguish between the personal prerogatives of the Queen, as Sovereign, and the political prerogatives, not all of which will require the participation of the Queen. The latter may be exercised by the Queen's Ministers — perhaps by her Prime Minister. In such situations the prerogatives are exercised by the Government of the day, and we can conveniently describe these actions as those of the Crown.

DEFINING THE ROYAL PREROGATIVE

As with many other areas of your constitutional law course, it is useful to have a prepared definition available. This will assist in answering questions since you can always begin by defining what it is you are asked to consider. This is not the only reason, however, for there may be many more exciting ways of beginning your answer than with a definition. A definition forces you to direct your mind to the nature of the subject. This is useful if only because many examination questions are of the type that begin with a definition of prerogative and ask you to consider it. Because a definition is intended to set you thinking, it does not actually matter if the definition is not complete or perfect. You only need look at the amount of time textbook writers spend offering you different definitions of the subject as a whole (in constitutional law, tort, equity, etc.) to realise that perfection is an impossibility. So you should regard your definition as a peg upon which to hang more useful information about the subject under scrutiny.

The most common definition in relation to the royal prerogative is far from complete. Most writers begin with Blackstone, and the flaws in the definition stem from the changing nature of the prerogative since Blackstone's time (Blackstone's Commentaries were published in 1765). His definition (paraphrased here) was of a particular pre-eminence vested in the King, over and above all other persons, arising out of the common law, but outside its ordinary course. Since this was written, the scope of the royal prerogative has diminished, and the definition gives no hint of this. In addition there is little clue to the relationship between prerogative and statute. As we shall see, this is significant because statutes can replace that ground traditionally occupied by the prerogative. Indeed, the vast majority of powers now vested in the Crown stem not from prerogative, but from statute. Nonetheless, those which remain are not insignificant. Thus when the Argentinians invaded the Falkland Islands and the Thatcher Government took the decision to dispatch troops to the Islands, this was done under the exercise of prerogative power. As our definition suggests, this was a legal action in the sense that the Crown had a positive legal power to do it. It is not a question of the deployment of troops being in the hands of the Government as a matter of convention (see chapter 4). However, comparison with conventions is a useful one, for the courts will recognise the existence of both prerogative powers and conventions. Unlike conventions, the courts will be more often drawn into scrutinising the extent and scope of prerogative powers, and there have been suggestions of late that the courts will review the workings of a prerogative power. (See *Council of Civil Service Unions* v *Minister for the Civil Service* [1985] AC 374 — considered below along with other case law and referred to hereafter as the *GCHQ* case.)

It is questionable whether our definition takes account of this most recent development, since although we are told that the prerogative arises out of the common law we are also told that it exists outside its ordinary course. We could quibble with both elements of this. Technically, prerogative powers are the residues of royal powers rather than common-law creations as such (cf. the *dicta* of Lord Haldane in *Theodore* v *Duncan* [1919] AC 696), which may explain the view that nowadays the only new powers of the Crown must emanate from statute (see the judgment of Diplock LJ in *British Broadcasting Corporation* v *Johns* [1965] Ch 32). Moreover, whilst it must follow that they fall outside the course of the common law (in the sense that they were the particular property of the Monarch), if they are now considered reviewable by the judges, then it may be difficult to separate them out from the common law generally.

RECOGNISING PREROGATIVES

All of this has shown how difficult it is to define the prerogative, but the attempt has been worth while since we have learnt something along the way. However, none of this tells us how to recognise a prerogative power, and it seems vital to be able to do this if only because a problem question in an examination, involving governmental action, may centre around the royal prerogative. Identifying prerogative powers is not easy because of their residual nature. Technically any ancient power which has not been superseded by statute remains as part of the prerogative. It follows from this that the Government could send a few soldiers to share your hall of residence or student flat for a month or two, for the right to quarter troops, at least in time of emergency, seems to be a long-established and undisturbed power of the Crown. If this is so, worse things might happen. At the time of the Gulf war you could have been impressed into the Navy without the necessity of the Government passing a statute permitting conscription.

This line of argument follows if you accept (as did Lord Reid in *Burmah Oil Co. Ltd* v *Lord Advocate* [1965] AC 75) that the way to recognise a prerogative power is to delve back into history. In that case the problem was that there had been only two cases raising the issue of the Government's power to requisition property over the centuries. However, Lord Reid did not accept that the power had become extinct by reason of its disuse. It simply rendered the scope of the power more difficult to identify. On this analysis, it would not avail you to argue that the quartering of troops in your household was outmoded or anachronistic. A preferable solution, and one suggested by counsel for the Burmah Oil Company in that case, was that the prerogative rights of the State are founded on necessity. Thus one could look to the purpose for which a particular power was claimed and the nature of that power in order to decide whether this power ought to be allowed to the Crown. However, prior to the *GCHQ* case, the courts not unnaturally shied away from this, for it comes close to arguing that rather than simply recognising the existence of a prerogative power they might review its exercise. It remains to be seen whether, post-*GCHQ*, if the Crown ever did try to invoke an obsolescent prerogative power, the courts might take a functional rather than an historical approach to determining its existence.

PREROGATIVE AND STATUTE

Problems also arise where a prerogative power and a statutory power exist alongside each other. In such a case, the Crown will generally be taken to have acted under the statutory power, and will therefore be considered bound by any limitations or restrictions in the statute. This will be true even if, prior to the statute, the prerogative power could have been exercised unconditionally, for this must follow from the doctrine of parliamentary supremacy. However, since Parliament is supreme, the statute may preserve some or all of the prerogative power; equally it may abolish it expressly. The real problems begin when it does neither of these things. You should read the case of *Attorney-General* v *De Keyser's Royal Hotel Ltd* [1920] AC 508 to discover more about this, but there you will note the differing language of the judges when discussing what happens to a prerogative power for so long as a statutory power occupies the same ground. For Lord Sumner the prerogative is abated 'at least for so long as the statute operates' (at p. 561); Lord Atkinson talks of 'abeyance', and argues that the statute 'abridges the Royal Prerogative while it is in force' — he rejects the notion that the statutory and the prerogative power are 'merged'; Lord Moulton does not feel that the prerogative is 'abrogated' but sees 'no excuse for reverting' to it. All of these views suggest very strongly that although a statute will always be assumed as the authority for Crown action, where prerogative power exists alongside that statute it must always spring back to life when the statute is repealed. However, this must be open to some doubt, for where a statute has replaced ancient and anomolous prerogatives, are we to assume that, in repealing that statute, it is the intention of Parliament to restore the powers to the Crown?

Another problem arises in trying to discover whether the prerogative and statute occupy the same ground. In *Laker Airways Ltd v Department of Trade* [1977] QB 643, it was thought that reliance on the prerogative power claimed would prove inconsistent with the statutory regime. This led to the conclusion that the executive had to observe the implicit restrictions placed there by Parliament. The case is also important for the views of Lord Denning that although the court would not interfere with the proper exercise of discretion, it would do so if the discretion were exercised mistakenly or improperly (there is more about this in the final section of this chapter). It is open for the courts to reach the opposite view on the facts. When the Home Secretary sought to provide chief police officers with CS gas without the approval of the local police authority, the view of the court was that the action was an exercise of the prerogative power to keep the peace. Such a power had not been replaced by s. 4 of the Police Act 1964, which empowered local police authorities to equip their forces for emergencies. Nor did that statute place the prerogative power in abeyance (see *R v Secretary of State for the Home Department, ex parte Northumbria Police Authority* [1989] QB 26).

One interesting case illustrating the significance of statutory interpretation in relation to the prerogative is *Pearce v Secretary of State for Defence* [1988] AC 755. In that case the plaintiff was a former member of the Royal Engineers who had taken part in the testing of nuclear weapons on Christmas Island in 1958. By 1973 the rights and liabilities relating to nuclear weapons were transferred, under the Energy (Weapons Group) Act 1973, to the Ministry of Defence from the Atomic Energy Authority. Pearce brought an action in 1985 to claim damages for tissue damage and cancers said to be caused by exposure to nuclear weapons whilst serving as a soldier. The Ministry of Defence sought to rely upon the protections available to the Crown against claims for personal injuries suffered by soldiers. These protections arise out of the Crown Proceedings Act 1947 (considered below). The House of Lords held that the Crown could not rely on the 1947 Act. The 1973 Act had transferred liabilities to the Crown, and it would be inconsistent if these liabilities could be retrospectively evaded by reliance on the 1947 Act. All in all, there remain many grey areas in relation to the coexistence of statutory and prerogative powers. And beware — grey areas are the habitat of the examination question.

SCOPE OF PREROGATIVE

It may be useful to make yourself a list of the prerogatives. Since, as is explained above, many of these are of questionable status and relevance today, you need only include those which are most common. The remainder of this section provides a suggested list. It does not claim to be exhaustive, and if you have covered others in your course (perhaps because your lecturer wrote his or her doctoral thesis on prerogative powers in respect of swans!), then you should add these to the list. Below each heading is a short explanatory note in order to clarify the scope of the prerogative. However, you will need to refer to the detail of your own notes for revision purposes. Prerogatives are categorised in different ways in different books, but here you will find a simple divide — the prerogative as it relates to domestic and to foreign affairs.

Domestic Affairs

(a) *The Sovereign is the fountain of honour.* In theory this is a personal prerogative of the Queen. However, in relation to (for example) peers, their appointment has obvious political significance. Therefore the Queen acts on the advice of the Prime Minister, who in turn is advised by a Political Honours Scrutiny Committee made up of Privy Councillors. This leaves certain other honours (e.g., the Order of the Garter) in the hands of the Queen, but it seems obvious that ministerial advice is increasingly prominent in the conferment of all honours.

(b) *The Sovereign is the fountain of justice.* Judges and magistrates are in theory appointed by the Queen. In practice the appointment is on the advice of the Prime Minister and/or the Lord Chancellor. In relation to criminal justice, many activities are carried on in the name of prerogative. One of the most significant of these is the discontinuance of a prosecution, at the instance of the Attorney-General, by entering a *nolle prosequi*. In 1987, the desire of the parents of a mentally handicapped minor that she undergo a sterilisation operation led to a claim that the courts had a residual *parens patriae* jurisdiction arising out of prerogative (see *Re B (A Minor) (Wardship: Sterilisation)* [1988] AC 199). Although the issue did not arise directly in that case, because the court could exercise its wardship jurisdiction, it seems likely that there is a *parens patriae* power to intervene to protect any person within the jurisdiction incapable of exercising legal rights on their own behalf (see *T v T* [1988] Fam 52 and *Re Eve* (1986) 31 DLR (4th) 1). These cases all raise the interesting issue (considered above) of the coexistence of statutory and prerogative powers.

The other famous prerogative under this head is that of pardon of a convicted person. This is exercisable in a number of forms, on the advice of the Home Secretary (or the Secretaries of State for Scotland and Wales). A pardon may be absolute, or it may be conditional in that it may substitute an alternative penalty to that declared by the court. Thus at the time of the death penalty the Home Secretary would often be under pressure to commute the sentence to life imprisonment — that is, to exercise the prerogative of mercy. In modern times some of the prerogative has been replaced by statute (*R v Foster* [1985] QB 115). Nonetheless the absolute nature of the Home

Secretary's discretion in this area is illustrated by the court's refusal to review the refusal to award compensation to a person wrongfully imprisoned — see *R v Secretary of State for the Home Department, ex parte Harrison* [1988] 3 All ER 86, considered below. Non-amenability to review the exercise of the prerogative of mercy was recently illustrated in the case of *R v Secretary of State for the Home Department, ex parte Bentley* [1994] QB 349.

There is a final point which causes some difficulty. In essence there is still a prerogative power to establish common-law courts. The courts have regarded the establishment of a Criminal Injuries Compensation Board as the exercise of a prerogative power (see *R v Criminal Injuries Compensation Board, ex parte Lain* [1967] 2 QB 864). However, the Board is not a court, and Diplock LJ has argued that this is government, 'by public statement of intention made by the executive government instead of by legislation'. There is no doubting the residual legislative power arising out of (for example) orders in council, but the extent to which wider powers exist is uncertain. We might be prepared to accept these where, as in *ex parte Lain*, they are used to confer benefits on citizens, but what if they deny rights or restrict freedoms? For this reason, Munro's analysis (*Studies in Constitutional Law*, p. 160) is to be preferred. There is nothing specifically referable to the legal attributes of the Crown in a scheme to offer payments to victims of crime — in his words, 'anyone might have done the same'.

In due course the Criminal Injuries Scheme was codified in the Criminal Justice Act 1988. Certain parts of the Act were not brought into force. The courts could not compel the Minister to bring the sections into force, but the House of Lords held (by a 3:2 majority) to continually review whether their implementation was appropriate, see *R v Secretary of State for the Home Department, ex parte Fire Brigades Union* [1995] 2 All ER 244. It followed that when the Home Secretary decided to effectively repeal the sections in question by introducing new tariffs for criminal injuries, he acted in excess of prerogative power. As Lord Browne-Wilkinson said 'it would be surprising if, at the present day, prerogative powers could be validly exercised so as to frustrate the will of Parliament expressed in a statute . . .'. It follows that this case is important not only in relation to the narrower issue of the power to found tribunals but also on the wider question of the interplay between prerogative and statutory powers.

(c) *Crown not bound by statutes.* This benefit of the Crown is now subject to the doctrine of parliamentary supremacy, with the result that an express or implied indication from Parliament will be sufficient to bring the Crown within the scope of the statute. This is well illustrated by *Pearce v Secretary of State for Defence* [1988] AC 755. Thus much of the Crown's privilege was removed by the Crown Proceedings Act 1947 (see (d) below, and earlier as to the relationship between statutes and the prerogative). In many other statutes the application of the statute to the Crown will be spelt out (see e.g., s. 48 of the Health and Safety at Work etc. Act 1974). Where this is not done and there is no necessary implication that a Crown service (such as a hospital or health authority) will be bound, then it may be assumed that they are exempt (see *Pfizer Corporation* v *Minister of Health* [1965] AC 512; *Hills (Patents) Ltd* v *University College Hospital* [1956] 1 QB 90). Something to look out for, however, is that the Secretary of State may choose to apply substantially the provisions of a statute which does not bind the Crown, by administrative action.

In practice the importance of the principle is often to leave the Crown immune from taxation and this will cover not only government departments (although, since 1993, not the Queen personally). To levy taxes on departments would be a grossly inefficient process, as they would be later paid back from public funds. However, notwithstanding this, publicly funded bodies such as public corporations or nationalised industries may not enjoy Crown immunities on the basis that their functions are not governmental in nature (see *British Broadcasting Corporation* v *Johns* [1965] AC 32).

(d)   *The Queen can do no wrong.*   This is the prerogative of perfection (as opposed to that of protection). In England (although not historically in Scotland) it was impossible to sue the Crown in tort, and difficult to do so in contract (though something called a petition of right made this possible). However, in 1947 the Crown Proceedings Act attempted to unify principles of civil liability in respect of the Crown and citizens generally, whilst leaving the personal immunity of the monarch untouched. In *M* v *Home Office* [1994] 1 AC 377, the House of Lords held that an injunction might lie against a minister (who here had decided not to arrange for the return of an alien following an *ex parte* court order). However, the order for contempt was made against the Secretary of State in his official capacity. Lord Templeman stated that to say that the executive obeyed the law as a matter of grace would reverse the result of the civil war! It is possible that your course will contain a discrete section on 'Crown proceedings' or 'governmental liability' in which civil proceedings both by and against the Crown will be discussed. In particular you may consider the problematical area of public interest immunity (once termed 'Crown privilege') and the claim by the Crown that certain evidence should not be produced before the court if to do so would offend the public interest. If you do cover these areas in your course remember to cross-refer back to prerogative, though at the same time note that appeals to the public interest may not only be made by the Crown (see *D* v *NSPCC* [1978] AC 171).

(e)   *Dissolution of Parliament/appointment of Prime Minister.*   These are said to be political rather than personal prerogatives (one of the 'divisions' which we discussed at the beginning of this section). These labels are a little confusing. The Queen does exercise the power of dissolution and of choice of a Prime Minister personally. But they are not personal in the sense that they do not rest upon claims concerning the monarch's powers — e.g., the Queen can do no wrong. The description of them as political prerogatives is self-explanatory. They do involve the most vital exercise of power at the most crucial points of constitutional history.

However, much of this is a theoretical power, for, by convention, the Queen will always accede to a request to dissolution. Much of this material has been dealt with in chapter 4, but you may have learnt from the material there that there are no guarantees that the Monarch will not become involved in tricky political decisions — e.g., if an election produced a hung Parliament. Rapid growth of a third, alliance party in the 1980s produced literature on these issues (e.g., Butler, *Governing without a Majority* and Brazier [1982] PL 395 (choice of Prime Minister)), and as you saw in chapter 4, it is easy to envisage realistic scenarios in which the exercise of the prerogative powers would demand solutions which constitutional conventions do not always provide.

A warning: if you cover this topic in depth — and some courses do — you will need to revise both the material on prerogative power and that on conventions in order to be sure of providing an adequate examination answer.

(f) *Disposition of troops.* Clearly, this may involve more than purely domestic matters and extend into the realm of foreign affairs, but it is correct to designate this power as domestic since it arises from a personal prerogative of the Monarch, namely that she is commander of the armed forces. As with many other prerogative powers, the theoretical power of the Crown has been removed — in this case by the Bill of Rights 1689, which demands parliamentary consent for the maintenance of an army in peacetime. However, the significance of the retention of the prerogative power is that it may limit the scope for judicial interference with decisions to deploy troops. Thus in the case of *Chandler* v *DPP* [1964] AC 763 (which is discussed in chapter 11) Lord Reid expressed the unequivocal view that: 'the disposition and armament of the armed forces are and for centuries have been within the exclusive discretion of the Crown and ... no one can seek a legal remedy on the ground that such discretion has been wrongly exercised'.

In spite of increased judicial activism one feels that unless there is some statutory opening for challenge (this is explained by Scrutton LJ in *China Navigation Co.* v *Attorney-General* [1932] 2 KB 197), this must remain good law.

(g) *Emergency powers.* In *Burmah Oil Co. Ltd* v *Lord Advocate* [1965] AC 75 Lord Reid considered carefully the extent of prerogative power in emergency. You should read this carefully. You will find that it accepts the existence of prerogative emergency power at a time of war, but points to the fact that in all recent emergency situations, statutory powers have been involved to permit emergency action. Nonetheless, where statute did not cover the situation, prerogative power ought to fill the gap. In that particular instance, Burmah Oil's property and installations had been lawfully destroyed to prevent their use by the advancing Japanese army. This was considered to be the lawful exercise of prerogative power but Burmah Oil were entitled to compensation (until the War Damages Act 1965 was passed to deny them retrospectively). Thus it seems a clear rule of common law that where property rights are interrupted or disturbed by this prerogative, compensation should be paid. At the time of the Falklands war, ships were requisitioned under terms governed by statutory instruments.

External Affairs

(a) *Treaties*. We have considered the place of treaties in UK law in chapters 5 and 6. You may recall that the conclusion of treaties is a matter for the Crown alone. Indeed, there have been challenges to the exercise of the prerogative treaty-making power in relation to the EC. In *Blackburn* v *Attorney-General* [1971] 1 WLR 1037, a declaration was sought that by signing the Treaty (of Brussels) acceding to the Treaty of Rome, the Government would be in breach of the law by signing away sovereignty. An application to strike out succeeded, and it was held in the Court of Appeal that the exercise of the prerogative in signing a treaty, even of such paramount importance, could not be challenged in the courts. In *R* v *Secretary of State for Foreign and Commonwealth Affairs* [1994] 2 WLR 115, it was held that Title V of the Treaty of European Union, which establishes a common foreign and security policy apparatus among Member States, was an exercise and not an abandonment of prerogative powers. The case, however, did not determine whether prerogative powers might be transferred.

As with the EC Treaty, any rights, duties, obligations, etc., which may be exercisable under a treaty will require incorporation by legislation in order to have effect in UK law.

However, the subject-matters of many treaties may not be of this type and will deal with matters such as cultural exchanges or defence agreements between two or more States. In such cases the treaty will become effective when ratified by the Executive, and although the text of the treaty will be laid before both Houses of Parliament (cf. delegated legislation — chapter 9) their approval is not generally required or received. It may be obvious from the above that declarations of war and termination of hostilities are matters for the Crown (see further *R* v *Bottrill, ex parte Kuechenmeister* [1947] 1 KB 41).

(b) *Sovereign immunity and prerogative power*. You may cover these matters in detail in your course or not at all. Essentially, much of the material in this area surrounds the reluctance of the courts to wander too far into legal issues which might have political ramifications involving other States. This was amply illustrated when the fickle Mr Albert Baker turned out to be the Sultan of Johore! (See the extraordinary case of *Mighell* v *Sultan of Johore* [1894] 1 QB 149.) However, you might find it simpler to consider the situation in which there is a coup in a foreign State, and some question of law turns upon whether the new regime in that State is to be recognised as legitimate. Not surprisingly these are considered matters for the Executive, so that it will be for the Crown to determine the extent of relations between the UK and the new regime and subsequent questions of recognition.

This is yet another area in which prerogative power is largely superseded by statute. Section 21 of the State Immunity Act 1978 provides that a Foreign Office certificate shall be conclusive evidence as to the existence of a State for the purposes of that Act. This can place the courts in the awkward position of (for example) grappling with whether to recognise the laws of the former German Democratic Republic when the Foreign Secretary has issued a certificate refusing recognition (see *Carl Zeiss Stiftung* v *Rayner & Keeler Ltd (No. 2)* [1967] 1 AC 853 and the distinctions to which the court was driven). It may also involve weighty jurisprudential reflections on the very concept of 'state' and 'law' (see the judgment of Lord Denning MR in *Hesperides Hotels* v *Aegean Turkish Holidays Ltd* [1978] QB 205).

Section 1 of the 1978 Act restates the common-law rule that a prima facie and recognised foreign State has absolute immunity from the jurisdiction of the UK courts. However, ss. 2 to 11 set out the rules whereby the government of an independent State and its public property can no longer claim immunity. However, a Head of State and family remain immune (s. 20). The detail of such rules will be beyond the scope of most constitutional and administrative law courses. Wait for 'conflicts' or private international law in the final year!

Other forms of immunity also exist. The most notorious, for those who try to avoid London traffic obstructions, is diplomatic immunity. This is governed by a series of statutes (see Wallington and Lee, *Public Law Statutes*) but note that the prerogative power still plays a part. Diplomatic status is determined by the Secretary of State's certificate as provided for in the statutes. However, these certificates are regarded as conclusive, involving as they do the exercise of the prerogative.

(c) *Act of State.* Many of the actions referred to above can be described as acts of State, for they are policy decisions or actions by the Executive affecting the relations with another State. However, if you read the judgment of Lord Wilberforce in *Nissan* v *Attorney-General* [1970] AC 179, you will find that the concept of 'act of State' could be said commonly to signify two broad rules:

(i)   The Crown (or its servants) will have a defence to torts or crimes committed outside the jurisdiction if it can be shown that the act was that of the Crown or was authorised or, at least, ratified by it.

(ii)   The United Kingdom courts will not generally question actions authorised by the Crown or by a foreign government once convinced that the action constitutes an act of State.

You will immediately note that this second formulation very much begs the question: what is an act of State? We are back where we started! Rather than focusing on definitions, it might be easier to ask when the courts will permit the assertion of act of State to be invoked. Clearly the courts will guard against their jurisdiction being ousted by anyone merely happening to make the claim. So we can say from the outset that only acts involving or attaching to significant policy of the Government are likely to prove acceptable to the courts.

In large part this is because there will often be individuals who will suffer detriment and be denied a remedy as a result of the act of State — as you will find on reading the problem questions! De Smith covers many of these situations in a list of what are described as 'tentative' observations. It would be a useful idea to incorporate these into your notes, since they deal with specific questions of the sort which may arise in problem questions: e.g., whether an act of State can be pleaded against a 'friendly alien' within Crown territory (answer: no). The section also notes authority for the propositions which it advances (in the above instance, *Johnstone* v *Pedlar* [1921] 2 AC 262). You should read and note the cases. Many of them are inherently interesting and will bring this difficult subject to life.

Incidentally, many students seem to be put off de Smith because it offers little information of the facts of cases, in comparison to (for example) Wade and Bradley, which insets case-notes in small print into the body of the text. Both are excellent books, but there are times when the analysis in de Smith is unsurpassed. You should not ignore its availability simply because it will demand more of you. Indeed, for many lecturers that is its strength.

But returning to acts of State, we must say finally something of the relationship between this and prerogative power. In spite of the inclusion of act of State under the umbrella of prerogative, there are subtle differences between the two concepts with which you will need to be familiar. This is because there may be a real possibility of an essay question — either in the examination or for course work — which will explore the boundaries of each concept. Unfortunately, in the most likely source of an answer, the House of Lords decision in *Nissan* v *Attorney-General* [1970] AC 179, the judges either evade the issue or fail to agree. Clearly they did not find the subject easy either! The lesson is beware of simple distinctions. Thus in *Nissan* it was posited that prerogative powers would not operate outside Crown territories. But what about the deployment of troops overseas? Conversely, an act of State does not always refer to external actions of the Crown, for they may involve aliens within the UK — see *R* v *Bottrill, ex parte Kuechenmeister* [1947] 1 KB 41. You will not be helped in any attempt to chart the distinctions by the fact that case law seems at times to refer to the two concepts interchangeably.

However, it is possible to work your way through this difficult assignment if it is set you. Probably the way to do it is by asking questions of both prerogative powers and acts of State which will expose the differences between the two. Thus:

    (i)   Are all exercises of prerogative power acts of State? (answer: clearly not — at the very least they must concern external affairs).

    (ii)   Are all acts of State the exercise of prerogative powers? (answer: probably not since the act of State may claim its validity in a statutory power).

Then we might try:

    (iii)   Can an action (e.g., for damages) be brought against the Crown in respect of an act of State? (answer: no, but if a British citizen brought the action, the claim of act of State is likely to be rejected (see *Walker* v *Baird* [1892] AC 491 and *Nissan* v *Attorney-General*).

    (iv)   Can an action (e.g., for damages) be brought against the Crown in respect of the exercise of a prerogative power? (answer: no, but compensation may be payable even for the lawful exercise of the prerogative (see *Attorney-General* v *De Keyser's Royal Hotel Ltd* [1920] AC 508).

You could ask the questions considered in the previous paragraph as to whether the two are exercisable inside Crown territories, and then, outside Crown territories. In this way you gradually fill in the details of your essay. It is very painstaking. It is not helped by the lack of clarity in the case law. But some subjects on the syllabus are more difficult than others, and at these points there is no substitute for, or alternative to, hard work.

REVISION

The above section seems to have wandered very much into the area of revision. You may also be able to draw upon material from chapters 4 and 7 in devising your revision strategy. There are close links between conventions and parliamentary privilege, especially in relation to the role of the courts. But you might find other similarities, as a student revising the topics; once again you will be dealing with wide-ranging lists of (in this case) powers of uncertain scope.

    Because prerogative powers occupy so wide an area, you must be attuned to the emphasis within your own course. This may focus very closely on external powers and act of State or it may concentrate on some much smaller aspects of the domestic powers, such as dissolution of Parliament. Obviously, tailor your revision to suit your course. Note also that in an era of strong executive government, prerogative power has become a much more contentious issue. There has been some rapid development, especially in relation to judicial review of prerogative power. This topic will be considered in the section which follows. Clearly other materials you study on judicial review in your course will have to be brought into your revision at this stage.

Because judicial attitudes towards review of prerogative powers are slowly changing, there will be a number of issues which will remain unresolved. For example, in *Nissan* v *Attorney-General* [1970] AC 179 the majority view was that the court could assess the validity of the claim that an act was an act of State, but that there was no scope to question the propriety of an act of State. In 1970 this would have placed judicial review of act of State and of prerogative power on the same footing. However, following the *GCHQ* case (considered below), ought this view to be reconsidered?

It is open questions such as this which make the subject an attractive one for the examiner. Here we have not merely a grey area, but one of high topicality. In addition to this, it is sometimes asserted that law lecturers stand some way to the left, in political terms, of law students. Is this true of your tutors? Because if it is, remember that the lack of parliamentary accountability involved in the exercise of prerogative power makes the subject politically contentious. Cases which involve the banning of trade unions, or the arming of the police, may have left a deep impression on your politically aware lecturer and may surface when at some point (s)he faces the unwelcome task of writing the examination paper.

THE EXAMINATION

On a 1988 university examination paper, the following question appeared:

> To what extent is the exercise of the powers claimed under the royal prerogative reviewable by the courts?

This type of question, straightforward and apparently requiring a purely descriptive answer might seem, to anyone ignorant of the law involved, almost too simple for a degree level question. To those familiar with the areas it is apparent that the student is to be cast adrift in uncharted waters. More than that, the question itself was entirely predictable, concerning as it does the aftermath of the *GCHQ* case.

An article by Walker which had appeared not long before in *Public Law* on prerogative and review ([1987] PL 62) would have placed the examinee in pole position had its main arguments been read and digested. But let us suppose you are not so lucky. How would you structure your answer? Unless you have sat through the lectures with your Walkman on, you must have grasped the indications that judges have begun to shift their ground on questions concerning the reviewing of the exercise of prerogative power. Armed with this information, an essay plan is obvious.

You begin by outlining the traditional stance of the courts. That was that they would determine the existence of the prerogative, and then its extent. Remember to use case law. This is not a problem for you. To the first of these matters — determining the existence — you can refer to *British Broadcasting Corporation* v *Johns* [1965] AC 32 discussed earlier in this chapter. If you have read the judgment of Lord Diplock as suggested, you will have the information at hand — and probably a useful quotation or two. You can also put in some of the material on reorganising prerogatives here. As you know, the courts will not accept novel powers as a genuine exercise of the prerogative. There must be some ancient, common-law basis for the power claimed. You have covered all this in *Burmah Oil Co. Ltd* v *Lord Advocate* [1965] AC 75. Cite it! Never hesitate to use authority.

This case is also useful in the second task showing how the court will consider traditionally the extent of a prerogative power. There are others: *Nissan* v *Attorney-General* [1970] AC 179; *Re B (A Minor) (Wardship: Sterilisation)* [1988] AC 199; *R* v *Secretary of State for the Home Department, ex parte Northumbria Police Authority* [1989] QB 26 — choose one or more examples. There may be some which you have studied in other contexts. Perhaps you will have read *Malone* v *Metropolitan Police Commissioner* [1979] Ch 344 (see chapter 4) for a seminar on freedom of expression.

Once this is done you can also make brief mention of the relationship between prerogative and statute. This is significant because it will affect the ability of the courts to intervene. The statute may determine the basis on which the power can be exercised, but the prerogative power itself may be subject to common-law limitations or demands — e.g., to pay compensation (refer to *Attorney-General* v *De Keyser's Royal Hotel Ltd* [1920] AC 508).

Having covered the traditional doctrine you are free to consider the revision of it of later. Primarily you will need to devote your time to the GCHQ case, but you will certainly gain extra marks if you mention that there was a precursor in the form of the judgment of Lord Denning in *Laker Airways Ltd* v *Department of Trade* [1977] QB 643 (considered earlier). In discussing an important case like GCHQ you can afford to spend some time on the facts. However, the important facts are that the exercise of a prerogative power withdrew trade union rights without consultation. (For a full account of the whole saga see Drewry (1985) 38 *Parl Affairs* 371.) Later it was claimed that considerations of national security had demanded such action. Because the claim was one of national security, it was felt that the matter was one entirely for Executive discretion and not with the jurisdiction of the court to review. The more important part of the case, however, lies in the *dicta* concerning judicial review of the prerogative. Lord Diplock extended Denning's view in *Laker* to outline the scope of judicial control. Here you should dredge your memory of your notes of the case and recall the following: illegal; irrational; and procedurally improper. These sorts of actions might be reviewable, since it would be odd if an Order in Council under the prerogative lay beyond review yet an order under statute did not.

So far so good, but a number of other questions arise. Will any assertion of national security suffice to exclude the courts? Are all prerogative powers reviewable (see especially the judgment of Lord Roskill)? For instance, it appeared that certain powers were not amenable to review: these included treaty-making; defence; honours; the dissolution of Parliament, and the appointment of ministers. What about the application of review to acts of State? Perhaps you can think of other such open questions. (There is a useful consideration of the basis for the distinction between matters which are justiciable and those which are not in Alder, *Constitutional and Administrative Law* (1989).) You need not answer all of these, however, this is an area of considerable judicial activity of late, and you should demonstrate some familiarity with post *GCHQ* case law. In addition to *R* v *Secretary of State for the Home Department, ex parte Ruddock* [1987] 1 WLR 1482 considered below, the case of *R* v *Secretary of State for the Home Department, ex parte Harrison* [1988] 3 All ER 86 which we have discussed already is highly influential. There the court said that in the absence of fraud or bias, they did not feel that it was open to them to intervene in the Home Secretary's refusal of compensation to the victim of false imprisonment, nor did the Home Secretary need to give reasons. This seems to have been on the basis that although the Home Secretary had a discretion to award payment, there was no legal basis or requirement for him to do so (cf. *McInnes* v *Onslow-Fane* [1978] 1 WLR 1520 considered in chapter 10).

This setback to proponents of judicial review of executive action is to some degree off-set by the decision in *R* v *Secretary of State for Foreign and Commonwealth Affairs, ex parte Everett* [1989] QB 811. In that case the Court of Appeal seemed persuaded that the issue of passports, though a prerogative power, was reviewable following the *GCHQ* case. In fact the Court found the actual policy followed to be sound, but stated that reasons should have been given for a refusal of a passport. Note that no remedy would have been available here except for judicial review, and that the courts do seem to bear this in mind. In *R* v *Civil Service Appeal Board, ex parte Bruce* [1989] ICR 171, the availability of remedies for unfair dismissal seems to have influenced the refusal to review the termination of a civil servant's employment. This case may be compared with *McClaren* v *Home Office* [1990] ICR 824 in which the suspension, without pay, of a prison officer was said to raise issues of private law. This was because the power to appoint arose out of statute rather than from the prerogative. You may not be able to cover all of these post *GCHQ* cases, but an indication of knowledge of them may be sufficient to show that you recognise the significance and dynamism of this area of the law.

Just to show that many of these issues can be recast in the form of a problem, consider the following:

Abbas, an Iraqi national, runs a mink farm adjoining an RAF base at Bamsville. He writes a letter to the *Bamsville Bugle* complaining about aircraft noise and jets flying too low, in which he refers to 'the Air force warmongers'.

Two weeks later a military operation is held at RAF Bamsville, and Abbas's land is occupied for two days while the SAS fire guns and explode bombs on his property.

This is in the middle of the mink breeding season and many of his minks miscarry. Abbas's request for compensation is rejected on the basis that the operation was necessary to allow the storming of hijacked aircraft in the light of a spate of such incidents by Islamic fundamentalists.

Discuss.

Hopefully you see immediately the act of State point. Although the events take place in the UK, they involve an alien. Is this a friendly or an enemy alien? A crucial point this, because an act of State cannot be pleaded against the former (*Johnstone* v *Pedlar* [1921] 2 AC 262) but can against the latter (*R* v *Bottrill, ex parte Kuechenmeister* [1947] 1 KB 41). Assuming that we are no longer at war with Iraq, we might assume Abbas to be friendly. The deciding factor is whether Abbas owes allegiance to the Crown. If this is established he will be placed effectively in the position of a British subject (see the judgment of Viscount Finlay in *Johnstone* v *Pedlar* and cf. *Buron* v *Denman* (1848) 2 Exch 167). This means that no act of State may be pleaded, but the person may be subject to the exercise of prerogative power.

Is there a prerogative power here? Yes, the deployment of troops is involved (see above; you may wish to cite *Chandler* v *DPP* [1964] AC 763). But given that there is some hint that the action is malicious, since it follows Abbas's complaint, is this reviewable? If it is malicious then according to Lord Diplock in *GCHQ* the courts would be prepared to intervene, except that Lord Roskill expressed the view that certain prerogative powers — including those in defence of the realm — were inappropriate for review. In any case would this not fall within consideration of national security? None of this itself determines Abbas's right to compensation — since this is not an act of State, Abbas is not prevented from suing for compensation (*Nissan* v *Attorney-General* [1970] AC 179) and in this type of case, even the valid exercise of prerogative power may imply a right to be compensated (*Attorney-General* v *De Keyser's Royal Hotel Ltd* [1920] AC 508) (and see also *R* v *Secretary of State for Home Department, ex parte Weekes* (1988) *Independent* 18 February 1988).

CONCLUSION

Easy isn't it? Well, not really, but by now you may realise that there have been a host of well publicised cases involving significant political issues, and this means that however troublesome you may have found this topic you cannot afford to ignore it. The *Northumbria Police* case involved the provision of CS gas against the wishes of the police authority. Then in one of the *Spycatcher* cases, *Attorney-General* v *Guardian Newspapers Ltd (No. 2)* [1990] 1 AC 109, the Master of the Rolls appeared to suggest that the prerogative might be invoked to protect actions which otherwise might be subject to criminal proceedings, saying that: 'it is absurd to contend that *any* breach of law, whatever its character, will constitute such "wrongdoing" as to deprive the service (MI5) of the secrecy without which it cannot possibly operate'. This line of thinking led to questions in Parliament (including questions concerning the procedure for criticising members of the judiciary) and to a House of Lords debate on the accountability of the secret service.

In *R* v *Secretary of State for the Home Department, ex parte Ruddock* [1987] 1 WLR 1482, members of CND had alleged that their telephones had been tapped contrary to published guidelines. Taylor J held that notwithstanding the lack of necessity to issue or adopt such guidelines, once they were adopted they gave rise to a legitimate expectation that they would be followed. The judge refused to decline jurisdiction on grounds of national security and was prepared to examine ministerial action to seek misfeasance or irrationality in the issue of the warrant. He found none. This case is clearly significant in its furtherance of the role of judicial review as espoused in the *GCHQ* case. But it has another significance. Both of the above cases concern issues which are highly contentious and which were widely reported at the time in radio and television broadcasts and in national newspapers. Even if you were not a law student you might reasonably be expected to know of such events. Once you are a law student, more is required. You must be able to state the basis on which such issues were resolved. If you find studying the royal prerogative cumbersome, then you might hope that it will not be included on the examination paper. As long as such newsworthy events as those above take place, this seems rather a forlorn hope.

FURTHER READING

Allan, T. R. S., (1994) *Law, Liberty and Justice* (Oxford: Oxford University Press). See Chapters 8 and 9.

Blackburn, R., (ed) (1992) *Constitutional Studies: Contemporary Issues and Controversies* (London: Mansell). See Chapter 5.

Griffith, J., 'The Political Constitution' (1979) 42 MLR 1.

Griffith, J., 'Judicial Decision-Making in Public Law' [1988] *Public Law* 564.

9 DELEGATED LEGISLATION

It seems curious to isolate delegated legislation as a single topic. In reality this is but one form of law-making which might be considered alongside the primary legislative process, and perhaps together with the judicial functions of interpreting statutes and developing the common law. Nonetheless, the constitutional law syllabus will often separate out delegated legislation for particular attention, and the examination paper may well reflect such treatment of the subject-matter. Why is this so, and what peculiar qualities of delegated legislation attract the attention of the constitutional lawyer? The answer to such questions lies at the heart of a successful understanding of the subject-matter.

Essentially the interest in this topic results from a constitutional dilemma. Notions of supremacy dictate that Parliament is the sole source of legislation but at the same time it is clear that the ability of Parliament to legislate is limited by a series of practical considerations. The solution is to delegate law-making power to individuals or institutions. This is done by specific and restricted authorities, and subordinate law-making will need to be subject to careful scrutiny. Such scrutiny falls within the ambit of administrative law, if only because the delegation is usually to some other arm of central or local government. Underlying a consideration of the principles of administrative law is a concern that delegated legislation manifests a tendency in government which, in so far as it reduces the legislative ability of Parliament, is anti-democratic and offensive to the idea of the separation of powers. Yet the volume of legislation continues to increase.

The consequences of this for the law student are threefold. To begin with, delegated legislation is an important topic to study, irrespective of constitutional issues, simply because it is increasingly common and, therefore, would-be lawyers ought to have a complete understanding of its nature and its role. Secondly, it may be apparent from what has been said that delegated legislation is viewed as a necessary evil. Clearly it is essential to be able to make some form of assessment of the extent to which it is evil, as some would claim, or is necessary as others would have us believe. Finally, the whole question of control is increasingly vital. This is an issue which is widely debated by academics, and it is important for the student (a) to understand the range of controls which exist, and (b) to be able to make some form of assessment of how effective such controls are in practice.

In fact it is highly likely that any examination question will concern the pros and cons of delegated legislation or the problem of control or (quite possibly) an amalgam of both issues. It is not so difficult, then, to prepare this topic for an examination, but a word of warning is necessary. Simply to say that it is possible to highlight the type of question which may be asked is not to say that it is easy to answer such a question, or that the material itself is straightforward. Some of the issues are extremely technical, especially in relation to judicial review. You may be studying judicial review of administrative action as a separate topic within your syllabus in which case it is important to link the two bodies of material together. There is no separate consideration of judicial review in this book (other than in relation to natural justice) but the principles will be considered in so far as they relate to the possibility of challenging the validity of delegated legislation.

A final reason for the difficulty with this subject results from the variety of rules, regulations, by-laws, orders etc. which may be classed as delegated or subordinate legislation. Few students bother to acquaint themselves with examples of each type, or to seek to understand their subtle differences. Later in your law degree studies you will become fully familiar with these legislative devices, and gain an understanding of the role which they play. Thus, labour law students cannot ignore the dramatic changes introduced by regulation (see, for example, the Transfer of Undertakings (Protection of Employment) Regulations 1981, or the Equal Pay (Amendment) Regulations 1983) and the fact that an employee's right (such as the qualification period for unfair dismissal) may be altered by statutory instrument. They must appreciate the consequences of codes of practice on subjects such as picketing and the closed shop. However, if you study constitutional law early in your course you may be forced to study delegated legislation before you are aware of its practical importance. The remedy lies in your own hands. Familiarise yourself with Acts of Parliament containing enabling provisions and find examples of delegated legislation made under such authority. Precisely because you are at an early stage in your legal scholarship, references to concrete examples are likely to impress an examiner.

THE NATURE OF DELEGATED LEGISLATION

Because Parliament is supreme, in theory, there is no limit upon the type or scope of authority delegated or upon the choice of body to whom the legislative ability is delegated. Although we shall see later that there is careful scrutiny of delegated legislation which is unusual or extensive in nature, the bulk of delegated legislation falls into certain well-defined groups. Apart from the examples from European Community law discussed in chapter 6 these include:

(a) *Statutory instruments.* This is a rather complex expression which is simply a generic term intended to encompass those forms of delegated legislation which are the subject of the Statutory Instruments Act 1946. There are three broad categories of legislative powers within the scope of the Act:

(i)   Powers conferred by statutes, after 1947, upon the Monarch in Council (Statutory Order in Council).
(ii)   Powers conferred on Ministers or rule-making bodies by statutes before 1948.
(iii)   Powers conferred on Ministers or rule-making bodies by statutes after 1947.

The rule-making bodies referred to above would include, for example, statutory rule committees empowered to make rules of practice and procedure for the Supreme Court and County Court. The 1946 Act contains provisions for the numbering, printing and publishing of statutory instruments as well as procedures for their scrutiny by Parliament.

(b) *Prerogative Orders in Council.* These differ from (a)(i) above in so far as the authority for their existence lies not in statute but under the royal prerogative. However, as with statutory Orders in Council, they will require the assent of the Monarch in the Privy Council.

(c) *Local authority by-laws.* By-laws (or byelaws as they are referred to in statutes) may be created by local authorities to apply to a particular locality, perhaps to solve a purely local problem. They have effect as binding law within the area which they are intended to cover, but they will generally be subject to the confirmation of a central government department, and they may be subject to wider grounds of challenge than are statutory instruments.

(d) *Local authority orders.* An example of a local authority order authorised by statute is the compulsory purchase order, but there are a variety of others which might similarly affect the rights of individuals within the locality. These orders are subject to ministerial confirmation.

(e) *By-laws of public corporations etc.* The power to make by-laws may be delegated not only to local authorities but also to public corporations, other governmental agencies, and occasionally to bodies independent of government (e.g., the National Trust).

THE PURPOSES OF DELEGATED LEGISLATION

The above section goes some way towards explaining the purposes of delegated legislation, but a little more needs to be said because it is possible to appreciate fully why delegated legislation is an inevitable part of our process of government. It is possible to suggest a number of functions which can only sensibly be carried out by the use of delegated legislative powers.

(a) *Technical regulations.* Members of Parliament are not selected or elected on the basis of particular expertise, although many do possess or develop a particular skill or body of knowledge. Nonetheless it is nonsense to imagine that meaningful debate could be carried out on many of the technical issues which are currently the subject of delegated legislation — even if parliamentary time allowed this. Indeed, it is much more efficient to carry out that debate between experts within central government and within the particular field which is the subject of a legislative proposal. This can be done by the consultation process which is an inherent part of the implementation of delegated legislation (see below). It is possible to think of many areas (food and drugs, health and safety, building standards, for example) in which the regulations are extremely technical, and it is no bad thing to skip through a number of these in the library in a free moment, simply to further your understanding of the difficulties.

(b) *Postponement.* Increasingly, Acts are not brought into force upon receiving royal assent, but their implementation is delayed. There are a number of reasons for this. Constraints on parliamentary time dictate that if a particular matter is the subject of legislation, because it may be some time before Parliament will be able to devote its attention to that subject in the future, the Act should be as comprehensive as possible. It may contain provisions which are not yet appropriate therefore but which deal with a forthcoming problem. More commonly, a short delay will be needed while the necessary administrative machinery required to implement, supervise, or enforce the Act is created. Perhaps consultation with pressure groups on a particular matter is not complete, and further time, following royal assent, becomes necessary. The easy way to deal with all or any of these problems is to provide that certain sections of the Act shall come into force on a day appointed in a statutory instrument, or the section may simply take the form of an enabling provision allowing a Minister to present regulations to Parliament at a later date.

(c) *Future problems.* Parliament will be aware when legislating on a particular subject that a host of difficulties may arise in the future. It would obviously be ridiculous if, in an area concerned with welfare provisions, for example, when it became obvious that a high rate of inflation, a growing level of unemployment, or a housing shortage was causing considerable hardship to a certain sector of the population, there was a lengthy wait for new primary legislation before the hardship could be relieved. Equally, an Act may operate in a manner unforeseen by Parliament so that a certain provision requires some alteration, or it may be obvious to Parliament from the outset that certain provisions will need constant updating. Delegated legislation is ideally suited to this task.

(d) *Emergency action*. At the time of a national emergency, it may be necessary to empower the government to act promptly. The classic example is the wartime Emergency Powers (Defence) Act 1939, s. 1 of which allowed 'such regulations ... as appear ... [to His Majesty] to be necessary or expedient for securing the public safety, the defence of the realm, the maintenance of public order and the efficient prosecution of any war'. It should not be thought, however, that regulations allowing emergency action apply only in wartime. They may be necessary to deal with natural disasters, and increasingly there has been criticism that delegated legislative powers within the field of economic regulation go as far as the doctrine of parliamentary supremacy might allow (see e.g., Korah (1976) 92 LQR 42).

SAFEGUARDS

De Smith comments that 'the most effective safeguard against the abuse of delegated powers is not to delegate them in such terms as to invite abuse'. There is no doubting the wisdom of this and consequently he categorises safeguards into two: contraceptive and antenatal. By this he means that there are a whole variety of safeguards to ensure that when a Bill is drafted it does not contain delegated powers which might offend constitutional principles or allow an undesirable degree of power to pass into the hands of a single individual. The presence of such 'contraceptive' safeguards is fully consider- ed in de Smith and is mostly certainly an important factor of which you ought to be aware. Concentration on the 'antenatal' powers is more usual, however, if only because most problem questions hardly lend themselves to a consideration of the policies of an interdepartmental committee of Cabinet, or the actions of the parliamentary draftsmen.

Publication

Not all statutory instruments are subject to publication, since they may have limited application, or their size may make publication undesirable, or the Minister may certify that publication would be contrary to the public interest. The majority, however, are numbered, printed and sold by Her Majesty's Stationery Office. This Office lists the date of issue of a statutory instrument, and the Statutory Instruments Act 1946 states that the listing provides conclusive evidence of the date on which the statutory instrument was published. The significance of this is that under the 1946 Act it is a defence to a prosecution for non-compliance with a statutory instrument to show that it had not been issued at the date of the alleged offence.

If, however, it can be shown that at the date of the offence reasonable steps had been taken to bring the statutory instrument to the attention of the public in general, those members of the public likely to be affected by it, or the defendant in particular, the defendant may be convicted notwithstanding the non-issue of the instrument. Thus for example in *R v Sheer Metalcraft Ltd* [1954] 1 QB 586, because the court was satisfied that reasonable steps had been taken to notify those affected by a statutory instrument, a conviction for non-compliance was upheld. The onus of proving that the statutory instrument was sufficiently well publicised falls upon the Crown (see *Simmonds v Newell* [1953] 1 WLR 826).

Consultation

Unless the parent Act makes it compulsory, there is no general duty to consult interested parties with regard to proposed statutory instruments. Having said that, it is widely accepted that central government departments take great care to consult those bodies likely to be affected by the proposal. There are a number of reasons why this makes good sense. Not only does it help bringing expert assistance to the department on technical issues, but it has obvious public relations advantages. The consultation process is aided by the fact that the text of the proposed regulation may be shown to those consulted (this is not true of the text of proposed Bills).

If the parent Act does demand consultation, this may take a number of forms. Consultation may be required of particular bodies or the parent Act may demand consultation but allow the Minister to decide upon those bodies to be consulted. In such case, the courts will be the arbiters of whether or not the duty to consult is fulfilled. Thus in *Lee v Department of Education & Science* (1967) 66 LGR 211, the statute (Education Act 1944, s. 17(5)) required the Minister to hear representations from the local education authority and 'any other persons appearing to him to be concerned with the management of the school' before varying the articles of government of a school. In the opinion of the court, although this could include a teacher, a parent had no legal right to be consulted. Similarly in a more frequently cited example, *Agricultural Horticultural & Forestry Industry Training Board v Aylesbury Mushrooms Ltd* [1972] 1 WLR 190, the Industrial Training Act 1964 required the Minister to consult any organisation 'appearing to him to be representative of substantial numbers of employers'. The failure to consult the Mushroom Growers' Association rendered an order made under the Act *ultra vires* in so far as it sought to apply to members of the Association.

The duty to consult implies that reasonable time be given to those whose advice is sought to express their views (see *R* v *Secretary of State for Social Services, ex parte Association of Metropolitan Authorities* [1986] 1 WLR 1). Note also that in the *Aylesbury Mushrooms* case the Court did not strike down the whole regulation, but the invalid part only. In *DPP* v *Hutchinson* [1990] 2 AC 783 the Secretary of State for Defence had issued by-laws relating to Greenham Common which were *ultra vires*, offending rights of common (i.e., rights to use the Common). The lower courts had attempted to re-write the by-laws so as to omit the offending part and render them lawful. The House of Lords said they could not be severed in this way. They were *ultra vires* and void. They could only be severed if what then remained was unchanged in legislative purpose, operation and effect. This was not the consequence of the re-writing. Hutchinson and various others had their convictions for offending against the by-laws quashed.

Parliamentary Scrutiny

The doctrine of the legislative supremacy of Parliament is further reinforced by the approval of Parliament of the greater proportion of delegated legislation. The parent Act will usually state that delegated legislation made under the Act, or under a particular section of the Act, shall be laid before one or both of the Houses of Parliament, and may be subject to either affirmative or negative resolution (see further [1983] PL 43). If the parent Act does no more than require that a regulation be laid before Parliament, this is purely to allow members to be informed of the regulation which does not require their approval (indeed it might even be in force). However, members, especially Opposition members, might avail themselves of the usual avenues (questions, calls for debate etc.) to promote a consideration by Parliament of a regulation.

The regulation will be laid before Parliament for 40 days. In the case of an affirmative resolution this will be the time allowed for a positive resolution in favour of the regulation. This may be compared with the more popular negative resolution procedure under which the regulation would come into force unless challenged within the 40 days, and annulled by a negative vote (see further Statutory Instruments Act 1946, ss. 4 and 5).

Action in Parliament using these procedures may be prompted by the Joint Committee on Statutory Instruments. This committee represents both Houses and is chaired (by convention) by a member of the Opposition. Its duty is to consider all instruments laid before Parliament and to draw attention to delegated legislation which:

(a)   Imposes taxation.
(b)   Excludes the possibility of challenge in the courts.

(c)   Is retrospective in effect (without the mandate of the parent Act).

(d)   Has been subject to an unjustifiable delay in publication or laying before Parliament.

(e)   Has been the subject of an unjustifiable delay in the notification to the Speaker where an instrument has come into force before being laid before Parliament (see the proviso contained in s. 4(1) of the 1946 Act).

(f)   Makes unexpected use of the power in the parent Act.

(g)   Requires elucidation.

(h)   Is defective in its drafting.

One matter specifically excluded from the ambit of the Joint Committee's review is the policy underlying the delegated legislation. The function of the Committee is to highlight legal defects or constitutional improprieties. It will be obvious looking at some of the list above (particularly (f), (g) and (h)) that if the defects are not remedied by Parliament, they may give rise to litigation before the courts. Although the Committee may make adverse reports to Parliament concerning a particular instrument, it will attempt, at first instance, to remedy the problem by allowing the department concerned to explain its actions. Rather than risk an adverse report, the department may then choose to reconsider the instrument. This may be why there are relatively few adverse reports. Even if an adverse report is produced, there is no automatic effect. The most that may happen is that it will lead, for example, to a challenge under the negative resolution procedure.

Judicial Review

In spite of their inability to challenge the validity of an Act of Parliament, the courts have a crucial role to play in supervising delegated legislation. This they do by means of the doctrine of *ultra vires*. Most commonly, this will mean that the instrument, although approved by Parliament, falls outside or goes beyond the power delegated by the parent Act. Hence there may be a direct challenge to the instrument by an application to the High Court for judicial review on the basis that the regulation is *ultra vires*. Alternatively the instrument may be the subject of a less direct challenge if a person charged with the breach of a criminal provision contained in delegated legislation alleges that this was *ultra vires* the parent Act (sometimes referred to as collateral challenge).

An example of this is the case of *McEldowney* v *Forde* [1971] AC 632 which concerned the validity of emergency regulations made under a Northern Ireland Act of 1922 (now repealed). The Act delegated powers to make regulations 'for preserving the peace and maintaining order'. One regulation created a criminal offence of belonging to a 'republican club' or to 'any like organisation howsoever described'. In spite of the lack of any public order disturbance, the appellant was convicted of belonging to such a club. By a majority of three to two, the conviction was upheld. The *dissenting* members of the House of Lords stating that the regulation was not merely *ultra vires* the 1922 Act, but too vague to be enforceable.

The appellant's argument in this case was that the regulation provided an example of *substantive ultra vires*. That is to say that the substance of the delegated legislation falls outside, or goes further than, that permitted by the parent Act. Thus in *Customs & Excise Commissioners* v *Cure & Deeley Ltd* [1962] 1 QB 340, a wide enabling power under a Finance Act was used to allow the Commissioners to determine the tax due in the event of a failure to provide an adequate tax return. Unless the Commissioners could be convinced within seven days that a different sum was due, the sum determined by the Commissioners was 'deemed to be the proper tax due'. In the view of the court, such regulations were *ultra vires* and invalid since in effect they substituted the rate of tax decided upon by the Commissioner for the true rate sanctioned by Parliament. Moreover the right of the taxpayer to have liability to taxation assessed in the court was effectively curtailed. *Cure & Deeley* is a useful case, therefore, since it demonstrates the vigilance of the courts to guard against implying a power to regulate so as to impose taxation (as in *Attorney-General* v *Wilts United Dairies Ltd* (1922) 91 LJ KB 897) or infringe the rights of the citizen (see *Chester* v *Bateson* [1920] 1 KB 829).

In order to decide issues of *ultra vires*, it may be necessary to construe delegated legislation in the context of the parent Act, so that if that Act states an underlying purpose, the regulations will be measured against that purpose. In *MacFisheries (Wholesale & Retail) Ltd* v *Coventry Corporation* [1957] 1 WLR 1066, the appellants were found not to have committed an offence relating to handling food so as to risk contamination because there was no evidence to show that the contamination would be injurious to public health. The enabling Act stated that regulations could be made for the 'protection of public health'. In such a case, the regulations are not necessarily *ultra vires*, they simply cannot apply to the appellant when read in tandem with the parent Act.

The importance of a careful reading of the parent Act is that it will determine the width of power given to the Minister. Thus in *R* v *Secretary of State for the Home Department, ex parte Brind* [1991] 1 AC 696, even an argument that the minister had issued restrictions under the Broadcasting Act 1981 which breach the European Convention on Human Rights were of no avail. The judicial caution is clearly evident in the words of Lord Ackner. He was concerned that there be no 'wrongful usurpation of power'. Thus the grounds of challenge to the lawfulness of the exercise of discretion are limited, for '[t]o seek the court's intervention on the basis that the correct or objectively reasonable decision is other than the decision which the minister has made is to invite the court to adjudicate as if Parliament had provided a right of appeal against the decision — that is, to invite an abuse of power by the judiciary'. It would have been necessary to show bad faith or unreasonableness (under the so-called *Wednesbury* principle: that restrictions are so unreasonable that no reasonable Minister would have imposed them — *Associated Provincial Picture Houses Ltd* v *Wednesbury Corporation* [1948] 1 KB 223).

Apart from challenges to the substance of the regulations, it may be that the procedure demanded by the parent Act is not followed in making the instrument with the result that the courts may declare it void. We have already considered two forms of *procedural ultra vires* in relation to publication and consultation (the *Aylesbury Mushrooms* case being an obvious example). It should be noted that procedural errors will invalidate the instrument if the procedure demanded by the parent Act is mandatory, but not if it is simply directory (and does not oblige, say, a Minister). Most case law examples concern issues such as consultation, but a serious procedural error could occur if, by an oversight for example, regulations were not laid before Parliament (this happened in the early 1940s with a series of regulations under the Fire Service (Emergency Provisions) Act 1941).

In late 1985 the London Borough of Greenwich challenged an order setting their maximum rate, which ought to have been served, under the Rates Act 1984, after the Rate Support Grant Report had been laid before Parliament. That Report had been laid before the Commons only, and the Greenwich order had been served prior to this. The Court of Appeal dismissed Greenwich's appeal against the refusal of judicial review. The Local Government Planning and Land Act 1980, which required the Report, demanded only that it be laid before the Commons. Moreover, if the order had preceded the Report this was a mere technicality not warranting the discretionary remedy of *certiorari* (see *R* v *Secretary of State for the Environment, ex parte Greenwich London Borough Council* (1987) 27 RVR 48). Documents referred to in statutory instruments need not themselves be laid before Parliament (*R* v *Secretary of State for Social Services, ex parte Camden London Borough Council* [1987] 1 WLR 819).

One final form of *procedural ultra vires* might be subdelegation. If delegated legislative power is given to a Minister, it is taken for granted that officials will exercise those powers in practice. If, however, the Minister chose to delegate to a separate authority without the approval of Parliament, there seems little doubt that the courts would hold that the power must be exercised by the particular person or body specified in the parent Act in the absence of an express or strongly implied approval for further delegation contained in that Act. For an example of a form of subdelegation see *R* v *Secretary of State for Social Services, ex parte Cotton* (1985) *The Times*, 14 December 1985. See also *R* v *Secretary of State for the Home Department, ex parte Oladehinde* [1991] 1 AC 254 in which the Court of Appeal said that it might be necessary for the Minister to delegate the management of certain affairs (in this case the issue of deportation orders) but that it could not be correct if the delegation of the power to issue such orders was to the immigration officers responsible for the investigation of illegal entry. the House of Lords agreed with this view. The court refused to find that the Secretary of State had acted *ultra vires* by acting in a disproportionate manner.

REVISION

If it is true, as suggested above, that the types of question available to an examiner wishing to question a student about delegated legislation are limited, this makes the task of revision much simpler. To begin with you might care to rehearse opening paragraphs to an answer. These might present the obvious dilemma of the growing necessity for and ever-increasing use of delegated legislation in spite of its essentially less than democratic nature. Suitably worded, this might provide an easy and appropriate introduction to a whole range of questions. At the same time it ought to be possible to arrange your notes to ensure that they contain points which might well be called for in an answer. Thus, if you are questioned on the necessity of the process, or given a quotation which roundly condemns the increasing use of delegated legislative powers, you ought to have the lines of attack drawn up well in advance. In reality you are being asked for little more than the advantages and disadvantages of subordinate legislation. It is generally important to cover both, for a question containing a quotation which is highly critical of delegated legislation will expect a carefully considered answer which also deals fully with its merits.

Your notes should therefore contain a section which deals with the pros and cons of delegated legislation. Ideally this should contain two columns — one with arguments for and the other with arguments against. Perhaps you could try to balance those out so that you choose (say) six major arguments in favour and six against. This is a great aid to memory, as is some form of shorthand which will assist you to recall each of the six points. Thus, if one point in favour of delegating legislative power is that the content of many statutory instruments is uninspiring and it would be extremely tedious for any legislature to deal with it, you could express this point by the one word in your notes — 'boring'. The chances are that you will remember this word appearing in your notes and it ought to spark off a complete recollection of the point which you wish to make.

However, it is important to remember that six points for, and six against is not an answer in itself. To begin with you must be certain that material of this sort will expand into a full answer. If you can say little other than 'Parliament is short of time to legislate' (or whatever) for each point, your answer will hardly prove impressive. Factual information on the use made of delegated legislation, examples of its abuse, etc., will assist in improving the breadth and quality of your answer. Even then, an answer which simply discusses six points for and six against, however well, might not be unusual in an examination but it will seem to have a rather artificial structure. Therefore, you ought to attempt in advance of the examination to devise methods of linking the pros together with the cons. Ideally this would allow you to answer each point in favour of a particular stance with an even more telling point against. It is this kind of answer which cannot help but impress the examiner. It looks as though you have been able to marshal a complex body of argument, and to produce a more carefully structured assault on the question than those of your fellow examinees, in the very limited time allowed. You have succeeded in pulling the wool over the marker's eyes. Rather than achieving so much in 45 minutes, you took the trouble to do so over two or three hours' revision, some days in advance of the examination.

Nor need the list of advantages and disadvantages be entirely your own. Most textbooks include a section of this kind. Indeed, you ought sometimes to beware of devising novel arguments. Generally, if a particular line of argument carries great merit, it will have been written up in books or articles already. Bizarre solutions to legal problems or complex, convoluted contentions may not serve you so well as the obvious, but manifestly correct reasoning offered in classes during the year. This is especially true in problem questions, since few examiners would seek to set a question which requires highly imaginative solutions if it is to be answered in so short a period of time. It matters not so much whether you have taken your arguments from books and journals, but much more whether you have understood those arguments and used them to answer the examination question in a manner which is appropriate.

The subject-matter of this chapter, and of the next one, forms part of administrative law. In law degree courses some administrative law is generally included within the constitutional law syllabus to satisfy the demands of the professional bodies who offer exemptions from their examinations for students who have studied a certain core of material. Administrative law will generally be offered as a separate subject later in the degree course. One advantage of this is that there is ample opportunity for a constitutional law student to follow these topics in greater depth by referring to texts on administrative law if they feel sufficiently confident. Thus, if you are putting together notes on the merits and demands of delegated legislation, you may find additional arguments in the more advanced texts, and certainly the material on safeguards against abuse will be covered in greater depth. Providing you have absorbed the material on your syllabus, never be scared of reading ahead by following cases, journal articles, or other reading, footnoted in the texts chosen for your course. It is most satisfying for an examiner to find a reference in a paper which must be the product of the student's own wider reading.

However, before doing this do make sure that you have covered in your revision all of the basic material which you will need to complete an answer. Think carefully what this might include. We have seen already that there is an obvious link between delegated legislation and judicial review of administrative action, so that both issues might need to be considered in order to answer a problem question. It is amazing how many students will answer a problem question on delegated legislation and write that a regulation appears to be *ultra vires* the parent Act, but go no further than that, failing to consider the question of remedies even though the character in the problem is being prosecuted for breaching the regulation. Much depends on the detail of your own course, but this seems an area in which a knowledge of remedies in administrative law is vital.

THE EXAMINATION

Let us take the type of question discussed in the previous section which refers to the merits of delegated legislation:

'In spite of supposed justifications, delegated legislation offends traditional constitutional principles and is open to obvious abuse.' Discuss.

Two preliminary points may be made about this question. Firstly, it is very tempting to follow its drift and produce an outright condemnation of delegated legislation. Beware. Anyone who considers the issue with any care is likely to conclude that, whatever the demerits, it would be absolutely impossible to manage without delegated legislation. To that extent the presence of delegated legislation must be accepted as part of our constitu-tional structure. The second point is that the question does not say 'What are the advantages and disadvantages of delegated legislation?' although it would be no surprise to find students answering the question as though it did say that. Taking the question apart, it says that in spite of justifications (discuss these) delegated legislation offends constitutional principles (such as what?) and is open to abuse (how?). Beyond a discussion of advantages and disadvantages, we have to consider constitutional theory and control of abuse of delegated power.

At this point a plan becomes necessary. There is no magic formula, but suppose that we decide to deal with pros and cons before deciding to what extent delegated power is open to abuse and concluding with a reconciliation between delegated legislation and constitutional principles. Begin jotting down the justifications (presumably using material from your revised notes). Remember that in a sense the purposes of delegated legislation provide the justification also. Thus if one purpose is to allow swift emergency action to be taken, then one advantage of delegated legislation is that it allows swift emergency action. . . . Match against these the criticisms of delegated legislation. For example, most writers agree that skeleton legislation is undesirable. By this they mean an Act of Parliament which has little substantive content but which gives wide legislative powers to another body. However, this might be acceptable, exceptionally, in an emergency situation. Consequently you could construct your argument to state that:

> Whilst it might be difficult to achieve efficient emergency action through the parliamentary legislative process, delegated legislation allows a prompt and flexible response. In consequence, wide powers of regulation are sometimes delegated in a state of emergency. It would be less satisfactory, however, to find such a width of delegation through skeleton legislation outside of an emergency, and there are few formal controls to prevent this if Parliament is so unwise as to enact primary legislation.

In this way, pros and cons may be linked with a little imagination and not too much difficulty. Notice that the objection to delegated legislation here is not to the practice of delegation as such but to a particular kind of abuse which may arise. In fact this is true of many of the criticisms which you may find so that, to a large extent, the adequacy of controls upon abuse becomes significant. This leads neatly to the next part of the question.

Of course it is unrealistic to attempt a complete explanation of the various safeguards against abuse in answer to a question of this kind — time would not allow it. What is needed is an assessment of the effectiveness of safeguards in controlling abuse. It may be possible to tie this in within the other part of the question which concerns traditional constitutional principles. If you consider which principles might be offended by the notion of delegating legislative power, two are immediately obvious: namely the supremacy of Parliament and the separation of powers. It might be possible, therefore, to link up these principles with parliamentary scrutiny of delegated legislation. For example, you could argue along the lines that executive initiative is the dominant feature of primary legislation as well as secondary legislation, so that it is a little naive to argue that the delegated powers are particularly more offensive to the idea of the formal separation of powers. Moreover, it may be argued that Parliament frames the powers in the parent Act and has an effective scrutiny process which asserts the supremacy of Parliament rather than denies it.

It is by no means vital to argue in this particular direction, but it can be seen that, suitably embellished, this line of thinking brings together a series of relevant points. There is some value in being a pragmatist on occasions. It may happen that it is quicker and simpler to adopt a particular stance, rather than to promote a view which, although more acceptable to your own thinking, would take much longer to present effectively.

To conclude it might be possible to shape an argument covering the entire question by stating that many of the arguments against delegated legislation are actually aimed at particular misuses, whereas there are obvious advantages. Therefore if these misuses can be avoided, and scrutiny, particularly by Parliament, allows this, then there is no obvious objection to delegated powers. Rather than offend constitutional principles, the process reinforces the supremacy of an independent legislature, if only because it leaves Parliament free to deal with the major matters of government.

A Problem Question

What follows is a relatively straightforward problem question in which you are asked to advise upon regulations which for a number of reasons appear to be *ultra vires*.

> The Control of Rabbits Act 1999 provides that, in order to curtail rabbit-rot virus, the Minister may by statutory instrument make such rules as he thinks fit for the purpose of controlling the size of the rabbit population. The Act obliges the Minister to consult such bodies as appear to him to be representative of rabbit owners.
>
> Subsequently, in the face of a rapidly increasing bill for the import of lettuces to replace those eaten by rabbits, the Minister, Warren, makes regulations under the Act prohibiting the keeping of two or more rabbits of opposite sexes on the same premises. In addition all owners of pet rabbits are required to obtain a licence costing £100 per rabbit per annum. Finally, Warren authorises the Rabbits Veterinary Society (RVS) to draw up guidelines under which RVS inspectors may order the destruction of unhealthy or infirm rabbits.
>
> Buck is Secretary of the Bunny Breeders of Britain (BBB), the largest association of rabbit owners in the country. He is invited to give his views on the new regulations, but only two weeks before they were laid before Parliament, and the executive body of the association was unable to meet, in order to prepare a response, within this time.
>
> Buck owns two rabbits (one of each sex), Himm and Hare, which are kept on the same premises. He is upset because he cannot afford the licence fee for Himm, and Hare has been condemned as unhealthy by an RVS inspector acting upon RVS guidelines.
>
> Advise Buck.

In an earlier chapter the point was made that problem questions have the advantage of providing a framework for an answer in so far as they introduce issues, and all the student need do is locate the major legal difficulties and provide the relevant advice as required. Thus, even if the question above seems extraordinarily difficult to begin with, by breaking down the first two paragraphs it is possible to isolate the points which require consideration. For example:

(a)   The power is to control the rabbit population in order to curtail disease. Will the measures control population, and are they designed to restrict the disease in question?

(b)   The Minister is obliged to consult representative bodies. Was this done and was the consultation adequate?

(c)   The Minister introduces control by licences and inspection. Are these measures *ultra vires* for any reason?

In effect, these broad questions cover the possible difficulties which may arise. The first is obviously central to the whole question, and it might be easy to then deal with the other issues of substance arising out of point (c) before dealing with the procedural issue of consultation at the end.

Earlier it was said that the regulation must be read together with the parent Act (and *MacFisheries (Wholesale & Retail) Ltd* v *Coventry Corporation* [1957] 1 WLR 1066 was cited as an example). Applying this to the first of our three points, the power is to control the rabbit population in order to prevent the spread of disease. It seems clear that if the parent Act does express a purpose, the expectation of the courts will be that the regulation should further that purpose. If the regulation is designed to achieve some other purpose, this may render it *ultra vires*. This is clear from a Privy Council case of *Sydney Council* v *Campbell* [1925] AC 338, in which a compulsory purchase power for the purpose of redevelopment was wrongly exercised by a local authority to acquire land likely to increase in value so that the city council could enjoy the benefits. In such a case there is no doubting the good faith of the authority, but the action may amount nonetheless to a misapplication of a power. There is no doubt that this principle governs the exercise of delegated legislative power. Consequently, on this ground alone, the regulations seem to be *ultra vires* the parent Act.

However, having discovered a ground which itself might offer Buck a sufficient remedy, it is necessary, nonetheless, to deal with other grounds. This is expected of you. Turning then to the licence, why might the imposition of the £100 licence be objectionable? The most obvious reason is the rule of construction, used by the courts to interpret delegated powers, that express words are necessary in order to raise finance (see *Attorney-General* v *Wilts United Dairies Ltd* (1922) 91 LJ KB 897). If the courts were convinced that such a large licence fee was tantamount to a taxation upon rabbits, then there is little doubt that they would intervene and declare the regulation void. Certainly they would wish to ensure that a licence fee of this size was necessary in order to control the rabbit population since the courts have shown themselves ready to enquire closely into the exercise of powers couched even in strongly subjective terms (see, e.g., *Congreve* v *Home Office* [1976] QB 629).

The point relating to the inspection of rabbits is perhaps the least obvious. You may look at this and decide that the destruction of unhealthy rabbits falls squarely within the purpose of the Act. Before concluding that this must be the case, however, remember that such a point is hardly likely to have been placed in the question unless the examiner wished to raise a specific point. Perhaps you have addressed yourself to the wrong question. Check mentally through your notes as to the types of *ultra vires* exercise of powers. What about subdelegation? We saw earlier that there are few examples in English law. However, if the effect of the Minister's action is to further delegate his powers so as to allow the RVS to decide the grounds upon which rabbits should be destroyed, there seems little doubt that, in the absence of an express power in the parent Act, this would lead to the court holding that the RVS guidelines are invalid.

The *Aylesbury Mushrooms* case [1972] 1 WLR 190 ought to assist in relation to the question of consultation. The only problem is that some attempt at consultation takes place, but it is extraordinarily hurried. The answer lies in the case of *Rollo* v *Minister of Town & Country Planning* [1948] 1 All ER 13, in which it was said that consultation must be made with a 'receptive mind' and that a 'sufficient opportunity must be given ... to tender advice'.

Two final points arise. So far we have dealt with judicial control, and this decision may be justified since it appears, from the question, that the legislation is in force. However, in view of the unusual purpose to which the regulations are put (curbing imports of lettuce) and in view of the heavy licence fee, it might be appropriate to express surprise that the Joint Committee on Statutory Instruments either did not report adversely upon these regulations, or, if they did, that Parliament sought neither to refuse approval (we are not told the appropriate resolution procedure, if any) nor seek to force the Minister to withdraw the regulations. This is not a significant point, but it does show that you are alert to the various forms of control.

The second point is rather more important. So far we have still not met the demands of the examiner. We must advise Buck. Your conclusion ought therefore to recap upon the *ultra vires* issues and advise as to the possibilities of direct challenge (by means of judicial review) or indirect (collateral) challenge (as a defence to criminal charges, perhaps for keeping male and female rabbits together) and as to the remedies available to Buck. This indirect challenge can provide an inexpensive and effective remedy; see, for example, Winder's defence of *ultra vires* to possession proceedings for his flat in *Wandsworth London Borough Council* v *Winder* [1985] AC 461 (but cf. *Avon County Council* v *Buscott* [1988] QB 656 where this course of action proved ineffective for trespassing gypsies complaining of a local authority's failure to provide sites for them as required by statute). It is surprising how many otherwise good answers stop short of the question of remedies — the importance of which is obvious, at least as far as Buck is concerned!

CONCLUSION

Potentially the subject area covered by delegated legislation is huge. A full understanding of the range of delegated powers and of the controls placed upon the exercise of those powers, particularly the judicial controls, could fill a sizeable textbook. However, most courses will confine the material to a manageable amount, and questions will centre upon the most obvious problems relating to the topic. At the same time it is likely that some administrative law material will be examined upon your course, because of the demands of the professional bodies. A (suitably measured) treatment of delegated legislation within the syllabus has the advantage of fulfilling the demand for administrative law materials, whilst confronting the student with constitutional issues which have a practical importance.

The type of questions outlined above may be legitimately expected therefore. There is little to fear from them. It is possible to anticipate the ambit of such questions, and relatively straightforward to prepare for them. Moreover, a thorough knowledge of the workings of delegated legislation gained early in your course will pay dividends in later years.

FURTHER READING

Baldwin, R. and McCrudden, C.,(1987) *Regulation and Public Law* (Law in Context Series) (London: Weidenfeld & Nicholson). See Chapter 4.

Hartey, T. C. and Griffith, J., (1981) *Government and the Law* (Law in Context Series) (London: Weidenfeld & Nicholson). See Chapter 16.

Hayhurst, J. D. and Wallington, P., 'The Parliamentary Scrutiny of Delegated Legislation' [1988] *Public Law* 547.

10   NATURAL JUSTICE

The phrase 'natural justice' is used often by laymen, usually when complaining of something which they feel is unjust. To the lawyer, the phrase is quite specific since it refers to a set of common law rules which seek to ensure the operation of fair procedures. Originally of application to courts of law, the rules have been extended to apply to judicial and quasi-judicial processes of statutory bodies and other (non-statutory) organisations. The rules can be condensed into two convenient tags which are still often expressed in the Latin: *'nemo iudex in causa sua'* often written *'nemo debet esse iudex in propria causa'* (no one can be judge in his own cause) and *'audi alteram partem'* (hear both sides). Sometimes you will hear these referred to as 'the rule against bias' and 'the right to be heard'. The principles of natural justice form one part of a much wider subject, namely judicial review of administrative action. Often, however, as part of the administrative law content of constitutional law courses, natural justice is taught as a self-contained topic.

Thus far, the subject seems easy — two simple rules which apply to decisions taken judicially. Indeed it may be that many students make the mistake of believing that the subject is quite straightforward. In fact, a host of complexities arise when you begin to study the precise content of the principles of natural justice. To begin with, when do the principles apply? What is meant by judicial and quasi-judicial decisions and how can you identify (in a problem question, perhaps) a situation in which the principles may be invoked? Then, as regards the principles themselves, the *nemo iudex* rule does not apply only to situations in which a person seeks to gain a direct advantage from the decision. Similarly, the *audi alteram partem* rule comprises a host of specific rights relating to the conduct of hearings. Finally, the waters are well and truly muddied by the concept of the duty to act fairly, the relationship of which to the principles of natural justice is uncertain — even to the judiciary!

Consequently, it is important to develop a clear knowledge of what the principles of natural justice are, and of when the principles are applicable. A detailed understanding of the case law is indispensable. When faced with a problem question, you will be able to arrive at solutions by making analogies with decided cases. Thus, suppose there is a problem question in which a local councillor is not selected to contest a local government election in his own ward. You may not know whether he is entitled to a hearing, or know of any cases which would assist you, but a case such as *John v Rees* [1970] Ch 345 (which concerned the suspension from a political party of a local constituency party) may provide you with ammunition with which to attack the problem. It helps therefore to ensure that your notes contain a fund of examples on which you are able to draw, and which may be used to add authority to your answer. Of course, the basis of any answer must still be a bedrock of legal principle upon which the cases may be laid in order to construct a solid answer. In other words, your cases must fit into a carefully prepared framework of how the rules of natural justice operate. The operation of those rules is now considered.

THE APPLICATION OF THE RULES OF NATURAL JUSTICE

Thus far it has been said that the rules apply to certain quasi-judicial functions of various bodies. Although this is designed to distinguish purely administrative functions, two problems arise: (a) it is not easy to separate judicial from administrative functions in all cases, and (b) even in purely administrative decision-making, the law may demand a duty to act fairly.

The duty to act fairly is considered below, but let us deal briefly with the judicial/administrative distinction. Obviously not every exercise of a legal power will give rise to the application of the principles of natural justice (though we will see below that the effect of the power on the individual may be a significant factor). This is particularly true in an age in which there exists a highly developed and complex administrative structure. At first the courts were slow to recognise that, outside the formal judicial structure, the rules of natural justice could operate to safeguard individual rights. At best they required good faith in decision-making. Thus in *Local Government Board v Arlidge* [1915] AC 120 a closing order was served by the Board on Arlidge's property following an inquiry before a housing inspector. Arlidge did not see the inspector's report; nor was he given an oral hearing before any official of the Board. The House of Lords thought that the Board were free to follow such procedures which they described as free from bias and allowing a sufficient opportunity to be heard.

Although cases such as *Arlidge* were not the invariable rule (see *Errington v Minister of Health* [1935] 1 KB 249 below) the courts showed themselves to be particularly timid in challenging administrative decisions, which involved matters of policy, as the 20th century witnessed the increasing influence of government decisions on the lives of many individuals. This was true even where, on the face of it, a government minister had closed his mind to possible objections (see for example, *Franklin* v *Minister of Town and Country Planning* [1948] AC 87 and compare *Fairmount Investments Ltd* v *Secretary of State for the Environment* [1976] 1 WLR 1255). The turning-point came with *Ridge* v *Baldwin* [1964] AC 40 (considered below) in which the judges seemed to recognise the desire on the part of many to extend the application of the principles of natural justice in order to match the increasing powers of administrative agencies. Since 1964 this has happened. The following situations provide some guidelines as to when the principles may or may not apply. Often they provide examples of decisions which are quasi-judicial, but with which the courts are reluctant to interfere. It goes without saying that because these are difficult areas, they are commonly selected by examiners drafting problem questions.

Statutory Restrictions

A statute might restrict the operation of the rules of natural justice by its express words. In addition the courts may imply an exclusion. For example, a statutory procedure which permits written representations might be read by the courts so as to exclude the right to oral representations.

Disciplinary Proceedings

It is sometimes said that the rules of natural justice will not apply to disciplinary proceedings within prisons, the forces, or services such as the police. The authority generally cited for this proposition is *Ex parte Fry* [1954] 1 WLR 730, which concerned the disciplining of a fire officer for refusing to obey an order. However, of late, cases such as *R* v *Hull Prison Board of Visitors, ex parte St Germain* [1978] QB 678 illustrate that this exclusionary rule is not absolute, and ought not to apply to the more formal hearings of the prison visitors for example. What the courts seemed anxious to avoid was the necessity of intervention on each occasion that a prison governor or a chief officer had cause to reprimand a prisoner or lower-ranked officer (see the judgment of Lord Denning MR in *Becker* v *Home Office* [1972] 2 QB 407, also *R* v *Deputy Governor of Camphill Prison, ex parte King* [1985] QB 735). However in *Leech* v *Deputy Governor of Parkhurst Prison* [1988] AC 533 the House of Lords overruled the *Camphill Prison* case, and stated firmly that disciplinary actions of a prison governor were amenable to review, and that the key to intervention was the seriousness of the prisoner's rights allegedly breached.

Dismissal from Employment

The courts may be reluctant to intervene to demand the observance of the rules of natural justice in the process of dismissal from employment. If the dismissal is unfair the employee will generally have a remedy of unfair dismissal, and a dismissal may be unfair notwithstanding the merits of the employer's case due to procedural irregularities. The reluctance of the courts to intervene pre-dates unfair dismissal legislation, however, and may apply irrespective of a statutory remedy (see *Vidyodaya University Council v Silva* [1965] 1 WLR 77).

Having said that, the absence of private law rights may prompt the courts to review a decision to dismiss. A recent example of this is the case of *R v Secretary of State for the Home Department, ex parte Benwell* [1985] QB 554 which involved the dismissal of a prison officer. A prison officer holds the rank of constable, rather than working under a contract of employment, and the vulnerability of the applicant to dismissal without legal redress (otherwise than by judicial review) clearly influenced the court.

The fact that a prison officer holds the office of constable is significant. In *Ridge v Baldwin* [1964] AC 40 the Chief Constable of Brighton was acquitted in a criminal trial, only to find himself dismissed, without a hearing, by the local Watch Committee. The House of Lords granted a declaration on the basis that the principles of natural justice applied. As a holder of an office (and removable for particular cause) a police officer was entitled to the protection of the rules of natural justice, and to a declaration that a dismissal is invalid. *Ridge v Baldwin* proved a turning-point in the history of natural justice, and given the lead by the House of Lords, the courts have been willing to expand the scope of natural justice generally, and also in relation to the question of dismissals from office.

Thus in *Malloch v Aberdeen Corporation* [1971] 1 WLR 1578 the local authority had the power, under statute, to dismiss Scottish schoolteachers at pleasure, subject to prior notice to the teacher before passing a resolution to dismiss. The House of Lords was prepared to accept that the prior notice must by inference include some opportunity to be heard following the service of the notice. Some discussion concerned the problem of whether or not the teachers might be considered office-holders, and two members of the House dissented on the basis that they could not be so considered. However, at least two members of the majority indicated their preparedness to accept the application of the principles of natural justice to a wider range of public employees than the strict category of office-holders. (The courts have also stated that the doctrine can apply to the expulsion of students! See *R v Board of Governors of the London Oratory School, ex parte R* (1988) *The Times*, 17 February 1988.)

Nonetheless, the law is less than clear here. One area of doubt concerns the distinction between ordinary employees (who may be restricted to statutory or contractual remedies) and office-holders or others with an available public law remedy. This is a tricky area indeed for a first-year student, not having studied employment law. Faced with a problem question regarding the application of natural justice to a particular dismissal, the best that can be done is to state the principles and work from whatever case law seems helpful. However, an examiner choosing a dismissal from work for the topic of a question may seek to assist by choosing an example not dissimilar to a well-known case, or one included in the syllabus and the teaching.

Licensing

Particular problems arise in relation to licensing, especially as regards the application of the *audi alteram partem* rule. Clearly it might prove a great burden if every application for some form of licence entailed the right to an oral hearing. Statute may lay down procedures for tribunals dealing with licensing matters, but this is not always the case. Local authorities have a wide range of licensing functions, many of which date back to ancient, private Acts of Parliament. In *R v Barnsley Metropolitan Borough Council, ex parte Hook* [1976] 1 WLR 1052, the revocation of a market trader's licence (for urinating in public) was quashed for a breach of the rule against bias (the market manager who made the allegations was present during the adjudication). However, it seems clear from this case that a denial of the hearing would have provided equally good ground for challenge. In Lord Denning's view the action was 'too severe a punishment' and there can be no doubt that the Court of Appeal were very much aware that the loss of the licence was the loss of the trader's livelihood.

The same principles may not pertain to the refusal of licence application, however, as is clear from the case of *McInnes v Onslow-Fane* [1978] 1 WLR 1520. This involved the refusal of the British Boxing Board of Control to allow an oral hearing of an application for a boxing manager's licence. It was sufficient in the view of the court that the Board had acted fairly and honestly even though reasons had not been given for the decision. The court did make it clear, however, that where the refusal to issue a licence might damage an applicant's reputation or cause excessive financial dislocation, a hearing might well form part of the duty to act fairly. An interesting extension of the right to a hearing within the field of licensing is the case of *R v Liverpool Corporation, ex parte Liverpool Taxi Fleet Operators' Association* [1972] 2 QB 299 (not to be confused with *R v Liverpool City Council, ex parte Liverpool Taxi Fleet Operators' Association* [1975] 1 WLR 701) in which the Association were held to be entitled to a hearing in the face of a proposal to increase the number of taxi-cabs. As Lord Denning MR pointed out a decision along such lines would be adverse to the interests of the Association's members, and if they would be entitled to a hearing if licences were revoked, it is hard to see the logic of denying a hearing when an increase in new licences would devalue those already in existence.

Investigation

Although a duty to act fairly may apply to an investigation, at this preliminary stage in the process, the rules of natural justice may not be thought appropriate. Thus in *Lewis* v *Heffer* [1978] 1 WLR 1601 a suspension without a hearing might well be upheld if that suspension is part of an investigative process which will proceed to a full inquiry in due course. There are a variety of cases under company law involving investigations into the affairs of companies by the Department of Trade. On the whole the courts have not favoured the application of the rules of natural justice, but the courts have shown concern that a report which contains serious allegations against an individual ought not to be published if that person is in ignorance of the allegations and has no facility to answer them (see *Re Pergamon Press Ltd* [1971] Ch 388).

General Principles

What can be learnt from the review of particular situations which causes problems? The first lesson is the willingness of the courts to intervene in certain classes of cases, especially where reputation or livelihood is at stake. Also, although formally there is a separation between the judicial and administrative decision, in fact there is no easy dividing line, and one gradually changes shade to become the other. This is not so surprising; many administrative decisions involve an assessment of the merits of a particular case. One consequence of this is that there are different levels upon which the courts might choose to intervene. Thus, the courts would wish to see freedom from bias whatever the nature of the decision-making process. Here there may simply be a sliding scale between the *nemo iudex* principle and the notion of bad faith. Greater difficulties arise in relation to when a full right to be heard should be implied. Even here, however, the courts may demand a range of responses from a tribunal varying from the fullest application of the *audi alteram partem* principle to the requirement to act fairly. It is important to consider the substantive rules of natural justice in this light.

THE RULE AGAINST BIAS

Impartiality is at the heart of the judicial process. The danger of bias may clearly arise because of a direct pecuniary interest in which case a judge ought to stand down rather than hear the case. Such is the result of *Dimes* v *Grand Junction Canal* (1852) 3 HL Cas 759 in which the House of Lords set aside the decision of the Lord Chancellor who was a shareholder in the company appearing before him. However, it is not only a financial interest which may lead a judge to favour a particular party. Thus in *R v Sussex Justices, ex parte McCarthy* [1924] 1 KB 256 a solicitor was acting as clerk to the justices in the hearing of a traffic offence following a collision. His firm was due to act for the other party to the accident in civil proceedings. Although he was not asked to advise the justices on this occasion, the clerk did retire with them. An application, by the defendant, for a writ of *certiorari* to quash the conviction was granted. In the, now famous, words of Lord Hewart CJ: '[It] is of fundamental importance that justice should not only be done, but should manifestly and undoubtedly be seen to be done' (for similar instances see *R v Feltham Justices, ex parte Nye* (1985) *The Times*, 15 February 1985 and *R v Bristol Crown Court, ex parte Cooper* [1989] 1 WLR 879). Note, however, that in *R v Bristol Crown Court, ex parte Cooper* [1990] 1 WLR 1031 the presence, on the Crown Court bench, of a justice who had rejected a previous application for licensing of a wine bar made some six months earlier did not amount to a breach of natural justice given the requirements in Crown Court rules for justices with local knowledge.

This principle was applied in *Metropolitan Properties Co. (FGC) Ltd v Lannon* [1969] 1 QB 577, in which a chairman of a rent tribunal had fixed a rent for a property belonging to the landlords of his father's flat. In his work as a solicitor the chairman had been involved also in protracted disputes with the landlords. His determination of the rent was quashed by *certiorari* since 'right-minded persons' might think that there was 'a real likelihood of bias'. This objective test has generally found favour, with the result that in reviewing decisions of tribunals the courts have been willing to intervene even though it seems likely the judges themselves did not suspect bias on the part of the tribunal.

The objective test is clearly illustrated by *Hannam v Bradford Corporation* [1970] 1 WLR 973 in which a local education authority committee met to consider a recommendation to dismiss a teacher, made by governors of a school. Some of these governors were members of the relevant committee, and although they were absent from the committee meeting, it was held that the dismissal procedures contravened the principles of natural justice. It is not easy to reconcile this decision with another involving the same local authority. In *Ward v Bradford Corporation* (1971) 70 LGR 27 a girl student who was found to have had a man staying overnight in her room in a teachers' training college was expelled by the same body which had instituted disciplinary proceedings. The expulsion was upheld. As de Smith wrote: 'it seems better to regard *Hannam* as the rule and *Ward* as the exception'. The later decision in *R v Barnsley Metropolitan Borough Council, ex parte Hook* [1976] 1 WLR 1052 adds weight to this opinion.

In *R v Gough* [1993] AC 646, the House of Lords stated the objective test in terms of whether there is a real danger of injustice rather than a real likelihood, and said that this approach should apply generally. The case concerned a man who had stood trial for conspiring with his brother to commit robbery, though the brother had been discharged at the committal stage. The man was found guilty by a jury which included his brother's next-door neighbour, though the juror claimed that she had not realised the relationship until the brother protested from the public gallery after the verdict was announced.

THE RIGHT TO A FAIR HEARING

This right includes not just a hearing, but a reasonable opportunity to put forward a particular case. Moreover, a reasonable opportunity must also include prior notice of any charges which a person must face, or of the case against the person.

Entitlement to Be Heard

The reasons why prior notice of a hearing is important are obvious. Apart from enabling a person to arrange to appear at the hearing, time may be needed to prepare a case, or even if the person does not wish to attend a hearing, prior notice will allow written representations. Consequently, the *audi alteram partem* rule has been invoked on many occasions when the first knowledge a person has of a decision to condemn or penalise him or her in some way is the communication of the result. *Ridge* v *Baldwin* [1964] AC 40 was such a case. However, the right to prior notice may be offended in less obvious ways. For example, if a person is informed in advance that he faces charges on one set of grounds but the hearing actually acts upon another set of grounds of which inadequate notice was given, the courts will treat this as a denial of an opportunity to be heard (*Lau Liat Meng* v *Disciplinary Committee* [1968] AC 391). Similarly the Privy Council also declared void the decision in which the results of an inquiry formed the basis of a dismissal of a police officer to whom the inquiry report had not been disclosed (*Kanda* v *Government of Malaya* [1962] AC 322).

Indeed the courts are likely to quash decisions of tribunals which hear any evidence to which a party is not allowed to respond. Conclusions drawn from a property inspection, but not put to the landlord, in a rent tribunal hearing would come within this principle (*R* v *Paddington and St Marylebone Rent Tribunal, ex parte Bell London and Provincial Properties Ltd* [1949] 1 KB 666; *Taylor* v *National Union of Seamen* [1967] 1 WLR 532). The exception to this rule may be where it must be obvious to the party what the substance of the allegations is. In such circumstances, providing the hearing centres upon those allegations alone, the failure to elaborate further upon these allegations will not necessarily amount to a breach of the principles of natural justice (see *Sloane* v *General Medical Council* [1970] 1 WLR 1130).

As is noted above, statute may lay down the detailed requirements as to notice, as indeed might the procedural rules for tribunal hearings. This is particularly true in the areas of planning and land use. In general these will be specific in their demands in comparison with the rather more vague requirements of the common law. On the other hand, the courts may demand that the statutory requirements are strictly met. In a famous case, *Errington* v *Minister of Health* [1935] 1 KB 249, the Court of Appeal quashed a slum clearance order which they decided had been made in breach of the rules of natural justice and outside the powers in the Housing Act 1930. Private meetings between council officials and civil servants held after the public inquiry to which the plaintiff was not invited provided the grounds for challenge. In the absence of statutory requirements as to the period of notice required, the sufficiency of the notice will be a question for the court to decide, bearing in mind the nature of the allegations.

In deciding this, however, it is important to remember that the entitlement is to an opportunity to be heard and not to a hearing as such. Consequently it may not be unreasonable to proceed with the hearing if the party fails to attend, without taking an opportunity to offer an explanation of absence, or if the party produces some reason which appears wholly inadequate. Thus in *Annamunthodo* v *Oilfields Workers' Trade Union* [1961] AC 945 a refusal to attend a hearing because of a prior engagement to be a judge at a 'mock trial' sponsored by a girls' group was described by the Privy Council as 'a poor excuse'. And in *Ostreicher* v *Secretary of State for the Environment* [1978] 1 WLR 810 even though an objector's religious beliefs prevented attendance at an inquiry upon the day set, there was held to be no breach of natural justice when the hearing went ahead in view of a complete failure on the part of the objector to communicate the problem caused by the day which had been chosen.

The Form and Conduct of the Hearing

A right to be heard is not necessarily a right to be heard orally, since the matter may be dealt with adequately in writing. However, the more serious the nature of the proceedings, the more likely is the need for an oral hearing — especially if this is the express desire of a party (see *R* v *Army Board of the Defence Council, ex parte Anderson* [1992] QB 169). Similarly the strict rules of evidence need not always apply, but if the hearing is akin to that which might take place in a court of law, the courts will be more ready to uphold evidential rules, particularly when to fail to do so would effectively deprive a party of a hearing (see *R* v *Hull Prison, ex parte St Germain (No. 2)* [1979] 1 WLR 1401; compare *R* v *Commission for Racial Equality, ex parte Cottrell & Rothon* [1980] 1 WLR 1580).

However, an oral hearing in proceedings of a judicial nature will generally include a right to make a submission, call witnesses, and cross-examine witnesses or others making allegations (see *Tudor v Ellesmere Port and Neston Borough Council* (1987) *The Times*, 8 May 1987 (withdrawal of taxi driver's licence)). It may be different, however, if, rather than making allegations a witness merely gives evidence outlining a particular policy. Thus it was no breach of natural justice to refuse to allow the cross-examination of a civil servant explaining national road policies at a public inquiry (see *Bushell v Secretary of State for the Environment* [1981] AC 75).

One difficult problem concerns legal representation before domestic tribunals. It has been suggested by the Court of Appeal that the more serious the charges, and the consequences of the hearing, the more willing the courts will be to apply the rules of natural justice — as in *Pett v Greyhound Racing Association Ltd* [1969] 1 QB 125 in which a hearing into the doping of greyhounds might have lead to the loss of Pett's trainer's licence (but see also *Pett v Greyhound Racing Association Ltd (No. 2)* [1970] 1 QB 46). However, the courts seem prepared to accept that the internal rules of an association may legitimately exclude legal representation, as do the appeals procedures of the Football Association (see *Enderby Town Football Club Ltd v Football Association Ltd* [1971] Ch 591). Note also that in amateur sport, in which 'livelihood' may not be at stake, the courts may be less ready to intervene (*Currie v Barton* (1988) *The Times*, 12 February 1988 — amateur tennis). It has been said that the courts should act with restraint when faced with decisions of sporting bodies — *R v Disciplinary Committee of the Jockey Club, ex parte Massingberd-Mundy* [1993] 2 All ER 225. In that case although it was accepted that the Jockey Club was a body created under the royal prerogative (by royal charter) and had a monopoly of power in an area of wide public interest, the courts refused to review a decision refusing to appoint the applicant as chairman of race meetings.

Finally, there is no general right to reasons (see *Local Government Board v Arlidge* [1915] AC 120) although the rules of statutory tribunals may demand that these be made available. However, it may be that a challenge to a decision will produce reasons either because the decision-maker will need to prove the correctness of the decisions, or because reasons will become necessary as the basis of the appeal. Thus a failure to explain a course of conduct may lead to the implication that the decision was capricious and therefore *ultra vires* (see *Padfield v Minister of Agriculture, Fisheries and Food* [1968] AC 997). Note that a duty to give reasons may arise out of the broader duty, laid upon administrative bodies, to act fairly. Thus, in *R v Lambeth London Borough Council, ex parte Walters* (1993) 26 HLR 170, in an appeal against an offer of accommodation, which had been dismissed by the authority with no reason given, it was held that the authority was obliged to act fairly and that in such circumstances there was a general duty to give reasons.

THE DUTY TO ACT FAIRLY

Earlier we spoke of the development of the principles of natural justice to match the increasingly significant role of administrative agencies. The duty to act fairly represents the foremost development and, although rather vague in its scope, this allows a flexible response, on the part of the judiciary, to ensure (as the name suggests) that in terms of the procedures adopted, the exercise of administrative discretion meets at least the rudimentary requirements of natural justice. Note that to equate the doctrine with fairness, the courts will require a substantive breach; a technical breach would not suffice: see R v Chief Constable of the Thames Valley Police, ex parte Cotton [1990] IRLR 344.

Thus in a case such as R v Liverpool Corporation, ex parte Liverpool Taxi Fleet Operators' Association [1972] 2 QB 299 it is easy to see that the court reviewed the procedures adopted in an area which is likely to fall outside the traditional ambit of natural justice. However, since the scope of this duty is so vague, it is not always easy to find a consistent pattern. In Schmidt v Secretary of State for Home Affairs [1969] 2 Ch 149 the plaintiff was an alien studying at a college of scientology and was refused an extension to his residence permit without a hearing. In the words of Lord Denning MR: '[A] foreign alien has no right — and, I would add, no legitimate expectation — of being allowed to stay. He can be refused without reasons given and without a hearing. Once his time has expired, he has to go.'

Lord Denning reached his conclusion having considered the case of Re H.K. (An Infant) [1967] 2 QB 617. In that case Lord Parker CJ stated that an immigration officer was 'required to act fairly' in dealing with an immigrant from Pakistan to whom he had refused entry on the grounds that he appeared to be over 16 (at which age he lost the right to enter). Consequently, the immigrant ought to have been given the opportunity of satisfying the official as to his true age. The distinction between the two cases rested, in Lord Denning's view, upon the right of one party to enter if qualified, but the absence of any right to remain in favour of the other party except by leave of the Home Secretary. This does not explain why the duty to act fairly does not apply in the Schmidt case, even if it is obvious why it should apply in Re H.K. The worry is that the duty to act fairly may be sufficiently vague to allow the intuitive assessment of the merits of a particular claim on the part of the judiciary to become the governing factor in determining the procedures to apply in handling that claim. In R v Secretary of State for the Home Office, ex parte Awuku (1987) The Times, 3 October 1987, the failure to allow refugees the opportunity to comment on the reasons for refusal of entry was held unfair and contrary to natural justice (notice the terms being used side by side).

An excellent example of the scope of the duty to act fairly is provided by the case of R v Norfolk County Council, ex parte M [1989] QB 619. In that case a plumber was alleged to have molested a 13-year-old girl. Although he denied the allegations, the Social Services Department at his local authority, without consulting him, placed his name on a register of known child abusers. He succeeded in having this registration quashed by the courts. There had been a complete failure of fair procedure towards him and it was not sufficient for the local authority to describe its action as 'administrative' and not subject to review. The seriousness of the matter required a duty to act fairly, and the Court went so far as to describe the authority's action as unreasonable in the *Wednesbury* sense (see previous chapter). Note that had the courts not intervened no remedy would have been available to the plumber, here. This case may be compared with *R v Harrow London Borough Council, ex parte D* [1990] Fam 133 in which a similar decision of a local authority was upheld having given the mother in question the chance to account for injuries to her child.

REVISION

One problem which immediately arises in relation to revising natural justice is how to categorise the topic for revision purposes. In one respect the rules of natural justice simply provide an example of the wider *ultra vires* principle. The breach of the rules of natural justice, on this analysis, is the breach of a procedure implied into the exercise of a particular power. If your course has fitted the topic into this mould, then it might be reasonable to expect an examination question which presents a problem of *ultra vires* action generally — one aspect of which is that a principle of natural justice is offended. It would be dangerous, obviously, in such circumstances to treat natural justice as an entirely separate topic.

On the other hand, your course may adopt the view that the rules of natural justice are an identifiable and separate body of common law rules which provide a framework for judicial and quasi-judicial decision-making and have become increasingly suitable to govern the exercise of administrative powers. On this analysis, the rules of natural justice may be taught in close proximity to judicial review of administrative action, but considered as a self-contained topic. Consequently it becomes possible, even likely, that a question will arise upon natural justice alone. Having said that, there is a close link between the two topics, especially in terms of the consequence of a breach of natural justice, so that it might be foolhardy to revise one topic and not the other, if both are included in the syllabus.

One problem that many students seem to face when preparing this topic is that they view natural justice as a series of rather straightforward, if somewhat vague, rules which may be learnt in a list. Thus, they may include in their notes a section concerning rights to representation, and if a problem arises in which it is stated that a party is refused representation, they will fall back upon that section of their notes. A vital step has been omitted. It is important to ask whether, and to what extent, the rules of natural justice are applicable. Therefore, if the situation was one in which the courts would do no more than imply a duty to act fairly, then rights to legal representation may be entirely inappropriate. It is much more difficult to cope with the thorny question of when to apply the principles than to understand what the (sometimes rather nebulous) principles are. If anything, students should devote more time to the former task than to the latter, whereas some students concentrate exclusively on the latter task.

It is difficult, admittedly, to grasp such issues as the distinction between judicial or quasi-judicial and administrative decisions, but it is by no means impossible. The key lies in a careful reading of the relevant case law. Some areas within the constitutional law syllabus are not heavily dependent upon case law, but the principles of natural justice are common law rules and creatures of case law. The best way to understand the applications of the principles is to witness them at work in the law reports. There are more ways of revising a topic than memorising notes. Reading and rereading relevant issues will assist you in compiling a mental file of those situations in which the principles of natural justice will apply. Rather than seeking to learn a rigid distinction between judicial and administrative decisions, try to understand the reality — that one shades into another.

Bear in mind that there may not be a clear answer to every point. The point concerning legal representation is not capable of a succinct answer, for example. Nor have the courts dealt consistently with the duty to act fairly. Your notes should reflect this and allow you to present a range of possibilities, or even alternative approaches, in answer to a specific problem question. Examiners will generally base problems around particular areas which have generated litigation, which is another reason for ensuring that you possess a thorough knowledge of decided cases.

This is also a prime example of an area in which it might pay dividends to attempt to answer questions from previous examination papers or from tutorial sheets. Seminar sheets often contain problems taken from earlier examinations in any case. This is why preparation for, and attendance at, seminars is vital. You are given the opportunity of working through a question of the sort that will appear in the examination in the presence of your tutor. Regular attendance ought to enable you, in the course of your revision, to tackle past papers. In an area such as natural justice, in which a variety of situations may give rise to differing applications of the principles, practice at answering a range of questions should prove invaluable.

THE EXAMINATION

In each of chapters 4-12 an example is given of an essay and a problem question on the particular topic. In certain topics, a problem question may be much more likely than in others. This is true of the topics in the chapters which follow on public order and police powers, and it is true of this chapter. Indeed it is probably easier for an examiner to devise a chain of events in which some unfortunate character is the victim of a perverse decision-making process, which is seriously harmful to his welfare, than it is to compose a searching essay question on the topic of natural justice. Nonetheless, here is one such question:

'The duty to act fairly provides a convenient smoke-screen behind which judicial discretion is allowed to operate without hindrance.' Discuss.

This is a very difficult question for a first-year law student, but it is the type of question which may be asked not only in constitutional law but also in other subjects such as torts or criminal law. It asks not only about the substantive content of the relevant body of law, but also about its underlying policies. There is nothing unfair about this. It would be idle to pretend that judicial discussion were made in a vacuum, free from the pressures and influences of the society in which they are made. For example, we have seen already in the chapter that the rules of natural justice seem to have expanded in scope to meet the growing demands for the accountability of the bureaucracy.

Nonetheless, it is not always easy for a student, who is new to the study of law and struggling to understand basic legal principles, to look beyond those principles and develop a wider view. It is important, however, for many obvious reasons, that students learn to do this from the first year. But what is meant by a 'wider view' and 'underlying policies'? Indeed what are we to understand from the quotation contained in the question?

The quotation refers to a long-standing debate between administrative lawyers. If judges are in a position to check administrative action is this to be welcomed as a constitutional safeguard which necessarily restricts the power of the executive, or is this to be deplored as an unwarranted intervention by a non-elected judiciary? Many of the standard works implicitly adopt the first viewpoint, but one book which can be quickly and easily read at an early point in your first year of law is J.A.G. Griffith, *The Politics of the Judiciary*, 4th ed. (1991). This represents the latter view, and would seek political rather than judicial safeguards. Inherent in the question above, therefore, is a second question: Ought we to support the ready exercise of judicial discretion? If the answer to that question is yes, then the likely reaction to the question is that it is unfair to talk of smoke-screens — judges are performing a legitimate function by following and developing a particular line of case law. On the other hand, if we oppose such discretion, we might seek to undermine the view that the duty to act fairly is comprised of a consistent line of authority by claiming that it is tainted by ill-disguised judicial preference for certain actions, and distaste for other actions.

Once again, either line of argument is possible; it is likely that you will have met both views in your reading on the subject, and you ought to have considered, in the course of your revision, your reaction to this type of question. Your argument should then reflect your view, and should be expressed in a measured manner, considering alternative arguments but explaining the validity of your own standpoint. It is fair in a question which invites you to be openly critical, to take that opportunity, but your case will not be well-served if that criticism is ill-founded or if it derides other viewpoints. With this in mind, let us consider how an answer which broadly supports the proposition presented in the question might be structured.

It might be an idea to begin by explaining, as briefly as possible, the function and scope of the rules of natural justice. This would enable you to make the point that they involve the exercise of discretion by their very nature. Their purpose is to ensure the application of particular procedural rules which would not have existed otherwise. Whilst this does not allow the judges to substitute their own decision for that of another body, it does allow them to set decisions aside and to influence the decision-making process via the procedural demands which they make. Having explained the principles of natural justice you are also in a position to outline the nature of the duty to act fairly by pointing to it as a development of the established principles of natural justice. As is stated above, the duty to act fairly is a somewhat slippery concept to grasp, but you can help yourself by having prepared a short statement or definition, which identifies the duty in advance of the examination.

If the principles of natural justice allow the judiciary some scope to shape the administrative process, the duty to act fairly must offer even greater scope for this. There are two reasons for this which you should explain fully. The first is that the duty to act fairly has a wider application than the rules of natural justice. You could refer here to the dicta in *Ridge v Baldwin* [1964] AC 40 which was seminal in the development of the concept and offer *Re H.K. (An Infant)* [1967] 2 QB 617 as an early example of the intervention of the courts in the decision-making process beyond the realms of the 'judicial'. Secondly, the duty to act fairly is itself a vague concept — thus allowing the judges a rather free reign. This could be illustrated by the confused legal principles apparent within much of the case law. For example, in *Re H.K.* itself there is obvious confusion between the duty to act fairly, as propounded by Lord Parker CJ, and natural justice as spoken of by Salmon LJ, though both judges seem to accept the need for procedural fairness, however described.

Does it matter, however, if the concept is rather a vague one? There are obvious points to make here. The need for clarity seems apparent — especially because the courts are in effect offering guidelines for tribunals which are not always well-endowed with legal expertise. There are also a number of points which, although less obvious, deserve to be made nonetheless, and you should seek to introduce these. The first is that if a wide discretion is allowed to the judiciary, there is a danger that they may prove consistently in favour of particular values in situations in which the administrative process seeks to conciliate between competing values. Griffith would cite as examples cases in which the rules of natural justice have been rigorously upheld against trade unions exercising disciplinary functions (e.g., *Taylor* v *National Union of Seamen* [1967] 1 WLR 532) in comparison with similar cases involving universities and students (e.g., *Glynn* v *Keele University* [1971] 1 WLR 487) in which the courts have been much more reluctant to act.

Many students represent this view by saying that 'judges dislike trade unions'. The point is rather more subtle than that. The further judges wander from firm legal principles the more we must expect the exercise of discretion, and that involves choices which the judges cannot make in a vacuum. Their choices are the product of their own social and political perspectives, and, over a period of time, the danger is that these may come to dominate. Notice incidentally that the cases referred to above are cases involving natural justice and not the duty to act fairly. That does not matter. If the point is true for natural justice, it must be all the more true for the more flexible duty to act fairly.

A second point which might also be made is closely related to the point above. Discretion may involve pragmatism — *ad hoc* approaches to individual cases rather than groups of cases. This may be the only way to distinguish the two Bradford Corporation cases (*Ward* (1971) 70 LGR 27 and *Hannam* [1970] 1 WLR 973) referred to earlier — the former case revealing obvious judicial disapproval of the conduct of the girl student. Similarly in *Schmidt* v *Secretary of State for Home Affairs* [1969] 2 Ch 149 the wish to uphold the Government line against scientology is one way which might help reconcile this view with that in *Re H.K. (An Infant)* [1967] 2 QB 617. At this point you could include the type of discussion of the latter two cases that is contained earlier in this chapter. Of course a series of pragmatic decisions may undermine confidence in judicial review. (You could introduce here a discussion of *Council of Civil Service Unions* v *Minister for the Civil Service* [1985] AC 374 in terms of judicial review of procedural impropriety in administrative action and the limits of such review.)

It follows from this that the above two points are linked. Individual decisions may knit together to form broad patterns of judicial behaviour such as that predicted by Griffith. Indeed the judges allow themselves large measures of future freedom by means of judicial precedent. Thus you could point out that cases such as *Pett* v *Greyhound Racing Association* [1969] 1 QB 125 do not lay down general principles applicable to legal representation, but allow that much will depend upon how serious are the issues at stake in individual cases. In assessing the very significance of those issues, therefore, the judges inherently determine the rights which follow. It may be the case indeed, as Griffith observes, that judges give low priority to particular causes — such as the expulsion of students. An example of this might also be *R v Board of Visitors of the Maze Prison, ex parte Hone* [1988] AC 379 where prisoners charged with serious disciplinary offences were held to have been legitimately refused legal representation even though a defendant in a criminal court facing such charges would have been granted it.

In conclusion, it is possible to make out a case supporting the proposition in the question. A case opposing it is also possible and may be easier to argue (in terms of curbing executive action) and to support with examples of judicial intervention to prevent procedural excesses. However, it may be apparent from the above discussion that there is no point in addressing your mind to the issues for the first time in the examination room. An answer to this type of question requires wide reading, and a careful and ponderous consideration of the whole topic.

Problem Questions on Natural Justice

As is stated above, there is ample scope for the setting of problem questions in this area. These are not difficult providing that you take a logical approach to them. Indeed many of them will appear fairly similar in terms of the type of events which you will be asked to consider.

Green is a teacher at Rainbow Sixth Form College. The college articles of government provide for disciplinary action against staff, and this includes dismissal for misconduct following a hearing before the board of governors. The board of governors comprises the headmistress, four councillors and three lay members.

Green is accused by another teacher of having an affair with Rose, the head girl, and unknown to Green the headmistress has found a letter written by Rose to Green, which states that she cannot wait to be with him on Wednesday evening. Unknown to the headmistress, they are due to partner each other at the bridge club on that evening.

Green is suspended on full pay prior to a hearing before the governors. At the hearing Green requests the name of the teacher who made the original allegation and the right to question that teacher. He also asks to be represented by a union official.

As a result of the hearing, and on the evidence of the letter, Green is dismissed. Councillor Blue later admits to the press that his daughter, Violet, an unemployed teacher who acted as Green's replacement during his suspension, will probably apply for the full-time vacancy which has now arisen. Green is considering an appeal to the education committee of the local education authority, but fears that Blue, who chairs that committee, will not reinstate him in the circumstances.

Advise Green.

This area provides a clear example of why it is important not to begin your answer by starting off half-way through — for example, by beginning, 'Green should have been allowed a representative here'. A better plan is to consider whether the principles of natural justice and/or the duty to act fairly will apply. If the principles of natural justice apply, the next step is to examine why these principles may have been breached. Consider in turn the right to be heard and the freedom from bias. Even if the question centres upon one of these, do not forget to check whether the other applies. If you are dealing with the right to be heard, isolate the particular events which might offend the principle — was there notice of the charges, was an oral hearing allowed, etc? Finally consider the remedies available to the plaintiff (Green in our example).

It is wise to follow such a pattern no matter how obvious the question appears. Of course, you are not likely to be given a question in which no matter of procedural fairness arises. Nonetheless, show to the examiner that you are able to understand when the rules of natural justice are applicable. This need not necessarily entail a long discussion of whether (in our example) the board of governors act judicially. If you have considered particular problematic situations (as suggested earlier) you may be able to short-cut the system. Thus here we have a situation concerning dismissal from employment, do the rules of natural justice apply? You can directly incorporate some of the material on this point into your answer, including the highly relevant case of *Malloch* v *Aberdeen Corporation* [1971] 1 WLR 1578. It is important, however, not simply to include a portion of your notes, or a discussion of any particular decided case in your answer, but to relate that discussion directly to the question.

If you conclude that the rules of natural justice are not applicable either in this case or in any other answer, do not stop there. You may be wrong. (Indeed you would be foolhardy to conclude baldly that they are inapplicable in our example.) No matter how certain you feel, deal with the proposition of what would be the case if the principles did apply. An ability to 'plead in the alternative' is essential to a good lawyer, and in your case it may save you many marks. If you are wrong on the applicability of the principles, at least you show that you know what those principles are.

It matters little whether you deal with the rule against bias before or after the right to be heard. However, if there is a question which mainly concerns the right to be heard and has a single point on bias, it may be wise to deal with the latter point first. Then, if you run out of time, it is clear you have spotted both issues. In our example there are two bias points: the interest that Blue will have in the outcome of Green's case (his daughter's job) and the participation of Blue in different levels of the decision-making process. Note that the latter point is rather casually introduced into the last line. As regards the first point, you could use cases such as *R* v *Sussex Justices, ex parte*

McCarthy [1924] 1 KB 256 to illustrate that the interest in the outcome of a case does not have to be a direct pecuniary interest, and that the courts are concerned that justice be seen to be done. As regards the second point, *Hannam* v *Bradford Corporation* [1970] 1 WLR 973 provides an excellent and pertinent example of the principle involved here. Note, in fact, that in *Hannam* the issue was less obvious, since the committee was considering a recommendation to dismiss from the governors who were actually absent from the meeting.

As regards the right to be heard, the issues which arise here may be dealt with in turn. Ensure that you read the problem thoroughly and pick up all relevant points. For example, what right does Green have to know of the evidence against him, and how does this relate to the non-disclosure to him of the letter which has been found? This and other relevant issues are considered above and will not be repeated here, but do remember to introduce authority for each proposition you put forward in Green's favour.

Finally, it is important to deal with the remedies available to Green. However, there are problems here. What is the effect of a breach of the rules of natural justice in this type of case? *Ridge* v *Baldwin* [1964] AC 40 seems clear that the decision is null and void. What, therefore, is the appropriate remedy? The usual one would be a declaration that the dismissal is null and void, but there is a rather uneasy relationship here with a general refusal of the courts to give specific relief in the case of a breach of a contract of employment. To what extent ought Green to exhaust his internal remedies before seeking judicial review — i.e., should he appeal or not? You are asked to advise on this, but it may be that by now you are out of your depth. There is no need to worry. No examiner would wish you to struggle through points which you have not covered in class. Some of these issues you would not cover until final-year courses in administrative law or even employment law. Be guided by your syllabus, and by your tutor. You cannot be penalised for failing to cover points which lie outside the scope of your course.

CONCLUSION

The final point is an important one. Constitutional law is a first-year subject in many law departments. It will be followed later in the syllabus by a separate course in administrative law. As a first-year student you are not expected to possess final-year knowledge. It is sometimes difficult to know where to stop, especially if you read widely around the subject you are studying. If you are not careful you will find yourself swamped by a mass of detail, some of which is too complex for a first-year student possessing limited procedural and technical knowledge of law. The best advice is to read more widely by all means, but do not venture into areas not included in your particular syllabus. In such uncharted waters, there is a great danger of sinking.

On the other hand, do not convince yourself that natural justice is an easy topic to cope with, and that it is no more than a rag-bag of rights illustrated by very obvious examples in case law. As with the whole of judicial review, it poses particular challenges to the law student. In order to meet these, careful and diligent study may prove necessary.

FURTHER READING

Campbell, N. R., 'The Duty to Give Reasons in Administrative Law' [1994] *Public Law* 184.

Harlow, C., (ed) (1986) *Public Law and Politics* (London: Sweet & Maxwell). See Chapter 8.

Jowell, J. and Oliver, D., (eds) (1994) *The Changing Constitution*, 3rd ed. (Oxford: Clarendon). See Chapter 15.

Woolf, Sir Harry, (1990) *Hamlyn Lectures: Protection of the Public — a New Challenge* (London: Stevens).

11 PUBLIC ORDER

Because there is no written constitution in Britain, safeguards for our freedom are to be found largely in the common law. The scope and content of that body of common law will almost invariably form part of the constitutional law course. However, it will be clear from the material which follows that this is an area in which there has been significant legislative activity of late — especially in the Public Order Act 1986 and the Criminal Justice and Public Order Act 1994.

There is, of course, a range of individual freedoms worthy of protection — privacy, freedom of expression, freedom from discrimination, for example. This chapter considers one such freedom, that of assembly and association. Such a freedom is generally considered vital to a free society, if only because freedom of assembly implies the right to protest about particular actions of the State. At the same time, the State may claim the necessity of upholding public order by restraining these freedoms. As elsewhere within constitutional law, we find competing claims which give rise to both academic debate and a steady stream of case law. Hence, there is a likelihood of this area being singled out for examination purposes.

The whole area poses two problems for the student attempting to understand and learn the relevant material. The first is that there is a positive plethora of restrictions on the freedom of assembly. These are not always easy to memorise, and it may be quite possible to overlook quite obvious points in a problem question by failing to exhaust the possible restrictions on a particular form of action. It becomes important, therefore, to find some method of categorising the material — breaking it down into smaller parts which are far easier to commit to memory.

A second problem is that there is some overlap between this area and that considered in the next chapter — police powers. Thus although laws relating to public order will always impact upon powers of the police, they will generally be considered under this head. Here you may be guided by your lecturer, and follow his or her division of material. However, there are some topics, such as breach of the peace, which will fall just as easily into either category. Another example would be obstruction of a police officer under s. 51(3) of the Police Act 1964. This should be included as part of your revision on both topics, and the possibility of this offence must be considered when answering questions on either topic.

It follows from this that it is inadvisable to revise material relating to public order and not that relating to police powers. If a problem is set in which disorder occurs, it poses no particular difficulty for the examiner to introduce a point which relates, for example, to the validity of an arrest. That is not to say that a question will include both elements or that only one topic of the two will appear on the examination paper. As we shall see, there is ample scope for a question on each subject.

FREEDOM OF ASSOCIATION

Several significant individual liberties regarding matters such as organisation of labour and religious freedom will depend on the freedom to associate with other people and to join associations of various kinds. The stance taken by English law is not to guarantee freedom of association, but to permit individuals to behave as they wish subject to certain restrictions. It is these restrictions that interest the constitutional lawyer. In relation to freedom of association, the limitations are not great, but those which do exist are contentious.

The most obvious example of a measure designed to restrict freedom to associate is the Prevention of Terrorism (Temporary Provisions) Act 1989. Section 1 of this Act makes it an offence to belong or to claim to belong to a proscribed organisation. There are two proscribed organisations (sch. 1): the Irish Republican Army and the Irish National Liberation Army. However, the Home Secretary may add to the list by statutory instrument. There is some similarity between the provisions of this Act and ss. 1 and 2 of the Public Order Act 1936, which outlaw uniforms indicating political allegiances in a public place or at a public meeting and ban the organisation of private armies (see *R* v *Jordan and Tyndall* [1963] Crim LR 124).

This apart, many issues in relation to freedom of association tend to concern trade unions. Some involve issues of public order, but wider points of principle arise also. It is sometimes said that the closed shop policies of certain unions offend notions of freedom of association by denying the individual the freedom of choice not to join the union. This is an oversimplification, and the issues raised are beyond the scope of this book. One point which does arise in this context, however, is that art. 11 of the European Convention on Human Rights states that 'everyone has the right to ...

freedom of association with others including the right to form and join trade unions ...'. In *Young, James and Webster* v *United Kingdom* (1981) 4 EHRR 38, three former employees of British Rail had been dismissed for not joining specified trade unions as demanded under a closed shop policy. On an application to the European Court of Human Rights, claiming that (*inter alia*) their rights under art. 11 had been violated, the court decided that it was not necessary to consider whether art. 11 could also be read so as to protect the right *not* to join a trade union. Rather they decided that, on the facts, the compulsion inherent within the closed shop system attacked the very substance of the freedom which art. 11 sought to guarantee.

By 1980, however, the law on the closed shop had changed by virtue of s. 7(2) of the Employment Act 1980. This allows that:

> The dismissal of an employee [in such circumstances] shall be regarded as unfair if he genuinely objects on grounds of conscience or other deeply held personal convictions to being a member of any trade union whatsoever or of a particular trade union.

The Employment Act 1982 then introduced a scheme to compensate those dismissed without a remedy under the law relating to the closed shop between 1974 and 1980. These provisions form part of a political attack on the closed shop which seems to go further than the Strasbourg decision in *Young* would require. There is no doubt that, in that case, the court placed great emphasis on the fact that the applicants' employment pre-dated the closed shop, and that existing union membership was so high as to cast doubt upon whether rigid enforcement of a closed shop agreement was necessary.

Following this, Britain became involved in another case before the Court of Human Rights concerning art. 11 of the Convention. In 1984 it was announced in the House of Commons that the Government had decided to introduce new conditions of service for staff at the GCHQ at Cheltenham. These would forbid staff to belong to a national trade union. The Council of Civil Service Unions sought a declaration that such action was invalid since the Minister for the Civil Service had withdrawn a fundamental right of their members, without consultation. At first instance it was found that such consultation ought to have taken place, but on appeal by the Minister, the Court of Appeal held that the prerogative powers exercised were not open to judicial review, and that requirements of national security overrode any duty which the Minister might have had otherwise to consult the staff.

The Council's appeal to the House of Lords was dismissed (see *Council of Civil Service Unions* v *Minister for the Civil Service* [1985] AC 374). The House of Lords was not prepared to accept that a power of this kind, emanating from the prerogative, was immune from judicial review. Nor were they prepared to accept the mere assertion that national security justified a course of action without evidence that the action was indeed taken in the interests of national security. Moreover, the appellants had a legitimate expectation of consultation before being deprived of a benefit which they had long enjoyed, and the duty to act fairly would ordinarily oblige the Minister to consult. However, on the evidence presented, the House of Lords accepted that the interests of national security had led the Minister to conclude that consultation should be refused, and for that reason the appeal was dismissed. An application to the Commission under art. 11 of the European Convention of Human Rights failed on the basis of the art. 11(2) restrictions of freedom of association for members of the administration of the State (*Council of Civil Service Unions* v *United Kingdom* (1987) 10 EHRR 269). The whole episode was discussed in chapters 8 and 10.

PUBLIC ORDER OFFENCES UNDER THE 1986 ACT

Our history is littered with famous campaigns which have depended upon public demonstration, ranging from the widening of the franchise to nuclear disarmament. In general our history and our society are the richer as a result of these, although some have been pursued in a spirit of hatred rather than altruism. The public meetings, demonstrations and processions which have formed an integral part of all such campaigns, are quite lawful *per se*. Yet they may quickly become unlawful and fall foul of a series of offences designed to maintain public order. The duty to maintain order falls upon the Crown since the peace of the realm is part of the royal prerogative. In practice, however, the duty is delegated — usually to the police.

There is no right to assembly as such. Such a right might be inferred from common law and, following the Public Order Act 1986 (hereinafter 'the Act'), from the fact that for the first time the opportunity was taken in statutory form to regulate the holding of assemblies (as opposed to processions). The Criminal Justice and Public Order Act 1994 allows for their prohibition and one can now assume that the holding of assemblies which do not offend the requirements of these Acts is lawful.

Violent Disorder

Section 2 of the Act introduces this offence, which is intended to curtail serious outbreaks of disorder. For the avoidance of doubt, if you see it referred to in cases or older textbooks, this offence replaces the ancient common-law crime of unlawful assembly which was abolished by the Act. Under s. 2 a person will be guilty of an offence when:

(a) there are three or more persons,
(b) in a public or private place (see *Kamara* v *DPP* [1974] AC 104),

(c) using or threatening unlawful violence,

(d) where their conduct as a group is such as to cause a person of reasonable firmness, present at the scene to fear for his/her safety.

And note that the person charged can only be guilty if (s)he actually uses or threatens unlawful violence. In other words it is no offence to be part of a group which meets the conditions (a), (b) and (d) unless condition (c) is also met. However, it may be a sufficient element of participation to encourage or assist others in the use or threats of violence (see *R v Caird* (1970) 54 Cr App R 499 and also *R v Clarkson* (1971) 55 Cr App R 445).

The elements of the offence above are fairly straightforward. You may wish to compare them with riot (see below) since, for examination purposes, this may arise directly (in an essay which seeks a comparison between the two) or indirectly (in a problem where you have to decide which offence may be appropriate). We shall see later that riot has certain additional elements — a larger number of persons, a common purpose, and the actual use of violence.

The only other element of (a)–(d) above which requires immediate elaboration is that of 'violence'. This is defined in s. 8, although not very helpfully. It means 'any violent conduct'. However, the section does add that:

— violence may be directed at property as well as people;

— violence need not cause or be intended to cause injury or damage (so that throwing a bottle in the air could be violence even though it does not hit anyone or damage anything).

In addition, s. 6 of the Act allows that a person can be guilty if intending to use violence or aware that the conduct may be violent. You may deal with this issue of awareness in your criminal law course, for in one sense it is a novel concept in relation to *mens rea* (the mental element in a crime). However, it has close ties to the concept of recklessness, for s. 6(2) seems to suggest that where a person can foresee that violence may follow his/her action and yet still pursues that action then that person will be 'aware'. Thus, to take our example from above, to toss a bottle backwards over one's head, realising the possibility of injury but not bothering whether it resulted, would constitute an offence. By s. 6(5) self-induced intoxication (by whatever means) affords no defence.

In spite of the lessened mental element within the definition, the action itself must be violent — of extreme force — and abuse or intimidatory shouting would not be sufficient (see *News Group Newspapers Ltd v SOGAT '82 (No. 2)* [1987] ICR 181; *R v Chief Constable of Devon and Cornwall, ex parte CEGB* [1982] QB 458). Also the violence must be unlawful. Thus the actions of a group of police officers charging a group of soccer supporters who have invaded a football pitch may appear violent, but unless their conduct is excessive it is likely to be excused by (for example) s. 117 of the Police and Criminal Evidence Act 1984 (dealt with in the following chapter). This also raises the interesting possibility that one group of football supporters could claim to be using lawful violence against a rival group by acting in self-defence (this possibility is heightened by *R v Bird* [1985] 1 WLR 816).

A couple of other points concerning s. 2 may be worth noting because they could be relevant for examination problems. Must the prosecution prove that there were persons present who feared for their safety? The answer is no. The test of the person of reasonable firmness is well known to common law and is a hypothetical figure intended to provide an objective test (see *Dwyer* v *Metropolitan Police District Receiver* [1967] 2 QB 970). In relation to this test when applied to the old common law on affray, it had even been doubted whether the presence of a bystander was necessary to prove the offence (see the *dictum* of Lord Hailsham LC in *Taylor* v *DPP* [1973] AC 964 and the Court of Appeal decision in *Attorney-General's Reference (No. 3 of 1983)* [1985] QB 242). In relation to this offence and also riot and affray it is now made clear in the Act that there is no necessity for the presence of 'the person of reasonable firmness'. And can the police arrest for violent disorder? The answer is yes, since violent disorder is an arrestable offence (see the following chapter).

Riot

Prior to 1986, there were two common-law crimes called rout and riot. The former had fallen into disuse, and the latter, having long remained dormant, was invoked (unsatisfactorily from many points of view) at the time of the miners' strike 1984-85. These are now abolished in favour of a new statutory offence of riot (s. 1 of the Act) which requires the following in order to establish guilt:

(a)   being one of 12 or more persons,
(b)   in a public or private place,
(c)   using or threatening violence,
(d)   for a common purpose,
(e)   where their conduct is such as would cause a person of reasonable firmness, present at the scene, to fear for his/her safety,

providing that the person actually uses violence for the common purpose. Note that the nature of the offence concerns unlawful violence of a general character among such a crowd, and the threat of violence alone does not constitute the offence. This was discussed by the Court of Appeal in *R* v *Jefferson* [1994] 1 All ER 270, the facts of which arose out of disturbances in the town of Bedford after a televised football match (between England and Egypt).

Our discussion of violent disorder above may allow us some short-cuts here. Note that the number of persons is raised to 12 — a figure which has an historical antecedent in the repealed Riot Act 1714. With this raised number comes a problem. Suppose there is a situation (in an examination question, for example!) in which there are a number of incidents in an inner city area (of the type which occurred in the summer of 1981). The persons involved total more than 12, but at no one time are they present in the same location. The answer seems to be that they cannot constitute a riot since they are not 12 or more persons together in a public place. It may be possible, however, to argue that the public place is a housing estate and that the separate violent activities constitute a continuous riotous sequence. This type of argument was successful in the famous case of *R v Jones* (1974) 59 Cr App R 120, which you should read — but read it with some cynicism. The case involved a common law charge of unlawful assembly (see above) and it sits uneasily with the wording of s. 1.

The major additional element is that of common purpose. This remains from older common law definitions, although it has always proved an elusive concept, and significantly it is not defined in the 1986 Act. However, it does not necessarily involve pre-planning and probably means no more than the existence of a group of like-minded individuals (see *R v Caird* (1970) 54 Cr App R 499).

One final point on riot is that although it is an arrestable offence (see the following chapter), the consent of the Director of Public Prosecutions is necessary in order to institute a prosecution for riot. In the past, the reason for this was so that what is intended to be the most serious of the public order offences was not misused. However, it may also follow the difficulty in obtaining convictions to common law charges of riot. While this may seem a technical point, it will make a considerable difference to the answer to a problem question if you advise the Chief Constable of Greater Melchester to seek the prosecution of the football hooligans at the Rovers match by, or with the consent of, the DPP. This adds an air of accuracy and authority to your answer which is sure to be acknowledged in the marking.

Affray

In comparison with the offences above, affray is quite straightforward; a person will be guilty if found:

(a)   using or threatening unlawful violence towards another,
(b)   in a private or public place,
(c)   with conduct such as would cause a person of reasonable firmness present at the scene to fear for his/her personal safety.

The differences between this and the offences already discussed will be apparent. Most obviously, there is no mention of the necessary numbers of actors. At common law the crime of affray could be committed by one person alone (see *Taylor* v *DPP* [1973] AC 964). Although the common law offence has been replaced by the statutory offence described above and contained in s. 3, it seems clear that the new offence would apply equally to a single person. Thus an unprovoked attack by one man on another would constitute an affray by a single person. Theoretically this is true even if the other fights back — for (an attempt at) self-defence is not likely to involve *unlawful* violence.

There was a body of case law at common law concerning the presence of bystanders at an affray, and this point has been considered above in relation to violent disorder. The Act requires use or threats of violence, whereas at common law it might have been sufficient to have made an unlawful display of force. What would be the position of a football hooligan who runs along the street, perhaps chanting the name of his team, knowing that at the head of the crowd fellow-supporters are throwing bottles at rival supporters in retreat? In the (riot) case of *R* v *Caird* (1970) 54 Cr App R 499 encouragement to others to use or threaten violence was thought to be sufficient to amount to an offence by a person not actually using or threatening violence; it is not clear whether this can apply to affray. Certainly mere presence at an affray cannot amount to the offence (see *R* v *Allan* [1965] 1 QB 130).

Three other matters warrant comment. Firstly, in *R* v *Button* [1966] AC 591, the House of Lords resolved a long-standing problem of whether an affray could be committed on private property by upholding the convictions for an affray committed at a ticket-only darts league dance in the local scout hall. This ruling is effectively endorsed by s. 3(5) of the Act, which allows that an affray may be committed in private. Secondly, s. 8 states that for the offence of affray violence must be directed at persons and not property. Finally, s. 3(3) demands in relation to affray (but not the offences previously discussed) that the use of words will not alone amount to a threat. Thus the chant of 'you're going to get your ******* heads kicked in', which occasionally drowns John Motson's commentary, is not itself an affray. But what form of non-verbal threat will be sufficient — this chant accompanied by clenched fists raised in the air? This ought to make it clear to you that questions of interpretation of the 1986 Act are by no means resolved. Keep a look-out for relevant case law during your period of study. This will assist your understanding of issues and may well prove of direct relevance in the examination, bearing in mind what has been said about the topicality of questions.

Affray is not an arrestable offence, although there will be a s. 25 (of the Police and Criminal Evidence Act 1984) power of arrest available (see the following chapter). In addition to this, and more likely to be used, is a specific power of arrest, made available to any constable reasonably suspecting anyone of committing an affray, contained in s. 3(6).

Threatening Behaviour

Just as the three offences above contained common elements, the following four offences all relate to the use of threatening, abusive or insulting words or behaviour. The most famous of these is the widely invoked offence of threatening behaviour under what for many years was s. 5 of the Public Order Act 1936 and is now s. 4 of the 1986 Act. This rather complex provision states that a person (the accused) commits an offence if that person:

(a) in a public or a private place [but not in someone's home],

(b) uses towards another person threatening, abusive or insulting words or behaviour, or

(c) distributes or displays to another person any writing, sign or other visible representation which is threatening, abusive or insulting, and

(d) intends that other person to believe that immediate unlawful violence will be used against him or any other person [note that this does not have to be violence on the part of the accused], or

(e) intends to provoke the immediate use of unlawful violence by that other person or anyone else, or

(f) whereby that other person is likely to believe violence will be used, or

(g) whereby it is likely that violence will be provoked.

Assuming that you understand elements (a) (b) and (c) and presuming you find (for example, in a problem question) that they exist, there are four possible situations in which an offence will be committed:

(i) The speaker (or writer or actor) intends a person in the audience, X, to believe that unlawful violence will be used against X or someone else.

(ii) The speaker tries intentionally to provoke X or someone else (successfully or otherwise) to use violence there and then.

(iii) It is likely, given the speech, that X will fear violence.

(iv) It is likely that X or someone else will be provoked to the point of violence.

Note the different requirements of the latter two instances. There is no requirement for the prosecution to seek to prove intention. An indication of how this might work is available in a case brought under the original 1936 Act — *Jordan* v *Burgoyne* [1963] 2 QB 744. In this case Jordan made comments, in a speech in Trafalgar Square, which insulted Jews, applauded Hitler, and which resulted in a disturbance. Jordan's defence, that no reasonable person would have responded violently, was unsuccessful in the Divisional Court. The broad principle upheld was that a speaker must take the audience as he or she finds it. Note that although there is no requirement of intention, there must be some immediacy of violent reaction where it is alleged there is a likelihood of violence being provoked (consider the case arising out of Salman Rushdie's publication, *The Satanic Verses*: *R v Horseferry Road Justices, ex parte Siadatan* [1991] 1 QB 260).

There is no necessity for the section to be used only in relation to demonstrations, protest meetings and the like. In the case of *Ward v Holman* [1964] 2 QB 580 the Divisional Court rejected an argument that the words of the old s. 5 had to be qualified to accord with the title of the Act. It was thought that the words of s. 5 were plain enough to be used to preserve public order in a public place whether or not there was a public meeting or a large crowd present. This point is reinforced by the extension of s. 4 of the 1986 Act to private places and the section can be used to cover a wide variety of situations which may lead to disorder (see *Rukira v DPP* (1993) *The Times*, 29 June 1993). In *Brutus v Cozens* [1973] AC 854 problems arose during a Wimbledon tennis match. Brutus and other anti-apartheid demonstrators distributed leaflets and sat down on the court. He was arrested under the insulting behaviour head of s. 5. The Divisional Court, hearing an appeal by the prosecutor, directed that the behaviour was insulting if it affronted people, showed disrespect for their rights and was likely to lead to resentment. The House of Lords allowed Brutus's appeal. The question of whether behaviour was insulting was one of fact for the trial court to decide, but the behaviour had to be insulting — disrespectful conduct might not be sufficient — in the famous words of Lord Reid: 'An ordinary, sensible man knows an insult when he sees or hears it'.

However, in what must be regarded as a dubious extension of the scope of the Public Order Act, in *Masterson v Holden* [1986] 1 WLR 1017 the conduct of two homosexuals fondling each other in an Oxford Street bus shelter in the early hours of the morning was said to amount to 'insulting' (and see *Parkin v Norman* [1983] QB 92).

Two final points: you will need to incorporate the material on unlawful violence from the offences discussed earlier into your notes on threatening behaviour, and you may care to note, for problem questions, that s. 4(3) of the 1986 Act gives constables the power of arrest without warrant, and that the Act amends the Police and Criminal Evidence Act 1984 (see the following chapter) to give a uniformed constable a power of entry to and search of premises when effecting the s. 4(3) power of arrest.

Incitement to Racial Hatred

Under the 1936 Act, an additional section (5A) had been added to the s. 5 offence of threatening behaviour to deal with the problems which arise in what is now ss. 18 and 19 of the 1986 Act. These two sections are similar in language to s. 4 of the 1986 Act and it is convenient to deal with them here.

There are a number of other offences which are created by the Act to deal with racially inflammatory material in plays, recordings and broadcasts. These will not be dealt with here, as they are more likely to be covered elsewhere in the syllabus (perhaps under freedom of expression or censorship).

However, before discussing ss. 18 and 19, you should also note that the possession of written material or recordings, which are threatening, abusive or insulting, with a view to displaying it, is an offence under s. 23 of the 1986 Act if: either an intention that racial hatred should be stirred up can be proved; or it is likely in the circumstances that racial hatred will be stirred up. This is a paraphrase of s. 23, which you should look at. It seems obvious that a problem question can include a character who has not yet had the chance to distribute leaflets which have been prepared. However, you will find the language of s. 23 similar to that of ss. 18 and 19, which are now examined.

Under s. 18 a person is guilty of an offence if that person:

(a)   in a public or private place [but not someone's home],
(b)   uses threatening, abusive or insulting words or behaviour,

or

(c)   displays any written material which is threatening, abusive or insulting, *and*
(d)   intends to stir up racial hatred, *or*
(e)   having regard to all the circumstances racial hatred is likely to be stirred up and the person intends the words or behaviour or written material to be, or is aware that they might be, threatening, abusive or insulting.

So if conditions (a) and (b) or (a) and (c) are met, there will be an offence provided it can be proved that the person:

(i)   intended to stir up racial hatred, *or*
(ii)   intended the words, etc., to be threatening, abusive or insulting and in the circumstance racial hatred was likely to be stirred up, *or*
(iii) was aware that the words, etc., might be threatening, abusive or insulting and in the circumstances racial hatred was likely to be stirred up.

As to 'awareness', see the text above under violent disorder. The latter two possibilities cover the situation in which the speaker (etc.) is reckless as to the nature and/or consequences of the words spoken (etc.). The first possibility covers the situation of an intention to stir up racial hatred even though there is no likelihood of this happening. This is necessary in order to cover flagrantly racist activities delivered to audiences unaffected by them.

Section 19 of the Act states that a person is guilty of an offence if that person:

   (a) publishes or distributes written material, *and*
   (b) the written material is threatening abusive or insulting, *and*
   (c) the person intends to stir up racial hatred, *or*
   (d) having regard to the circumstances racial hatred is likely to be stirred
up.

Note that in the latter instance, it will be a defence if the accused can prove that (s)he was unaware of the content of the written material and had no reason to suspect and did not suspect that it was threatening, abusive or insulting.

In relation to these offences you can incorporate much of your material on s. 4 (e.g., in relation to the definition of 'threatening, abusive or insulting'). However, there will be new material which you will require. In particular you will need to know the meaning of racial hatred (see the definition in s. 17 of the 1986 Act). The word 'ethnic' in this definition has given rise to some difficulty, but you can go some way to resolving this by reading the judgment of Lord Fraser of Tullybelton in *Mandla* v *Dowell Lee* [1983] 2 AC 548. Similarly, for the purposes of s. 19 you will need to be able to define publication and distribution. However, s. 19(3) offers a definition (which is much wider than under the old law).

Some final procedural points: the consent of the Attorney-General is necessary for ss. 18, 19 and 23 prosecutions. There is a power of arrest for s. 18 offences (see s. 18(3)) and for s. 19 offences (s. 155, Criminal Justice and Public Order Act 1994, amending s. 25 of the Police and Criminal Evidence Act 1984 (see the following chapter). Under s. 23 (alone) there is a power of entry and search under warrant (see the following chapter).

Causing Harassment, Alarm or Distress

This offence, created by s. 5 of the 1986 Act, was entirely new. You may find it easier to abbreviate its label to 'disorderly conduct'.

   A person is guilty of an offence if that person:

   (a) in a public or a private place [but not someone's home],
   (b) uses threatening, abusive or insulting words or behaviour, *or*
   (c) displays any writing, sign or other visible representation which is threatening, abusive or insulting, *or*
   (d) uses disorderly behaviour, *and*
   (e) does so within the hearing or sight of a person likely to be caused harassment, alarm or distress by the conduct involved in (b) or (c).

Note that s. 4A has been added by s. 154 of the Criminal Justice and Public Order Act 1994, concerned with the intentional causing of harassment, alarm or distress. The measure seems aimed at serious and persistent (often racial) forms of harassment.

One problem in attempting any explanation of this section is that crucial phrases new to this section — 'disorderly behaviour' and 'harassment, alarm or distress' — remain undefined. Watch carefully for cases which will throw light on these elusive concepts. Read s. 5 in conjunction with s. 6(4), which outlines the requisite mental elements (basically *intention* that words (etc.) or behaviour be threatening (etc.) or disorderly; or *awareness* that this may be so). In one early case, *Lodge* v *DPP* (1988) *The Times*, 26 October 1988 it was said that it was not necessary that a person 'alarmed' for the purposes of this section was concerned with his own safety. He could be alarmed at the prospect of danger to a third party. A police officer could be 'a person likely to be caused harassment . . . etc.' under the section (*DPP* v *Orum* [1989] 1 WLR 88).

Note that in s. 5(3) three defences appear (see *Kwasi Poku* v *DPP* [1993] Crim LR 705). One relates to the exemption for homes in (a) above. It is also a defence to show that the accused had no reason to believe that there was anyone around likely to be caused harassment, etc. Finally, it is a defence to show that the conduct was reasonable. Time will tell whether this will avail the Rolls-Royce driver whose car has just been written off by a double-decker bus!

It might be thought that the s. 25 power of arrest (see Police and Criminal Evidence Act 1984 in the following chapter) might be ideal for dealing with this type of offence. Curiously, s. 5(4) has its own unusual arrest power without warrant for a constable who warns a person engaging in conduct likely to constitute a s. 5 offence ('offensive conduct') where that person then engages in further such conduct within a short time (whatever that is!) of the warning (see also s. 4A(5).

Applications of the Above Offences

The above offences are difficult enough to come to terms with, but you also need to know when they will be invoked. This information will generally be required by a problem question. It is important not just to know the trees (i.e., the specific offences) but also to be able to see the whole of the wood (i.e., to know the range of options available and when they will be used). In order to assist the following may prove helpful.

(a) *Riot* is the most serious of the charges. It can only be used if the numbers warrant it, but expect it to be a rare charge reserved for serious outbreaks of violent conduct. Remember that you will have to show 'common purpose' and that the consent of the DPP will be necessary.

(b) *Violent disorder* deals with group violence or threats of violence. This could be used as a riot develops but where no person has actually begun to use violence but has simply threatened it. It may occur in a wide range of problem scenarios involving football hooligans, demonstrations, picketing and the like. It carries up to five years' imprisonment, so that it is a fairly serious charge.

(c) *Affray* is commonly used for fighting, especially but not exclusively street fighting, but threats to fight, express or implied, (e.g., a group of football hooligans chasing a rival group) would suffice. The charge can be particularly useful in group situations where the particular roles of individuals are not easy to establish.

(d) *Threatening behaviour* was previously the most frequent of all public order charges. It has been used for more minor offences at demonstrations, on picket lines, and at football matches — often for the shouting of insults. The dividing line between this and harassment (below) will now need to be drawn.

(e) *Incitement to racial hatred offences* are self-explanatory. Note that there could be overlap between these and threatening behaviour, and, because this latter offence does not require the consent of the Attorney-General, it may be used on occasions to deal with racial insults.

(f) *Harassment, alarm or distress* could be used, for example, on the picket line, but was claimed to be for dealing with hooliganism and rowdy behaviour, for example by youths on a housing estate causing disturbances. This may be particularly so where the persons suffering as a result of the disturbance are unlikely to respond with violence (e.g., elderly persons).

Although it is not suggested that you learn these, some indication of the available penalties for these offences and the prosecution practices, may offer some indication of the seriousness of the charge. You can then ask yourself whether the gang who played football with Mr Jones's dustbin in the problem question merit a possible maximum sentence of five years (for violent disorder) or a fine of £400 (for harassment, alarm or distress). (The answer implied is the latter, but this may depend on your level of tolerance to noise!)

OTHER PUBLIC ORDER OFFENCES

Offences in Relation to the Highway

The right to use the highway is restricted to passage and other acts incidental to passage. Consequently, it is possible that any other usage might amount either to a trespass against the owner of the land, or to an offence at common law or under statute. The common law offence of obstructing a public right of passage is that of public nuisance. This may be any act or omission which, in the absence of a lawful excuse, obstructs or causes damage or inconvenience to the public in the exercise of rights common to all citizens.

One illustration of the law in this area is the case of *R v Clark* [1964] 2 QB 315, in which Clark was alleged to have led a large group of people through side-streets in Whitehall during an attempt to circumvent police cordons at a CND demonstration. The direction to the jury on the question of whether this amounted to a public nuisance was whether the streets were obstructed, and whether Clark incited the obstruction. This was successfully appealed on the grounds that it amounted to a misdirection in so far as it did not require the jury to consider whether the user of the highway was unreasonable. It may be obvious that there is an obstruction, but the question is then whether that obstruction is unreasonable. For a similar decision in relation to the statutory offence of obstruction of the highway, see *Hirst v Chief Constable of West Yorkshire* (1986) 85 Cr App R 143.

Public nuisance can also give rise to civil proceedings at the instance of either the Attorney-General or a private citizen able to show special injury. In *Hubbard v Pitt* [1976] QB 142, a picket of an estate agent's office in protest at the alleged harassment of local tenants was found to be unlawful, notwithstanding its entirely peaceful nature. In so far as it prevented the reasonable use of the highway, it constituted a nuisance. Lord Denning delivered a powerful dissenting judgment in which he argued that the right to protest ought to be recognised wherever it was exercised peaceably and in harmony with the law (c.f. *R v Chief Constable of Devon and Cornwall, ex parte CEGB* [1982] QB 458). One difficulty with the case is that it was decided at the interlocutory stage, so that a full hearing of the issues in relation to protests on the highway did not take place. Note also that peaceful picketing which is in contemplation or furtherance of a trade dispute and which takes place at or near the pickets' place of work is lawful by virtue of s. 15 of the Trade Union and Labour Relations Act 1974 (as amended) (see also the Code of Practice on Picketing and *Thomas v National Union of Mineworkers (South Wales Area)* [1986] Ch 20).

Lawful picketing should seek to peacefully persuade persons to work or (more usually!) to abstain from working. Action beyond this may well fall outside the protection of the section. In *Tynan v Balmer* [1967] 1 QB 91 pickets circling a factory gate and denying access to traffic constituted a public nuisance and an obstruction of the highway (see below). In *Piddington v Bates* [1961] 1 WLR 162 a police officer wishing to restrict the number of pickets outside a factory arrested a picket seeking to join the existing group. His conviction for obstructing a police officer in the course of his duty was upheld.

The offence of obstruction of the highway, referred to above, is contained in s. 137 of the Highways Act 1980, and consists of wilfully obstructing free passage along the highway without lawful excuse. In *Arrowsmith v Jenkins*

[1963] 2 QB 561 it was said that it matters not that no obstruction was intended, or even that the whole of the highway was not blocked and passage remained possible — any obstruction is sufficient (but contrast the case of *Hirst* v *Chief Constable of West Yorkshire* (1986) 85 Cr App R 143). Indeed, the offence has, for instance, been used to deal with ticket touts and others touting for business (see *Cooper* v *Metropolitan Police Commissioner* (1985) 82 Cr App R 238). Note here that a restricted offence of touting (related mainly to football matches) was introduced by s. 166 of the Criminal Justice and Public Order Act 1994.

Offences under the Public Order Act 1936

There are two offences which might be committed under the 1936 Act which have been retained post-1986.

(a) *Uniforms.* Section 1 of that Act makes it an offence to wear a uniform, indicating support of, or affiliation to, a political organisation, at a public meeting, or in a public place. In *O'Moran* v *DPP* [1975] QB 864 dark glasses, jackets and berets worn at the funeral of an IRA member were said to amount to a uniform (and see s. 3 of the Prevention of Terrorism (Temporary Provisions) Act 1989, discussed above).

(b) *Private armies.* These have also been referred to earlier. Section 2 of the 1936 Act bans their organisation or training. Training in the use of arms without legal authorisation will constitute an offence under the Unlawful Drilling Act 1819.

Offensive Weapons

The carrying of offensive weapons is not dealt with in law as a problem specific to public order, but is dealt with as part of the general criminal law under the Prevention of Crime Act 1953. In addition, the Criminal Justice Act 1988 deals with offences of manufacturing, selling or hiring offensive weapons (s. 141 and c.f. the Crossbows Act 1987) and makes it an offence to carry a blade in a public place (s. 139). In relation to this provision there is a stop and search power available to police constables.

Section 1 of the 1953 Act makes it an offence to have an offensive weapon in a public place without lawful excuse. An offensive weapon is defined as 'any article made or adapted for use for causing injury to the person, or intended by the person having it with him for such use by him'. This suggests two types of weapon: one made to cause injury (e.g., nails welded together into a ball); the other not ordinarily offensive but intended to be used to cause injury (e.g., a dart or a kitchen knife). The two categories differ in that the intention to cause injury is a necessary part of the offence if the person prosecuted had with him an article within the second category.

Thus, in *Woodward* v *Koessler* [1958] 1 WLR 1255, Koessler attempted to break into a cinema using a sheath knife, but when disturbed used it to frighten away an elderly caretaker. Two questions arose. Did the accused fall within the 1953 Act given that he had not necessarily taken the knife out in order to threaten the caretaker? And, if the accused wished only to frighten the caretaker, did this satisfy the requirements of an intention to 'cause injury'? The Divisional Court decided that for the purposes of this section it was sufficient for the accused to make use of the knife to cause injury once he had taken it out with him, and that 'causing injury' could include intimidation. On the latter point it is now generally accepted that such an interpretation goes too far, and that some physical injury must be intended — see, e.g., *R* v *Edmonds* [1963] 2 QB 142.

Obstruction of a Police Officer

Section 51(1) of the Police Act 1964 deals with assault of a constable in the execution of his duty, and s. 51(3) deals with wilful obstruction of a constable in the execution of his duty. There is a great overlap with police powers here, since one obvious question is whether the constable was acting in the execution of his duty. However, most courses will include the s. 51(3) charge of obstruction within the public order part of the syllabus — if only because the section is of immense value to the police in dealing with public order difficulties. Preventative powers in relation to public order are dealt with in the section on 'Revision' later in the chapter, but it is necessary to examine the elements of the offence. The case of *Duncan* v *Jones* [1936] 1 KB 218 is the classic illustration of the workings of s. 51(3).

In that case, Mrs Duncan intended to address a meeting in a cul-de-sac adjacent to a training centre for the unemployed. The meeting was organised by the National Unemployed Workers' Union and a previous meeting of theirs, in the same location, had led to a disturbance at the training centre. The police, therefore, asked her to move to another site within 200 yards of the original location. Upon refusing, Mrs Duncan was arrested for threatening a breach of the peace and eventually charged under a provision similar in wording to s. 51(3) of the 1964 Act. Note that on this occasion she had not provoked or committed a breach of the peace, but Humphreys J was of the opinion that: '... the respondent reasonably apprehended a breach of the peace. It then ... became his duty to prevent anything which in his view would cause that breach of the peace. While he was taking steps so to do, he was wilfully obstructed.'

The decision is open to a number of criticisms. Primarily, there was (as Humphreys J admitted) no previous authority for such a decision. Yet the case effectively created new preventative powers within the realm of public order. Indeed, as a first-year student faced with the question 'Do judges make law?'

in (for example) a legal system examination, you could do worse than cite *Duncan* v *Jones* as an example of overzealous judicial creativity. Of course, it remains open to the courts to question the reasonableness of a constable's apprehension of a breach of the peace and so control the preventive power allowed. However, cases such as *Piddington* v *Bates* [1961] 1 WLR 162 show that too often the courts are prepared to leave the police officer 'to take such steps as he thinks are proper' without any rigorous examination of the reasonableness of such action (and see *G* v *Chief Superintendent of Police, Stroud* [1987] Crim LR 269).

The powers effectively created by *Duncan* v *Jones* continue to grow. In *Willmott* v *Atack* [1977] QB 498 a question arose as to whether an interference in an arrest in order to assist the police, which actually had the effect of allowing the prisoner to escape, could amount to a wilful obstruction within s. 51(3) of the 1964 Act. The view of the Divisional Court was that it could not. Croom-Johnson J sought to construe the section as a whole, and concluded that some element of criminal intent — 'some form of hostility to the police with the intention of seeing that what is done is to obstruct' — was necessary. It was not sufficient to show that the police were in fact obstructed.

However, it is not easy to reconcile this approach with that taken in *Hills* v *Ellis* [1983] QB 680. In that case, the defendant, a passer-by outside a football ground, convinced that the police were in the process of arresting an innocent man, sought to grab the elbow of the police officer and draw his attention to the man's innocence. The passer-by was arrested, charged with obstruction, and convicted before the magistrates. It seems clear on these facts that hostility towards the police, as referred to in *Willmott*, was not present. On appeal, however, the Divisional Court distinguished the earlier case on the basis that the actions of the passer-by were intentionally directed at the police, they did seek to prevent an arrest, and did amount to an obstruction. There was no scope for allowing that the defendant acted with lawful excuse — there could be no lawful excuse for interfering with a lawful arrest. In the words of Griffiths LJ, this was 'as clear a case as we can have of obstructing a police officer in the course of his duty'. This would not be the case where the third party intervention relates to an unlawful arrest (see *Edwards* v *DPP* (1993) 97 Cr App R 301).

The reasoning of *Hills* v *Ellis* was applied in *Lewis* v *Cox* [1985] QB 509, and it seems clear that in the view of the Divisional Court, at least, an intentional act which will have an obstructive effect will constitute an offence if it makes the task of the constable more difficult, regardless of the underlying motive. Thus in *Lewis* v *Cox* even opening the rear door of a police van in order to ask an arrested friend where he was being taken, could amount to obstruction. *Lewis* v *Cox* goes much further than *Hills* v *Ellis* in its *ratio*; and there can be few situations in which a citizen may intervene at the time of the arrest of another person which will not amount to an obstruction. However, it may be that *Willmott* v *Atack* would still amount to such a situation.

The miners' dispute of 1984–5 saw widespread use of s. 51(3). Roadblocks were set up (in advance of the power to do so purportedly under s. 4 of the Police and Criminal Evidence Act 1984) in order to stop miners travelling to picket lines. If miners refused to turn away, they were charged under s. 51(3). This raised the question of the legality of arrest for imminent breaches of the peace but in *Moss* v *McLachlan* [1985] IRLR 76 Skinner J stated that: 'If the police on reasonable grounds believe a breach of the peace may be committed, the police officer is ... under a duty to take reasonable steps to prevent that breach occurring.' However, he further stated that the risk of a breach must be in 'close proximity both in place and time', so that the 'immediacy of the threat to the peace determines what action is reasonable'. On the facts of *Moss* v *McLachlan* (four collieries locally) there was arguably a sufficient proximity but the judgment must cast doubt upon many police actions in the dispute (e.g., preventing Kent miners picketing in the north of England by stopping them in the Dartford Tunnel).

Offences in Relation to Public Meetings

Part II of the Public Order Act 1986 allows that conditions may be laid down for open-air meetings of at least 20 persons. These are reviewed below. Failure to meet such conditions constitutes an offence. In addition, s. 1 of the Public Meeting Act 1908 makes it an offence to act in a disorderly manner (or incite others to do so) at a lawful public meeting, for the purpose of preventing the transaction of business for which the meeting was called. The Public Order Act 1936 amended the 1908 Act in order to allow a constable, at the chairman's request, to take the name and address of a person whom he reasonably suspects of an offence under the Act. Refusal or failure to give one's true name and address is an offence under the section. (Note that this section has been amended by the Police and Criminal Evidence Act 1984.) There exist similar offences under the Representation of the People Act 1983, s. 97. The section applies to a political meeting held between dates of issue of a writ (for parliamentary elections) and the date at which a return to the writ is made, and to a meeting held with reference to a local government election on, or within three weeks of, the election date.

One point which arises out of this is whether the police have the right to be present at meetings held on privately owned property, since, in general, entry on to property without the consent of the owner will constitute a trespass. This would apply to a police officer having no lawful right to be present so that (s)he may be asked to leave and be ejected if necessary (see *Davis* v *Lisle* [1936] 2 KB 434). However, the common-law rights of the police to be present at such meetings may be more extensive than those of the citizen, following the difficult case of *Thomas* v *Sawkins* [1935] 2 KB 249.

Thomas v *Sawkins*, rather like *Duncan* v *Jones* [1936] 1 KB 218, seems to rest upon little, if any, authority. The case suggests that the police are entitled to be present at a meeting held on private premises, if they have reasonable grounds for believing that either a seditious speech or a breach of the peace is imminent or likely. By an unhappy accident, the meeting which the police felt it necessary to attend in the *Thomas* case happened to be demanding the dismissal of the Chief Constable! (See also in the context of entry on to property *R* v *Chief Constable of Devon and Cornwall, ex parte CEGB* [1982] QB 458.)

NEW STATUTORY DEVELOPMENTS: TRESPASS

In recent years we have seen legislation directed at problems which have come into political prominence in a number of ways, and in quite unrelated areas, such as football hooliganism, and so-called hippy convoys, hunt saboteurs, and rave parties. The legislation in these areas has increased the range of criminal consequences for trespass and has implications that extend well beyond the immediate province of public order with which we are concerned.

A few examples from the Criminal Justice and Public Order Act 1994 will suffice. With an eye to the concerns of the authorities about so-called new age travellers and mass trespass to land, the police now have extended powers to order persons (and any vehicles) to move off land on which they are trespassers, under s. 61 of the 1994 Act (repealing the earlier incursion into this new area of the criminal law, in s. 39 of the Public Order Act 1986). Breach may involve commission of an offence and also enable the seizure of any vehicles (s. 62).

There are also new police powers, under s. 63, in connection with an arguably newer phenomenon, that of unlicensed 'raves' (trespassory or not), based upon gatherings of 100 persons or more on land in the open air, the noise from which is likely to cause serious distress to inhabitants (music being 'emission of a succession of repetitive beats', a definition which might voluntarily be extended to activities within the authors' homes!). Under the same section, directions to leave may be given, supported by criminal sanctions in the event of breach. Indeed, s. 65 empowers the making of directions to persons on their way to raves. There are provisions for seizure of vehicles or equipment (ss. 64 and 66).

There is also a provision which appears to be primarily aimed at anti-hunt saboteurs and other forms of direct action, such as demonstrations which seek to prevent development activities, such as the construction of new roads. Section 68 provides for an offence of aggravated trespass, involving the trespass on land in the open air with the effect of intimidating others to deter them from carrying on lawful activities, as defined, obstruction or disruption. There is a power in the police to order persons to leave, under s. 69.

Sections 72 to 74 of the 1994 Act extend the panoply of powers available against squatters. This goes beyond what is normally considered to be part of a constitutional law course and no comment is offered here (see the amendments to ss. 6 and 7 of the Criminal Law Act 1977, and new s. 12A, extending protection with respect of certain forms of re-entry; and offences by those who do not leave on request). Moreover, s. 76 provides for criminal consequences for disobedience to a new summary, civil interim possession order. The Act further enacts stricter provisions arguably directed at gypsies, with new provisions enabling the removal of unauthorised vehicular campers (ss. 77 to 79).

Note that, in ss. 70 and 71, the 1994 Act provides for the prohibition of certain assemblies, and this alters the law as previously contained in s. 14 of the Public Order Act 1986. This is referred to again below, where consideration is given to preventative powers under the Public Order Act 1986.

REVISION

The above sections deal with offences in relation to public order. As we shall see, it will be necessary to deal with preventative powers in relation to public order, since these may be vital in answering an examination question. It may help, however, to divide the material in this way so that it does not appear as one huge mass of notes awaiting revision. There is no doubt that public order is a difficult topic to revise. It has an inherent interest, and the majority of students find it easy to relate to (if only because it is generally possible to participate in demonstrations during student days). However, it can be quite difficult to grasp what is now a considerable body of statutory offences, and corresponding case law.

An obvious divide between the above offences is to form three groups: (a) the original common law offences now labelled riot, violent disorder and affray; (b) threatening behaviour, incitement to racial hatred, and disorderly conduct; and (c) other offences. In doing this you could arrange, perhaps, in the form of a table, the elements of the three offences in group (a). For example, you could form a grid with the names of the offences across the top, and, down the side, a list of the requisite conditions. Two such headings would be 'public place' and 'private place' and a tick would appear against each for each offence reading across the page. This shows that all three offences can be committed in both a public and a private place. Some points on this grid would have crosses. Thus against the heading 'Common purpose' a tick would appear against riot only. Under violent disorder and affray, neither of which requires an element of common purpose a cross would appear. Once you have digested the table you can learn the definitions and attributes of the requisite elements. In this way you need not learn material three times. You have one section on 'unlawful violence' to revise and you know that this element is relevant to all three offences. This may sound cumbersome explained here in print, but an example appears below showing how to do the same with the preventative powers for assemblies and processions.

If you are studying criminal law simultaneously, you may have already devised strategies for dealing with similar material in that area. It may also be helpful if you are allowed to take public law statutes into the examination room, but as stated previously, this does not dispense with the need to master the material. On the other hand, you may be offered no such assistance, and those elements of constitutional law concerned with personal freedom may contain the largest amount of statutory material in your first-year studies. For this reason you must maintain a checklist of offences, and you will then be able to run through these in any given problem question and decide which are relevant. Approaching the subject this way ought to eliminate obvious oversights. It may also assist with certain types of essay question — for example:

'It is open to question whether a public meeting on the highway could ever be lawful' (Lord Scarman). Discuss.

Even though you may know all the requisite elements of an offence it may not be necessary to detail all of them in an answer. Take s. 137 of the Highways Act 1980:

If a person, without lawful authority or excuse, in any way wilfully obstructs the free passage along a highway, he is guilty of an offence ...

Here the constituent elements of the offence are:

(a) obstruction of free passage along a highway;
(b) wilfully;
(c) without excuse.

When answering problem questions, it is not necessary every time the facts suggest an obstruction to repeat the details of s. 137. Often you will be able to suggest that the conduct of a particular party amounts to an obstruction, and it may only become necessary to mention the detail of the section if there is some doubt as to whether the conduct is in fact an obstruction under the Act, e.g., because the obstruction does not seem to be wilful. It follows, therefore, that rather than learning by heart the particular details of the various offences, it is more important to develop a broad understanding of the nature of the public order offences, and the ability to recognise how they may or may not apply in particular situations.

In short, it is wiser to divert some of the time, which you might have spent learning sections of the Acts of Parliament, to the consideration of past questions, perhaps with your textbook open, so that you can spot, in future questions, the type of conduct which might constitute an offence or enable the police to take specific action. This is particularly necessary with a subject like public order which may well give rise to problem questions. Such questions may end by asking you to advise a party to the problem. This may be the Chief Constable who is attempting to ensure order within a particular locality. Alternatively the problem may simply end with the command 'Discuss'.

In either case you will need to consider the preventative powers open to the authorities to cope with a situation which is likely to lead to disorder. Some preventative powers have been considered in the previous section, thus s. 51(3) of the Police Act 1964 and the common law power to enter premises on the authority of *Thomas* v *Sawkins* [1935] 2 KB 249 have obvious uses in handling disorder, or dealing with a situation which the police fear will lead to disorder. It is advisable, however, to consider the range of options available to maintain order so that complex problem questions may be readily answered. An illustration is now offered as to how this might be done in note form for the preventative powers in the 1986 Act. You may need to refer to the larger texts to understand the shorthand.

The provisions of ss. 12 to 14 of the Public Order Act 1986, concerning the placing of conditions upon processions or assemblies (ss. 12 and 14) and prohibitions of processions (s. 13), have been augmented by new ss. 14A, 14B and 14C, inserted by ss. 70 and 71 of the Criminal Justice and Public Order Act 1994. The new banning powers apply to newly defined trespassory assemblies. These involve at least 20 people, are held on land to which there is either no or limited right of public access, and without permission of the occupier of the land. An order can extend to four days and across an area whose radius is no wider than five miles. Just as in the case of processions, application for an order is made to a local authority for a prohibition. The powers are triggered by a reasonable belief by the chief officer of police that there may result serious disruption to the life of the community or significant damage to land, a building or monument, which is of historic, architectural or scientific importance. Criminal offences are provided on breach. Note that there still appears to be no requirement of advance warning to be given of assemblies, reflecting a political compromise reached on this issue. The terms applicable also differ, illustrated by the description briefly appearing below.

Preventative powers under the 1986 and 1994 Acts

For	Processions	Assemblies
Advance notice?		X
Included	Demos of support/Oppo to views or actions. Publicising cause/campaign. Marking/commemorating events.	
Excluded	Funerals Customary processions Not reasonably practical	
Notice?	Written details of route, time, organiser. Six days + in advance (or as soon as reasonably practical).	
Controls		
Included	Threatens: Serious public disorder, or	Ditto
	Serious damage to property, or	Ditto
	Serious damage to community life	Ditto
	or Purpose: intimidation of others with a view	Ditto
	to compulsion	
Excluded	All others	Ditto
By whom	Senior police officer with reasonable belief of threats above.	Ditto
Considerations	Time, place, circumstances, route	Time, place, circumstances
Type of control	Such directions as appear necessary excluding a ban but including any other conditions.	Directions imposing conditions on place, duration, numbers, only as appear necessary.
When	In advance/At the time	Ditto
Bans		
Requirement	*Requirement* to ban if s. 12 conditions believed insufficient to prevent serious public disorder.	Reasonable belief, trespass; may result in serious disruption to community or damage to monuments etc.
Included	All classes, specified in banning order.	All trespassory assemblies (including 20 +).
Excluded	All not within classes specified unless blanket ban.	Beyond five miles from specified centre/exceeding four days.
By whom	Chief Constable or London equivalent	
Procedure	1. Application to and approval by local council	Ditto
	2. Home Secretary's consent to council making order	Ditto
	or (London)	
	1. Consent of Home Secretary	
	2. Order by Commissioner.	
Failure to comply		
Advance notice	Offence by organisers if notice or inadequate notice given.	X

Defence	Did not know/Had no reason to suspect Circumstances beyond control Acquiescence of/with police.	
Control offences	Organisers' or participants' failure to comply with conditions.	Ditto
	Incitement to breach conditions.	Ditto
Defences	(Failure to comply only) circumstances beyond control.	Ditto
Banning offences	Organisation of or participation in banned procession incitement to participate and breach of direction not to proceed.	Ditto

This ought to give you the bones of what you need to know. Wider reading and familiarity with the statutes will fill in the gaps on matters such as advance notice procedures. Definitions, e.g., procession and assembly(!), will need to be learnt, and explanatory sections on the main elements incorporated into your notes with relevant case law included. No one should ever promise that studying law would be easy!

It is also important to bear in mind that these powers in the 1986 Act are not the only relevant preventative powers. Some significant inclusions appear below in (thankfully) more conventional prose.

Binding Over

This power derives from both common law and statute — the most famous of the statutory provisions being the Justices of the Peace Act 1361. A person may be bound over by magistrates following complaint against a named person, or following an arrest without warrant (at common law) for a breach, or apprehended breach, of the peace — see chapter 12. The order will require the person to enter into recognisance either to be of good behaviour or to keep the peace, or both. Generally, however, a person may only be bound over to keep the peace upon evidence of a fear for personal safety, whereas a surety to be of good behaviour is much wider (see further *Lansbury* v *Riley* [1914] 3 KB 229). The case of *Wise* v *Dunning* [1902] 1 KB 167 and the constraint of Pastor Wise provides a useful illustration of the purpose of this power. Although it will be clear from the above discussion that a person may be bound over with or without facing criminal charges, failure to observe the order is an offence punishable by imprisonment. For the avoidance of confusion, you should separate binding over from the somewhat dubious practice of attaching conditions to the grant of bail (prevalent at the time of the miners' strike) — see *R* v *Mansfield Justices, ex parte Sharkey* [1985] QB 613.

Section 1, Official Secrets Act 1911

It may seem strange to see this included as a preventative power in relation to public order. However, the section renders guilty of an offence any person who, for any purpose prejudicial to the safety or interests of the State, 'approaches, inspects, passes over or is in the neighbourhood of or enters any prohibited place'. The case of *Chandler* v *DPP* [1964] AC 763 illustrates the possibility that this power may be used to prevent particular types of demonstrations. Here anti-nuclear protestors attempted to invade a military airfield, but were prevented from so doing and were charged with conspiring to commit a breach of s. 1 of the 1911 Act. Their motives — that they wished to further world peace — did not amount to a defence, and the House of Lords refused to restrict the ambit of s. 1 of the Act to offences concerning espionage, despite the margin note in the Act which reads 'Penalties for spying'.

Injunction

The above powers are largely available to the police. However, it may be open to a citizen to restrain particular forms of protest which constitute a trespass or otherwise infringe his or her legal rights. The most famous example of this concerns the Court of Appeal decision in *Hubbard* v *Pitt* [1976] QB 142, which is almost better known for Lord Denning's strong dissent in favour of freedom of expression than for the majority decision. However, the case illustrates the availability of interlocutory injunctions for actions which are prima facie tortious, if serious damage might be occasioned to the interests of the plaintiff.

The use of injunctions has become a particularly important part of public order law in recent years, following events at Wapping in the News International dispute (see *News Group Newspapers Ltd* v *SOGAT '82* [1987] ICR 181), at Stonehenge, and during the miners' strike. To take the latter example, in *Thomas* v *National Union of Mineworkers (South Wales Area)*, working miners were granted an interlocutory injunction to restrain the NUM (South Wales Area) from organising picketing at certain colliery gates other than in numbers not exceeding six and for the purposes only of peaceful communication and persuasion.

Breach of the Peace

There is a section in the following chapter on breach of the peace. This can be defined as an act which causes harm to a person or to property in the presence of (at least) the property owner. Acts which threaten such harm or cause fear of such harm can be included — see *R* v *Howell* [1982] QB 416. For now it is sufficient to note the significance of the concept, as a ground of arrest, and the width of discretion given to police officers seeking to prevent an apprehended breach of the peace. Examples go back as far as *Humphries* v *Connor* (1864) 17 ICLR 1 and the removal of the protestant lady's orange lily, and include *Duncan* v *Jones* [1936] 1 KB 218. Note that, as in that case, refusal to comply may lead to charges of obstructing a police officer. Anyone in doubt of the width and significance of the power (notwithstanding the 1986 reforms) should refer to *Moss* v *McLachlan* [1985] IRLR 76.

THE EXAMINATION

By their very nature, freedom of association and freedom of assembly concern conflicts of interest. The conflict may be between opposing groups or between protestors and the State, but it will invariably exist. The reason for this is obvious. Ideally people will support the notion of freedom of assembly, but only up to the point that the furtherance of the objectives of a particular group are not at variance with their own. At that point they might seek to register their own objections or they may demand that the State intervene. The question, therefore, is where the line is to be drawn. And it is this question that will be repeated time and time again in essay questions in the examination paper.

Thus you may be given very wide questions such as:

The right of assembly is a crucial freedom, but one that can only be allowed so long as order is maintained.
Discuss.

This asks you whether the law succeeds in allowing protest, whilst at the same time maintaining order, and offers you the opportunity to make your assessment of whether (for example) the law goes too far in restricting freedom of action in the name of maintaining the peace. You could answer this question by pursuing some of the wide powers offered to the police, by statute and at common law, in relation to the maintenance of order.

Although this type of question is very common, it is not the only possibility. Some questions will be directed very particularly at certain aspects of public order (such as that incorporating the quotation of Lord Scarman, in the revision section). There is also available a middle path for examiners — an amalgam of these two varieties. This would be a question which is directed at a particular problem of public order but nonetheless allows you scope to deal with the questions of police discretion and of balance. This is perhaps the trickiest type of question, and the following is an example:

The general principle is that a lawful act does not become unlawful merely because other persons decide to offer unlawful resistance to it (de Smith).
Discuss.

In line with what was said in chapter 3, you may learn a good deal from the source of the quotation. Presumably the learned authors of de Smith do believe this to be the 'general principle' and it may be safe to assume that they are correct in this. However, the word 'general' does imply that there may be exceptions to such a principle. They do not talk of an invariable principle, and it may be that they are suggesting that conduct which is prima facie lawful may have to be restrained in exceptional cases, in order to avoid disorder which might be provoked.

Before examining this, one further comment may be made. The reason why this question is described as tricky (above) is because it tempts the student to dive into the question without first exploring its depths. *Beatty* v *Gillbanks* (1882) 9 QBD 308, in which the salvationists were bound over to keep the peace, is the classic illustration of lawful conduct opposed by unlawful means. Many an unwitting student reads the type of question given above, thinks 'hallelujah, I know this', begins a discussion of *Beatty* (usually by reciting the facts) and quickly realises that there is no obvious direction in which to proceed once the discussion of this one case is concluded. No matter how obvious the answer appears, produce a plan. Of course *Beatty* will be included in this discussion; indeed it may play a vital role, but it has to be placed in some context.

You may begin your essay with a short introductory paragraph. In line with previous instructions (chapter 2) you may have an introductory paragraph prepared upon the obvious theme of the competing values of freedom of assembly and maintenance of public order. That will serve excellently here. Note also the balance inherent in the circumstances in which statutory conditions or bans may be imposed on processions or assemblies (ss. 12-14, Public Order Act 1986, as amended by the 1994 Act mentioned above). If you are familiar with it, there is also a highly relevant case on the European Convention of Human Rights, article 11 of which upholds freedom of peaceful assembly. In *Christians against Racism and Fascism* v *UK* (1980) 21 DR 138 the Commission ruled that the possibility of violent counter-demonstration could not remove the right to organise a peaceful demonstration.

On the other hand, examine the offence of threatening behaviour. Under s. 4 of the Public Order Act 1986, as you will recall, an offence may be committed without intention where action which falls within that section is likely to provoke the use of violence. Therefore once there is some element of insulting behaviour, notwithstanding the underlying legality of the purpose of the action, the methods by which it is pursued and its likely results may render it unlawful. Thus behaviour which can provoke opponents can be unlawful. This is what is meant by the word 'merely' in the question. Of course action might be unlawful if its intention was to provoke resistance.

Thus few persons would seriously argue that it was wrong to bind over Pastor Wise (in *Wise* v *Dunning* [1902] 1 KB 167) following his behaviour in evangelising in his own peculiar and offensive manner in the Catholic areas of Liverpool. At the same time many would agree that on the facts of *Beatty* (and you should briefly outline these) it was correct for the Divisional Court to quash the decision of the magistrates' court binding over certain salvationists on the basis that they constituted an unlawful assembly.

Of course here we make value judgments as to the worth of the action of both parties. The type of value judgments which are inherent in cases such as

Wise and *Beatty* are repeated elsewhere. Thus in *Humphries* v *Connor* (1864) 17 ICLR 1, the activity of wearing a flower was prima facie lawful, but it is widely accepted that in the circumstances of the case the police officer had the power to remove it if it was an orange lily worn in a predominantly Catholic quarter of Ireland. Today many of these questions could arise in the context of s. 51(3) of the Police Act 1964, following *Duncan* v *Jones* [1936] 1 KB 218, which is considered above. Therefore the question is one of enormous practical importance, since the powers stemming from that Act can be ideally used in situations where disorder is anticipated. Similarly one cannot ignore the width and exercise of discretion relating to the various charges under the 1986 Act and to issues such as what may amount to disorderly conduct. The question asks you to provide some rationale for the legal powers and their operation, and this is an extremely difficult task.

Simply to say, as suggested above, that certain parties are more culpable than others because they provoke a reaction is fraught with difficulties. In a sense Pastor Wise no more caused disorder than did the salvationists, so that to say that the latter group ought to have the right to demonstrate their views, but Pastor Wise (or Mrs Duncan) ought not, is fraught with difficulties. It is possible to distinguish these cases on the basis that they arose in differing legal contexts — unlawful assembly, binding over, obstruction of a police officer, etc. However, such legalism is unhelpful when the underlying conduct is so similar. It is also possible to argue that certain of the cases are wrongly decided. Thus it is argued above that *Duncan* v *Jones* rested upon little authority. Or it is possible to argue that there is absolutely no reason why the Salvation Army did not amount to an unlawful assembly as the law then stood (but see *R* v *Chief Constable of Devon and Cornwall, ex parte CEGB* [1982] QB 458).

At the end of the day there is no obviously right or wrong answer to this difficult question. All that you can be expected to do is to examine both sides of the coin; those situations in which the protest is considered legitimate in spite of the opposition it provokes and those in which the protest is condemned because it provokes opposition. The value judgments here are enormous, as shown in the miners' strike when the police chose continually to escort single miners to work notwithstanding the difficulties of supervising the naturally angry picketing which ensued. Similar problems have recently arisen with regard to police escorts of lorries containing live animals bound for the mainland of Europe, during 1995. Your conclusion might be that the law has never succeeded in coming to terms with this problem, and that as a result the law is uncertain, but wide enough to allow variations to the general principle referred to in the question, so as to allow purely lawful action to be rendered unlawful in the face of determined opposition — perhaps rendering the 1986 Act unnecessary! And indeed the possibility is there that the police may as a matter of practicality choose to require the least blameworthy party to disperse in a particular clash and use s. 51(3) of the 1964 Act to reinforce this policy. Whilst this is unsatisfactory, it tells us a great deal about the dilemmas which are central to the problem of protest and order.

A Public Order Problem

If an examiner takes care in drafting a problem, then the problem ought to read as succinctly as possible. Long problems on an examination paper look daunting and can become very confusing. A good examiner will try hard to abbreviate the points and allow the question to read in a straightforward and unambiguous way. Because this is so, there are unlikely to be redundant words in the problem itself. It becomes important to ask yourself why particular events happen, or why particular detail is placed in the problem itself. Here is a question on public order:

> Blodwyn, a Welsh Nationalist MP, is due to arrive at Aberdung Railway Station at 8 p.m. to address a meeting of Welsh Nationalists in the Market Square of Aberdung. She is travelling on the train from London to Aberdung with a party of supporters, all dressed in red and carrying giant leeks.
>   George has organised an anti-Celtic demonstration — a torchlight procession — which is due to arrive at the station at 7 p.m. George has booked the station tea rooms and has placed an advertisement in the Aberdung Bugle inviting all people of anti-Celtic sentiment to attend. The meeting is scheduled to last one hour and will disperse on to the station forecourt at the same time as passengers travelling from London.
>   Advise the Chief Constable of Aberdungshire of any offences which may be committed, and outline any steps he may take to prevent disturbances occurring.

If what is said above is true, then one way to approach a problem question is to ask yourself why all of the particular facts are relevant. One idea is to underline all of the words which appear to elaborate upon the basic theme. For example: Why did the examiner make Blodwyn an MP? Is the time relevant? Why is the meeting in the Market Square? Does it matter that supporters are dressed in red and carry giant leeks? Similarly, there are a whole range of questions which apply to George, and they concern precisely the same issues — the status, timing, location and nature of his activity. To take one example, does it matter that the demonstration is 'anti-Celtic'?

For each question there is an answer, but these are best jotted down in rough notes first. Some of the issues may be obvious. For instance, you may see that the wearing of red might be taken to constitute a political uniform or you may grasp the point that the hire of the station tea rooms may raise issues concerning public and private places and the right of entry for the police under *Thomas v Sawkins* [1935] 2 KB 249. However, you may not be able to work out the relevance of Blodwyn's being a Member of Parliament or the fact that the times of the meetings are given. This is not something to worry about too much. As is said in chapter 1, few students manage to spot all relevant points in a problem, but even those who do would find it impossible to list all points immediately. The longer you work at a problem, the more you may find in it.

Many law teachers have experienced the rather curious process of drafting a moot problem, and then later hearing able students argue out the points raised. At that level of analysis arguments begin to emerge which had never entered the head of the teacher at the time of writing the problem. In an examination room this is unlikely to happen, but it is not surprising if new arguments occur to you, throughout the 45 minutes which you spend on an answer. Let us take one example from the problem which concerns the timing of the events. You see immediately that these will clash at 8 p.m. on the railway station, but why is the event set in the evening? At first you cannot understand why, so quite correctly you put that point aside and begin to answer the question.

At some stage you will consider the powers of the Chief Constable in relation to George's meeting and procession and Blodwyn's meeting. You will mentally run through the powers available. The first thing to note is that under ss. 12 and 14 of the 1986 Act the officer must have regard to time, place and circumstances since these factors may lead her/him to apprehend serious public disorder, etc. Having regard to these factors, he may impose 'such conditions as appear necessary' for the preservation of public order. Thus it may be possible to direct the organiser of the procession to reschedule the event — to move it to earlier in the day perhaps. Note also that many of these conditions could be imposed, probably, on the Market Square meeting, but it seems apparent that much of the trouble will occur prior to this at the railway station. Section 12 would also allow the re-routing of the procession away from the railway station. Note also the possible application of the powers applicable to processions (and now to trespassory assemblies) contained in s. 13 of the 1986 Act and ss. 14A, 14B and 14C of the 1994 Act (the station forecourt or platforms would seem prima facie to be 'public places' within the definition contained in s. 16 of the 1986 Act). Finally, s. 12 would seem to permit the prohibition of flags, banners and emblems in so far as is reasonably necessary to prevent serious public disorder, etc. Its predecessor (s. 3 of the 1936 Act) mentioned this specifically. This being evening, there is a torchlight procession. Could the provision be invoked to prevent the carrying of torches? Alternatively, could the torches amount to offensive weapons? So you see that an evening event does form part of a wider scenario, and eventually brings in particular problems of its own.

Once you have listed the points in your notes, and feel satisfied that you are able to begin writing, it is necessary to decide upon a strategy. You are asked to advise upon offences and preventative measures, and using your checklists you should have isolated in your notes all of those which are relevant. However, it is not necessarily wise to follow your instructions literally and deal with offences first and preventative measures second. The reason for this is that preventative measures fall into two types — those which may be exercised well in advance (like s. 12 of the 1986 Act) or those which will need to be adopted in much closer proximity, such as in relation to a breach of the peace. That being so, it makes sense to deal with the advance powers first, then the possible offences which might be foreseen or which might occur, and then the immediate powers to prevent disorder.

It is not intended to deal with the whole of these here — the earlier notes can serve as your own checklist — but a couple of points may be made. Firstly, there are two opposing groups here, so that the situation is similar to those discussed in relation to the essay question in this section. You are, however, asked to advise the Chief Constable, and therefore it is important to make some form of assessment as to the appropriate party to seek to restrict. Here it may be relevant to consider the party political nature of Blodwyn's visit and the fact that she is an elected MP, perhaps seeking to address constituents. This may be compared with George's racist notices and the fact that his action seems purposely designed to produce a clash with Blodwyn's arrival. Also as a purely practical matter, there are a number of obvious limitations which may be applied to George, but it is rather more difficult and considerably less convenient all round to prevent the train arriving in Aberdung.

The second, and final, point is this. If you are asked to advise the Chief Constable, that advice might need to be quite wide-ranging. George's racist motives are referred to above. Assuming that you anticipate the possible breaches of ss. 18 and 19 of the Public Order Act 1986 inherent in either the meeting or the advertisement in the Aberdung Bugle, it would make a considerable impression on the examiner if you advised also that a prosecution under this part of the Act is only possible with the leave of the Attorney-General. Even the fact that the meeting in the problem happened to be not an anti-foxhunting protest (for example), but an anti-Celtic demonstration, raises a host of points!

CONCLUSION

In Britain we are rather complacent about the safeguarding of our individual liberties. This is rather surprising, since in the absence of any written, constitutional guarantees, it might be thought that there would be concern as to the limits upon freedom of association and assembly. Perhaps many people in Britain regard the right to protest as unimportant, or believe the restrictions to be few. On either count they are wrong. The freedoms here are vital, but the available limitations are wide, and consist of a powerful armoury of statute and common law.

This tells us much about the nature of the subject. To begin with, it is one which the student can relate to as significant and relevant to society in general. This does not always appear to be true of all areas of law. In consequence, public order is generally a popular subject to study. Do not lose sight, however, that the area is complex. Coming to terms with it will not be easy, and you will need a careful and structured approach to handle the many events which might find their way into a problem question. The subject repays study, however, for in terms of the conflict between protest and order, the questions raised are fundamental to the very nature of our society.

FURTHER READING

Robertson, G., (1993) *Freedom, the Individual and the Law*, 7th ed. (London: Penguin). (See, in particular, Chapter 2.)
Smith, A., 'The Public Order Elements (of the 1994 Act)' [1995] Crim LR 19.

*extended
Police
Powers*

— *Police & Criminal Act   1984*

Codify & Clarify Police Powers

Arrest, Search, detention and evidence

Quasi legislation

12   POLICE POWERS

Personal liberties, such as those examined in the previous chapter, need to be considered in the light of the powers vested in the police to check, and detect, crime. In consequence this is an area which has long been central to the constitutional law syllabus and which became, if anything, more important after the extension of police powers in the Police and Criminal Evidence Act 1984 (hereinafter 'the Act'). There are a number of problems raised by that Act for the law student, but three in particular are crucial to the study of this area of law. To begin with, the Act represents an attempt to codify and clarify the law on police powers, but there is a complex relationship between the new statute law and the earlier common law authority on police powers which may prove significant in filling in the gaps in the legislation or answering points of interpretation. Second, it is a long Act, dealing not merely with arrest and search, but also detention at the police station and points of evidence. It may well be that there will be insufficient time to cover all of the Act on your course, so you will need to pay careful attention in class in order to determine which parts of the Act your teacher views as relevant. The third is that there are codes which amplify the Act. More is said about these later, but there is an opportunity to acquaint the student with what might be called 'quasi-legislation'.

In a sense, the Act has made police powers easier for the student. The powers exercised by the police may be categorised more logically, and certain difficulties apparent in the existing common law have been dealt with. At the same time, the subject appears much bigger than before. There is now a larger body of statutory material, as well as certain codes of practice, the status of which is not always easy to grasp. In addition, as stated above, the student will need to learn a certain body of case law decided both prior to and following the implementation of the Act. Having said this police powers is not a subject to be afraid of, for providing that you are able to organise your

Officers Acting out of Scope of duty Collins v Wilcock and Lindley Rutter

notes so as to include checklists of the powers available under various headings — arrest, search of premises etc. — there are few problems which are likely to cause you serious difficulty.

THE ACT AND THE CODES

Mention is made of codes of practice above, and a little needs to be said about these. They emanate from the Secretary of State (see ss. 60 and 66 for details of the codes and their coverage) and these will be considered as and when appropriate in the text which follows. The codes were extensively redrafted in the years 1989-1991 and again in 1995 following the introduction of the Criminal Justice and Public Order Act 1994. Failure to observe a code may render a police officer liable to disciplinary proceedings, but not to criminal or civil proceedings. However, as with most codes (e.g., the Highway Code) it is presumably open to a person to refer to breaches of the codes, as appropriate, as supporting evidence for a particular argument. Thus in a civil action against the police, a breach of the code may assist in arguing, for example, that the actions of the police amounted to a trespass, or in a criminal case, that, as a result of a similar breach, evidence ought to be ruled inadmissible.

However, there is a problem here, for example, it is quite possible for a police officer to have a power to stop and search, other than in public, short of arrest (see ss. 1 and 2 discussed below). If the police officer searches under a lawful power, but contrary to the code (e.g., because a male officer acting alone requires a woman suspect to remove her blouse) does this amount to a trespass? It is suggested that the answer to the question depends upon whether the police officer's action takes him outside the course of his duty. Cases such as *Lindley* v *Rutter* [1981] 1 QB 128 and *Collins* v *Wilcock* [1984] 1 WLR 1172, although not directly comparable, tend to suggest that the courts might be prepared to find that the police officer acted outside the scope of his duty. There are similar problems in criminal proceedings — will the breach of a code amount to oppression in the eyes of the court? We begin to see some of the huge problems which remain in spite of (or because of?) the Act. Nonetheless, let us examine its provisions.

ARREST

As a constitutional principle, the police pursue the law enforcement duties as private citizens, although, as we shall see, they do have wider powers of arrest than most citizens both at common law and under statute. Nonetheless it follows from this that a police officer may be sued for wrongful interference with a person's freedom since this will generally amount to a trespass. As a normal rule, apart from the stop and search powers of the early sections of the Act and the powers contained in the Criminal Justice and Public Order Act 1994 (see below), any detention will need to follow the exercise of a lawful power of arrest. There is no general power of detention short of arrest. The powers of arrest are now considered.

Power to Arrest

As we shall see in the section on revision, it is advisable to draw up a checklist of powers of arrest. The powers of arrest are:

(a) Arrest with a warrant.
(b) Arrest for a breach of the peace using common law powers.
(c) Arrest without a warrant for an arrestable offence.
(d) Arrest without a warrant for an offence not falling within (c) but for which there is a residual statutory power of arrest (see Schedule 2).
(e) Arrest without a warrant under s. 25 of the Police and Criminal Evidence Act 1984.
(f) Arrest without a warrant for the purposes of fingerprinting.

Broadly the Act changed the powers of arrest as follows. The powers contained in (a) and (b) are largely unchanged. The many statutory powers of arrest without warrant are reduced to certain specific powers contained in Schedule 2 to the Act (see (d) above) and many older powers were repealed by s. 26 of the Act. However, the definition of arrestable offence (see (c) above) is a wide one under the Act, and a general power of arrest provides for offences remaining outside categories (b), (c) and (d), subject to certain general conditions of arrest being fulfilled (category (e) above). This general power was introduced by the 1984 Act as was the power of arrest under (f) which seeks to facilitate fingerprinting at the police station. Let us examine these categories in turn.

Arrest with a warrant
A warrant is available from a magistrate acting upon the authority of a statutory provision (see, e.g., the Magistrates' Courts Act 1980, s. 1). A police officer will generally lay an information before a magistrate who has a discretion whether to issue a warrant or not. A warrant is generally thought appropriate where the matter would not normally be dealt with by summons (as with minor offences) and where the offence is punishable by imprisonment (see Magistrates' Courts Act 1980, s. 1(4)).

Breach of the peace
This is a common law power of arrest, and is unaffected by the provisions of the 1984 Act except in so far as the provisions of s. 28 apply (discussed below

under 'manner of arrest'). There is no statutory definition of breach of the peace, but this may include fighting, affray, menace, assault, or threats of violence (see chapter 11). It is unlikely to include domestic disturbances or activities which are merely noisy. Nonetheless a breach of the peace can take place on private premises, even though the disturbance involves only the persons on the premises, if other persons are likely to be disturbed (see *McConnell* v *Chief Constable of Greater Manchester Police* [1990] 1 WLR 364). Thus in relation to affray (see chapter 11) a person could arrest if the affray takes place in his or her presence, or if it had taken place and was likely to reoccur. For example, in one of the earliest authorities, *Timothy* v *Simpson* (1835) 1 Cr M & R 757, the plaintiff complained of the price of an article in a shop. An argument began in which a shop assistant struck the plaintiff and a struggle resulted. The proprietor of the shop sent for the police and had the plaintiff forcibly restrained until they arrived. No charges were made and the plaintiff sued the proprietor. It was held that the proprietor had a power of arrest in order to prevent a breach of the peace. This could last until things cooled down or until a police officer arrived. It did not matter that the plaintiff did not start the fight; all fighting persons could be arrested. Note that if a breach of the peace has occurred and is not likely to reoccur, then there is no power of arrest under this power (see *King* v *Poe* (1866) 15 LT 37) (and see, in relation to apprehended breaches of the peace, the section on obstruction of the police officer in chapter 11).

Residual statutory powers of arrest
As is stated above, most of the 126 separate statutory police powers of arrest without warrant which existed before the Act (see the report of the Royal Commission on Criminal Procedure) are repealed by s. 26. However, Schedule 2 preserves a number of such powers relating mainly to immigration offences, terrorist offences and the arrest of persons unlawfully at large. There are 21 statutory powers preserved by virtue of s. 26 and contained within Schedule 2. Certainly when there were 126 statutory powers it was unrealistic to remember them all for examination purposes, and this must still be the case (unless you receive contrary advice) even though they are reduced to 21. However, it might be useful if you pick out a couple of examples for illustrative purposes.

One difficult point is the relationship between the Schedule 2 statutory powers, and those elsewhere in the Act. To begin with, it seems clear that the remaining statutory powers are meant to be free from the conditions contained within s. 25 (below). This is important because there is an overlap between the s. 25 powers and those contained in the provisions referred to in Schedule 2. Thus driving when under the influence of drink or drugs (Road Traffic Act 1988, s. 4(6)) is the subject of a preserved power of arrest even though arrest may be possible in practice under s. 25 (in view of the likelihood of injury or property damage). Offences under the provisions mentioned in Schedule 2 may or may not be arrestable offences under s. 24, depending upon the available sentences, but, of course, it may be important to work out whether they are or not for reasons of the citizen's arrest or to decide whether the offence is a serious arrestable offence (s. 116).

Arrestable offences

These are now listed in s. 24(1) to (3) of the 1984 Act. If anything, the importance of recognising an arrestable offence has increased following the passage of the Act because the exercise of many other powers depends upon the offence being an arrestable offence. A serious arrestable offence (see below) must be an arrestable offence under s. 24. It may be of immense value to have statutory material available in the examination in order to check the offences listed in s. 24. Briefly they are:

(a)   Murder and treason (for which the sentence is fixed by law).

(b)   Any offence which may carry a sentence of a term of imprisonment for five years or more.

(c)   Customs and excise offences for which a customs officer could arrest.

(d)   Offences under the Official Secrets Acts which would otherwise not be arrestable offences.

(e)   Certain offences under the Sexual Offences Act 1956 — indecent assault on a woman; procuration of a girl under 21; and causing prostitution of women.

(f)   Certain offences under the Theft Act 1968 — taking a conveyance etc. (s. 12(1) of the 1968 Act); going equipped for burglary, theft or cheat.

(g)   Corruption in public office.

(h)   An attempt or a conspiracy to commit any of the above offences.

(i)   Inciting, aiding, abetting, counselling or procuring any of the above offences.

Under s. 24, the powers of arrest available both to police constables and private citizens are the same as those exercised previously under s. 2 of the Criminal Law Act 1967 (which is now repealed, but which you will see if referred to in the older textbooks). Broadly the powers in relation to arrestable offences are as follows:

(a)   Any person may arrest if he reasonably suspects another person to have committed an offence provided an offence has in fact been committed.

(b)   Any person may arrest a person whom he reasonably suspects is in the process of committing an offence.

(c)   A constable (but not a private citizen) may arrest a person whom he reasonably suspects is about to commit an offence.

(d)   A constable (but not a private citizen) may arrest a person whom he reasonably suspects has committed an offence even though that offence has not in fact been committed (providing that he reasonably suspects that an offence has been committed).

Powers under section 25
The general power of arrest created here is available to a police constable (alone) in the following situation:

(a)   The constable has reasonable grounds for suspecting that an offence has been, or is being, committed or attempted and has reasonable grounds to suspect a person of having committed/attempted, or being in the course of committing/attempting to commit, that offence, and
(b)   The constable forms the view that service of a summons is impracticable/inappropriate because
(c)   There is a reason which amounts to a 'general arrest condition' under s. 25.

The general arrest conditions fall into two basic categories. The first is where the police constable has difficulty in establishing the name or address of a suspected person. The second is in order to prevent certain undesirable consequences.
As regards the first of these, if the conditions satisfied in (a) and (b) above are met, then a constable may arrest if a suspect refuses to volunteer a name, but only if this cannot be readily ascertained by the constable. In addition, even if a name is given, an arrest may follow if the constable has reasonable grounds for doubting that the name given is that of the suspect. An assertion to the effect that suspects usually give false names would not suffice (*G* v *DPP* [1989] Crim LR 150). There is also a power to arrest (other conditions being satisfied) if the suspect fails to provide a satisfactory address for service of a summons or if the constable has reasonable grounds for believing that the address provided is satisfactory. Note that the address need not be the home address of the suspect, therefore — simply one at which the suspect will be residing for a sufficiently long period or one at which some other person (e.g., a solicitor) will accept service.
One problem that arises in relation to the whole of this area is that of detention. Although s. 25 is riddled with powers for the police constable who reasonably suspects a false name or address, there is no power to detain the suspect (short of arrest) whilst the veracity of a name or address is checked. Prior to 1984, *Rice* v *Connolly* [1966] 2 QB 414 represented the law in this area and denied the power of constables to require suspects to give their names and addresses. This is effectively swept aside, but the wider rule that there is no general power to detain for questioning remains (see *R* v *Lemsatef* [1977] 1 WLR 812).

An example of this principle is provided by the case of *Kenlin* v *Gardner* [1967] 2 QB 510 in which two police officers in plain clothes saw two boys calling at various houses. In fact they were trying to get together a rugby team, but the police officers became suspicious and approached them in an attempt to question them. Although one officer did show a warrant card, the boys (aged 14) either did not realise or did not believe that the adults were police officers. They tried to run away and a struggle ensued. The boys were charged with assaulting the police officers in the execution of their duty (contrary to the Police Act 1964, s. 51(1)). However, the court held that since the officers had no power of detention except by arrest, an attempt to detain the boys was itself an assault taking the officers outside the execution of their duty. One must imply now a limited right to detain for questioning (in order to render s. 25 workable) upon reasonable suspicion that the person has committed (in line with (a) above) a non-arrestable offence.

To some extent, this is in line with *Donnelly* v *Jackman* [1970] 1 All ER 987: 'It is not every trivial interference with a citizen's liberty that amounts to conduct sufficient to take an officer outside the course of his duties', and t is submitted that the facts of *Donnelly* would not cause the courts difficulty in view of the powers necessary under s. 25. This is not to say that the section will never cause difficulties. One open point is whether the constable could check the veracity of an address given. No such power is contained within the Act. Even if it is implied, how long should such a check take? And could a person be physically restrained during such a check. Such case law as there is suggests that police powers are not extensive in such events (see *Collins* v *Wilcock* [1984] 1 WLR 1172 and *Bentley* v *Brudzinski* [1982] Crim LR 825).

This covers the first broad category of general arrest conditions under s. 25. The second category covers what might be termed the preventative powers of arrest. As the name implies, there are certain evils which the constable must seek to prevent by arresting the suspect. These are as follows:

(a)   The causing of physical injury either to the suspect or to another person (which presumably includes the arresting officer).

(b)   The suffering of physical injury by the suspect (e.g., because he or she may be attacked as a consequence of the offence committed).

(c)   The causing of loss or damage to property.

(d)   The commission of an offence against public decency (although this is not defined it would clearly include, e.g., indecent exposure, importuning, or a variety of other sexual activity providing it took place in public).

(e)   The causing of an obstruction of the highway (see Highways Act 1980, s. 137, considered in the previous chapter — there is now no provision for arrest under s. 137(2) by virtue of s. 26 of the Act, but this power clearly extends to situations similar to that in *Arrowsmith* v *Jenkins* [1963] 2 QB 561).

(f)   Harm to a child or other vulnerable person (it is not clear who 'vulnerable' persons are, or why they are in need of protection, but the harm might be other than physical injury, since certain statutory powers of arrest in relation to sexual exploitation were repealed by s. 26(1)).

Arrest for fingerprinting
Section 61 of the Act lays down provisions relating to the fingerprinting of a person before or after being charged, or following conviction for a recordable offence (one recorded on national police records) if prints have not been previously taken. Section 27 seeks to enforce the post-conviction fingerprinting process by providing a power of arrest if a person does not attend a police station within seven days of being lawfully required to attend. There are a number of restrictions upon the use of this power, but these will not be considered here.

Manner of Arrest

This is another area in which the Act has adapted the existing common law rules, particularly those laid down by the House of Lords in *Christie* v *Leachinsky* [1947] AC 473. Broadly there are three conditions, breach of which might render an arrest unlawful, even though there is ample power to arrest either by warrant or without a warrant on the grounds considered above. These are:

(a)   The person arrested must be informed by the arrester of the fact of the arrest.
(b)   The person arrested must be informed by the arrester of the grounds for the arrest.
(c)   No more force than is reasonable in the circumstances must be used in effecting the arrest.

These are the broad rules, but they need to be considered in greater detail.

The fact of the arrest
An arrested person must be put in no doubt that an arrest has taken place, either at the time of the arrest or as soon as is practicable thereafter. A distinction is made between arrest by a constable and that by a private citizen, for a private citizen may be relieved from the duty to inform of the fact of the arrest if this is obvious in the circumstances. The requirement that the police constable inform the arrestee even here is a departure from the guidelines in *Christie*, and the only dispensation from this duty for the police officer is if the arrestee escapes before the information can be given. Problems may still arise similar to that in *Alderson* v *Booth* [1969] 2 QB 216 in which the words 'I shall

have to ask you to come with me to the police station' were held not to constitute an arrest.

In *R* v *Inwood* [1973] 1 WLR 647 it was said that on an arrest, it must be clear to the arrestee that there is a detention and that he or she is no longer free. In *Inwood* the suspect originally went to the police station as a volunteer, so that it seems likely that he did not assault the police officers whilst attempting to leave the police station where they had attempted to detain him. Section 29 of the Act now makes it clear that if a person attends a police station (or any other place) as a volunteer (i.e., without being arrested) then that person may depart at any time. If the constable wishes to prevent this, then this may only be achieved by an arrest.

The grounds of the arrest

The duties here are similar to those relating to the fact of the arrest with the same distinction being made between constables and private citizens (see s. 28(3) and (4)). Failure to state the grounds of arrest tenders the arrest unlawful and may leave the arrester liable to civil proceedings, but it will not generally invalidate subsequent charges (see *R* v *Kulynycz* [1971] 1 QB 367). In *Lewis* v *Chief Constable of South Wales* [1991] 1 All ER 206 two sisters were arrested on suspicion of burglary but given no reason for their arrest, until 10 and 23 minutes respectively after their arrests. They were held for five hours and then released. They successfully sued for wrongful arrest, but their damages were limited. In the court's view their wrongful arrest became lawful 10 and 23 minutes following their initial detention. In *Christie* v *Leachinsky* [1947] AC 573 it was said that technical language need not be used providing that the basic nature of the wrongdoing is brought home to the person arrested (see also *Gelberg* v *Miller* [1961] 1 WLR 153 and *Abbassy* v *Commissioner of Police of the Metropolis* [1990] 1 WLR 385).

An arrest may become unlawful as in *DPP* v *Hawkins* [1988] 1 WLR 1166. If reasons cannot be given until violent conduct by the defendant is ended, it is a breach if they are not given at that stage.

Use of force

Section 117 of the Act provides that where a power is conferred on a constable by the Act, and that power may be exercised even without the consent of another person, then the constable may use reasonable force in the exercise of the power. The use of excessive force would take police constables outside the execution of their duty (see the cases referred to above — *Donnelly* v *Jackman* [1970] 1 WLR 562; *Collins* v *Wilcock* [1984] 1 WLR 1172).

STOP AND SEARCH

Section 1 of the Act gives the power to stop, detain and search a person (or vehicle) without arrest. A code of practice on stop and search exists alongside the Act. The search must intend to uncover stolen or prohibited articles, and the power must be exercised in a place where the public has access.

Place of Public Access

As regards the latter condition, the Act isolates three types of places where the stop and search power may be exercised:

(a)   A place to which the public has access, at the time of the detention, as a matter of legal right or by permission.
(b)   Any other place which is not a dwelling but to which people have ready access at the time of the detention and search.
(c)   A garden, yard or land occupied with and used for the purposes of a dwelling providing that the constable reasonably believes that the person who is to be searched is not there with the express or implied permission of the resident of the dwelling.

Thus outside of the latter provision there is no power to search a person within a dwelling under this provision. However, a variety of buildings could be covered by (a) including pubs, cinemas, public libraries etc., and some could be included under (b) which might include, for example, a derelict building which has not been fenced off.

Stolen or Prohibited Articles

The constable must have reasonable grounds for suspecting that stolen or prohibited articles will be found as a result of the exercise of the stop and search power. Paragraphs 1.5 to 1.7 of the Code of Practice on Stop and Search offer guidelines as to what might amount to reasonable grounds for suspicion. There must be more than a mere suspicion or hunch by the police officer. The suspicion must be reasonable and have a concrete basis. This may lie in articles which a person appears to be carrying, or because there is some degree of prior knowledge (e.g., a description of a suspect). However, the fact that a person is known to have a previous conviction for an offence is not in itself sufficient, and the code of practice is careful to stress that dress, hairstyle and in particular colour of skin cannot of themselves provide a basis for reasonable suspicion. Finally the degree of suspicion necessary for the exercise of a stop and search power is no less than that required for an arrest without warrant.

The categories of articles which the constable must reasonably suspect will be found by a search fall into three broad categories:

(a)   Stolen goods;

(b)   Offensive weapons; there is some discussion of this phrase in the previous chapter and the definition in s. 1(9) of the Act is very similar to that contained in s. 1(4) of the Prevention of Crime Act 1953. Thus it can include weapons which are offensive *per se* (made or adapted for use for causing injury) and an article not necessarily or ordinarily offensive but intended by the person having it with him for use for causing injury to persons.

(c)   Articles for use in offences of dishonesty; an article amounts to a prohibited article if it is made or adapted for use in the course of, or in connection with theft, burglary, taking a conveyance, or obtaining property by deception (see the Theft Act 1968, ss. 1, 9, 12 and 15). An article is similarly prohibited (even if it is not specially made or adapted) if it is intended by the person having it with him for a use as outlined above either by him or by another person.

Note that the above powers do not include a power to stop and search for drugs or firearms. However, this is not necessary, since several stop and search powers which pre-date 1984 remain unaffected by the Act — including s. 47 of the Firearms Act 1968, and s. 23 of the Misuse of Drugs Act 1971. A most useful list of the available stop and search powers is contained in an annex to the code. You are advised to read (though not to learn) this.

The Manner of Search

The search powers under this provision apply not only to any person but also to any vehicle, providing the conditions referred to above are satisfied. The only qualification to this concerns a vehicle parked in a garden or yard or on land occupied with, and used for, the purposes of a dwelling. In such a case, the constable may only search the vehicle under this stop and search power if he has reasonable grounds for believing that the person in charge of the vehicle does not reside at the dwelling, and that the resident has not given express or implied permission allowing the vehicle to be put or kept there. The vehicle may be unattended, of course, in which case a notice should be left in the vehicle giving details of the search. Then the vehicle must be left secure if possible (see the code of practice) and, if necessary, compensation for damage may be payable. Finally, if a vehicle is searched, anything in or on the vehicle may be searched also.

As regards searches of the person carried out in public, the constable may only require a person to remove an outer coat, jacket or gloves. If a person refuses to cooperate when asked, reasonable force may be used (in accordance with s. 117 — considered above). There is no power to remove a hat or footwear in public. However s. 2(8) and the code of practice suggest that a more detailed search may be carried out at a nearby place out of public view.

Thus in the back of a police car, for example, a more thorough search could be carried out, but if items of clothing other than all of those listed above are to be removed, then this must be in the presence of an officer of the same sex if it is to accord with the code of practice. The thoroughness of the search will depend upon the article being sought. A crowbar ought to be fairly readily apparent, whereas a flick-knife might be more carefully concealed. The provision of the code to this effect is quite significant, because the Act speaks of removing clothing and does not prevent frisking or feeling inside clothing — embarrassing though this may be.

Articles found as a result of the exercise of the above powers may be seized.

Other Stop and Search Powers

Section 4 of the Act provides a power to set up road checks. There is a new power in s. 60 of the Criminal Justice and Public Order Act 1994 which enables uniformed police officers to stop and search pedestrians or vehicles for offensive weapons or dangerous instruments. Note that there is no requirement for an officer exercising the power to have grounds for suspicion of the individual (s. 1(3) of the 1984 Act). Authorisation is required from a senior officer who must reasonably believe that incidents involving serious violence may take place in a locality in the area. The authorisation may not exceed 24 hours (with provision for six hours' extension). This provision is clearly directed at concerns of anticipated violent conduct. Similar powers are contained in s. 81 with regard to the prevention of terrorism.

ENTRY AND SEARCH

Powers of entry to premises available to the police are numerous and rather complex, but broadly they fall into the following two lists:

(a) Entry by warrant:

(i) Entry by warrant issued under s. 8 of the Act in order to investigate a serious arrestable offence.
(ii) Entry by warrant following non-compliance with a production order (see Schedule 1 and s. 9).
(iii) Entry by warrant under other legislation.

(b) Entry without a warrant:

(i) Entry without a warrant under a statutory power.
(ii) Entry without a search warrant in order to arrest.
(iii) Entry without a search warrant following an arrest.

(iv)   Entry at common law (e.g., to prevent a breach of the peace).
(v)   Entry with the consent of the occupier.

Entry by Warrant

The Act introduces a new power of entry and search under s. 8 and then introduces limitations and safeguards which are to apply to the s. 8 power as well as to those statutory powers which pre-date (and are preserved by) the Act. Under the s. 8 power a justice of the peace may issue a search warrant on an application to a constable providing certain conditions are met. There must be reasonable suspicion that a serious arrestable offence (see below) has been committed and that there is material on the premises likely to be of substantial value to the investigation, which is likely to prove admissible at a subsequent trial. Moreover, for one of the reasons laid down in s. 8(3) it must be appropriate to proceed by way of warrant rather than with the consent of the owner. However, no search warrant can simply authorise a search for the following categories of material:

(a)   Legally privileged material: communications for the purpose of legal proceedings and other lawyer-client correspondence.

(b)   Excluded material:

(i)   Personal records of a trade, business, profession or other occupation, or for the purposes of any office, which are held in confidence (see further s. 12).
(ii)   Human tissue or tissue fluid taken for diagnosis or treatment and held in confidence.
(iii)   Journalistic material in the form of documents or records which are held in confidence (as to the meaning of held in confidence see s. 11(2) and (3)).

(c)   Special procedure material:

(i)   Journalistic material not already included within excluded material.
(ii)   Material not included in the above categories which is acquired or created in the process of any trade, business, profession, occupation or office and held in confidence.

This review of the workings of what is Part II of the Act raises two important questions. The first relates to the meaning of 'serious arrestable offence'. Any arrestable offence falls within this category if it has led or is likely or intended to lead to one of the following consequences:

(a) The death of any person.

(b) Serious injury to any person.

(c) Substantial financial gain or serious financial loss.

(d) Serious harm to state security or public order.

(e) Serious interference with the investigation of an offence, or with the administration of justice.

In addition to this, there are a number of arrestable offences which are always to be regarded as serious arrestable offences. These are listed in Schedule 5, which you should read. It is probably unnecessary to learn the full lists, but you might study the type of offences which are regarded as serious, and learn a few examples. The purpose of the lists is to cure historical anomalies which grew up prior to the Act — e.g., there was no power to enter (and search) premises whilst investigating murder or kidnap.

The second question is: what do the categories of privileged, excluded or special procedure material indicate? As the name suggests, legally privileged material cannot be searched for or (if found incidentally) seized. Excluded and special procedure materials will generally only be made available upon an order to produce the material issued by a circuit judge. Because an application for such an order will be served on the person in possession, the application for a production order will be *inter partes*, though until the application is dismissed the party may not dispose of the material. Failure to comply with a production order may amount to a contempt of court. However, a search warrant may be issued by a circuit judge on application where a person has failed to comply with a production order or where compliance would be impracticable. There are procedural safeguards relating to both the application for, and execution of, search warrants under ss. 15 and 16 of the Act and the Code of Practice on Search and Seizure.

Entry without a Warrant

Just as statutory authorisations for warrants which existed prior to the Act are preserved, so too are the statutory powers of entry without warrant, the most famous of which is perhaps the Misuse of Drugs Act 1971, s. 23(1). Again although it would be unrealistic to seek to learn the whole of these, you might choose specific examples, such as the one above, which could occur in problem questions. As we shall see other common law powers of entry without warrant are abolished with the exception of a power of entry where there is an actual or appehended breach of the peace (see s. 17(5) and (6) of the Act and *Thomas* v *Sawkins* [1935] 2 KB 249 discussed in the previous chapter).

However, certain powers which may have existed prior to 1984 are reformulated. Section 17 of the Act allows the constable a power to enter and search any premises in order to arrest either under warrant or for an arrestable offence. This power is extended to deal with public order offences under the Public Order Acts and where appropriate under the Criminal Justice and Public Order Act 1994 (e.g., raves under s. 64) and offences of entering and remaining on property contrary to the Criminal Law Act 1977 (a power of entry was previously contained in s. 11 of that Act). Finally there are powers of entry in pursuit of a person unlawfully at large, and to save life or prevent serious damage to property. Section 17 rationalises the law, but the powers largely existed prior to 1984 (see, e.g., s. 2(6) of the Criminal Law Act 1967 and *Swales* v *Cox* [1981] QB 849).

In *Jeffrey* v *Black* [1978] QB 490, Black was arrested for the theft of a sandwich from a public house. Prior to being charged Black was escorted to his home which he opened up, and the arresting officers entered and searched the premises where they found cannabis. The justices found, at a later hearing, that Black had not given his consent to the search and they ruled that the evidence was inadmissible. The prosecutor appealed, and the Divisional Court allowed the appeal sending the case back for a rehearing. The Divisional Court agreed that there was no authority to search especially if what was sought bore no relation to the offence charged. In other words it seems clear that on searching the flat the police did not expect to uncover a serious case of wide-scale sandwich theft. Nonetheless, the fact that the evidence was the product of an illegal search was not in itself sufficient ground for the trial judge to exercise a discretion to exclude evidence — such discretion should be exercised in exceptional cases. The conduct of the police in the case was later described as 'the high-water mark of this kind of illegality' (per Lord Diplock in *R* v *Sang* [1980] AC 402 at 435) and in *McLorie* v *Oxford* [1982] QB 1290, it was held that police officers seeking to enter premises without warrant subsequent to an arrest were acting outside the execution of their duty.

This whole area was recast by s. 18 of the Act. A constable may enter and search premises occupied or controlled by a person who is under arrest for an arrestable offence, if he has reasonable grounds for suspecting that the premises contain evidence (not subject to legal privilege) relating to that offence, or some other similar or connected arrestable offence. This may be done by taking the arrested person to the premises immediately following arrest if that person's presence is necessary for an effective investigation. Alternatively, the search may be carried out on the written authorisation of a police inspector (see s. 18(4) to (8)). Thus the conduct of the police in *Jeffrey* v *Black* would presumably remain unlawful, since sandwich theft and unlawful possession of cannabis cannot be said to be similar or connected arrestable offences. Of course, if in a situation like this of *Jeffrey* v *Black*, the person consented to the search of that flat, no question of illegality arises.

SEIZURE

Where there is a search power exercised in line with the powers considered above, there will generally be a power of seizure. Thus there are powers of seizure under the Act which may be exercised subsequent to the following search powers:

(a) Stop and search under s. 1 (see s. 1(6)) and s. 60 of the Criminal Justice and Public Order Act 1994 (see s. 60(6)).

(b) Search warrant under s. 8 (and see also Schedule 1).

(c) Search conducted under s. 18 (see s. 18(2)).

(d) Search upon arrest (see s. 32 and s. 54).

(e) Search or intimate search of a detained person (ss. 54 and 55).

In addition to these five powers, there are a number of statutory powers of seizure attached to powers of search. It would be unrealistic to try to remember all of these, but you could select pertinent examples, e.g., under s. 9(1) of the Official Secrets Act 1911 (as amended by s. 11(3) of the Official Secrets Act 1989).

However, in addition to the above powers, s. 9 of the Act introduces a wide-ranging power of seizure. This applies to a constable who is lawfully on any premises (whether or not he has power to search). He may seize anything which is on the premises if he has reasonable grounds to believe that it has been obtained in consequence of the commission of an offence, or it is evidence in relation to an offence (whether or not it is the one under investigation) and that it is necessary to seize it in order to prevent its loss, damage, destruction, concealment or alteration. The purpose of this section (like that of s. 18) is to clarify the previous common law powers (see *Chic Fashions (West Wales) Ltd* v *Jones* [1968] 2 QB 299 and, especially, *Ghani* v *Jones* [1970] 1 QB 693). Also like s. 18 the police have been given extensive powers in the process of this clarification.

Admissibility of Evidence

In *Jeffrey* v *Black* [1978] QB 490 it was said that 'it is open to the justices to apply their discretion and decline to allow the particular evidence to be let in' although it was stressed that this discretion should be exercised rarely, and Lord Widgery CJ spoke of trickery or oppressive or morally reprehensible conduct. However in *R* v *Sang* [1980] AC 402 in which the police allegedly incited the accused by acting as *agent provocateur*, the House of Lords said that the test was not whether the evidence was obtained by improper or unfair means but whether, in the opinion of the trial judge, the evidence should be excluded since its prejudicial effect outweighed its probative value. This test in *Sang* seemed to overrule the view in *Jeffrey* v *Black*, though even this was uncertain. However, s. 78 introduced a discretion to refuse to allow evidence (including confessions: see *R* v *Mason* [1988] 1 WLR 139) if it appears to the court that, in view of all of the circumstances, including the circumstances in which the evidence was obtained, the admission of the evidence would have such an adverse effect on the conduct of the trial that the court ought not to admit it.

Thus the harsh distinction in *Sang* between the means by which the evidence was obtained (which was irrelevant to the exercise of a discretion) and the use to which the evidence is put at the trial (which was relevant in terms of the prejudicial effect and probative value) is modified. Section 78 demands a review of the whole circumstances including those in which the evidence was obtained, although the effect on the conduct of the trial is still of primary importance. This might help clarify some of the conflicting dicta in *Sang* but for the problem posed by s. 82(3) which states that 'Nothing in this Part of this Act shall prejudice any power of a court to exclude evidence ... at its discretion'. The problem here is simply this. Since s. 78 offers a different basis for the exercise of a discretion to exclude evidence than *Sang*, is the effect of s. 82(3) to preserve the rule in *Sang* which, since it allowed a power to exclude evidence pre-dating 1984, seems to fall within the wording of the latter provision? If this is the case, then it is to be hoped that the *Sang* test will apply only in so far as it is more favourable to the accused — if it ever is.

This question is likely to be in issue in the context of police undercover operations. Whilst there is no defence of entrapment *per se*, where an allegation involving an *agent provocateur* is made, the discretion under s. 78 should apply: see *R* v *Smurthwaite* [1994] 1 All ER 898. Thus the fairness of the proceedings must be considered, including fairness to the public; and the activities entered into, including the nature of the entrapment, the officer's role and the evidence; and how far there was an unassailable record or other strong corroboration. Note that the codes may not apply, where discussion with undercover officers takes place (*R* v *Christou* [1992] QB 979). However, such operations should not be used in order to circumvent the requirements of the code (*R* v *Bryce* [1992] 4 All ER 567): see further *R* v *MacLean and Kosten* [1993] Crim LR 687. Perhaps if there ever were an area of the exercise of judicial discretion dependent upon a case's own facts, then this would be it.

Evidence may, for example, be admissible even if unlawfully obtained by trespass to land: see *R* v *Khan* [1994] 3 WLR 899, concerning trespass and tape-recording, where the interests to the public were held to outweigh any breaches (D's offence concerned the importation of heroin). See also *R* v *Bailey* [1993] 3 All ER 513, a case concerned with obtaining evidence by subterfuge, including the bugging of the appellant's remand cell. It was held by the Court of Appeal that allowing the taped evidence was a correct exercise of the discretion. Of the numerous issues discussed, it was interesting that the evidence here was held not to undermine the right to silence, for an involuntary conversation could not be equated with involuntary statements to the police.

Although the questions above are difficult, it is important to remember that your course is not a course on the law of evidence, but one concerned with individual liberties. It is therefore important to know, e.g., whether the fruits of an illegal search are admissible in evidence, since such questions touch on police powers and corresponding liberties. On the other hand, a detailed knowledge of the law of evidence is unlikely to be required.

DETENTION AND QUESTIONING

Once arrested the suspect should be taken by the constable to the police station as soon as is reasonably practicable (s. 30(1) and as to citizens' arrests see *John Lewis Ltd* v *Tims* [1952] AC 676) but the common law rule of *Dallison* v *Caffery* [1965] 1 QB 348 is preserved so as to allow a delay in order to investigate further along with the arrested person (e.g., check out an alibi). There may also be some delay if the person is searched prior to being taken to the police station. Such a search is permitted if a constable believes upon reasonable grounds that a person may present a danger to any person (including himself) or that the person has concealed evidence of an offence or an instrument which might be used to escape from custody. If the person is arrested at the police station, or elsewhere but is taken to the police station, then the police are required to ascertain the property that the person is carrying, and are able to search the arrestee in order to do this (see s. 54). However, intimate searches (examination of body orifices: see *R* v *Hughes* [1994] 1 WLR 876) are governed by separate rules (see ss. 55 and 62 as amended by the Criminal Justice and Public Order Act 1994, ss. 54 to 58 and sch. 10, paras 56 to 58). Note here that s. 59 of the 1994 Act amends s. 32, allowing a search of a person's mouth on arrest.

Detention at the police station is regulated by Part IV of the Act, and revolves to some extent around the custody officer. This officer (of at least the rank of sergeant) will be present at certain designated police stations which are able to accommodate detainees. On arrival at the police station, the person must be presented to the custody officer who will decide whether there is sufficient evidence to charge with the offence for which that person was arrested. If there is, detention for a period in which the person can be charged is permitted. If not, the person will generally be released either on or without bail. However, even if there is insufficient evidence to charge, the custody officer may believe, on reasonable grounds, that it is necessary to detain before charge in order to preserve evidence relating to an offence for which the suspect is under arrest, or to obtain such evidence. In such a case there is no requirement to order release, but the suspect must be told the grounds of detention.

Thus the Act introduced a novel concept into English law — the right to detain for questioning. This type of detention will normally carry a 24-hour limit, and even then it will be subject to regular review by the custody officer. However, a series of extensions are possible in the case of a serious arrestable offence (see above). These are:

(a)   An extension of detention beyond the 24 hours to 36 hours if authorised by a superintendent who has reasonable grounds for believing that such a detention is necessary in order to secure or preserve evidence or obtain evidence by questioning, and that the investigation is being conducted diligently and expeditiously.

(b)   An extension beyond 36 hours for a further period of 36 hours subject to a maximum of 96 hours' detention without charge. This is granted by a magistrate upon hearing evidence upon oath in the presence of the detainee. The information on oath will need to state the nature of the offence, the general nature of the relevant evidence, the present and future line of inquiry and the reasons for the necessity of further inquiries.

Once a detained person is charged, if not released, he or she must be brought before the court as soon as is practicable (see s. 46).

The so-called right to silence (not considered here in any detail) arises out of the duty on the prosecutor to prove the case beyond reasonable doubt. It is not for the accused to disprove that case. Amendments made by the Criminal Justice and Public Order Act 1994 allow inferences to be drawn by the court in specified circumstances from an accused's failure to give information. At the time of writing it is unclear how this will operate or even how the revised police caution will read. Many institutions will leave this material until a final-year evidence course, but if this is covered within your constitutional course then it is an area which you should consider and review carefully.

Rights during Detention

The custody officer must inform the detainee of certain rights. These include the reason for the detention, the right to consult the codes of practice, the right to have someone informed of the detention and the right to consult a solicitor upon request (s. 56).

When the codes were revised, some important changes were made to the rights of access to a solicitor. This right of access has always been the subject of an exemption covered by the Act which is amplified in paragraph 1 of Annex B of the code. Broadly this allows that where there is a detention in connection with a serious arrestable offence (see above) access to legal advice can be restricted where it is feared that it might lead to interference with evidence, harm or injury to persons, alerting confederates, or the recovery of property. Note that there must be some supposition that a particular solicitor will prejudice the interest of justice. In such a case, it may be that the services of another solicitor can and should be offered. Delay can only be for as long as is necessary and for no later than 36 hours after the relevant time (see s. 41).

Note that under the revised codes, it has to be made clear that legal advice is available *freely* to the detainee. Moreover, it is a new demand of the code that the detainee be told that there is a continuing right, lasting throughout custody to legal advice. If the suspect decides that legal access is not required, then there should be a signature on a waiver form on the custody record. Equally reminders of the availability of legal advice should be recorded. In particular, before any interview starts a reminder should be given.

Once access is required, consultation, if not in person then by phone, should take place as soon as is reasonably practical. It seems, however, that it is not necessary to delay the taking of breath, blood or urine samples in drink/driving cases: see *DPP* v *Billington* [1988] 1 WLR 535. Otherwise questioning will be delayed until consultation with a legal adviser takes place. In general, the police are prohibited from questioning a person who has asked for, but not yet received, legal advice. However, where there is a likely delay involving risk of harm to persons or property, or an unreasonable delay in the arrival of a solicitor, or where the solicitor cannot be contacted, and the suspect then declines the duty solicitor, questioning can begin. However, the police need to be careful, because continuing questioning in the absence of a solicitor may end in the confession being excluded: see *R* v *Samuel* [1988] QB 615.

There is no requirement, even in the new codes, for notification of the rights to legal advice prior to arrival at the police station. This is generally thought to be a gap, and it has been argued that the police are more often commencing questioning prior to arrival at the police station, perhaps in the hope of avoiding the recording procedures which will now need to be followed (see Hall, 135 SJ 601). It is often useful to read about police practice in these areas, and in relation to advice and assistance at the police station, there is an important report by Sanders (and others) summarised in [1990] Crim LR 494.

A tape recording requirement has applied since 1991 throughout England and Wales, and a code applies to the process. This innovation should result in a marked decrease in allegations of false confessions being made, and this in turn should affect the incidence of circumstances in which the court may be called on to consider the efficacy of confession evidence, under s. 76 (and s. 78) or the Act (see below). The person interviewed shall be given the opportunity to read this record, sign it as correct or indicate any apparent inaccuracies.

Note that there is a right to have someone informed of the arrest; whether or not this is a legal adviser, this person should be told of the place of detention. The code suggests that the arrestee may contact a friend, relative, or person likely to take an interest in the arrestee's welfare. Choices must be allowed. In the case of children and young persons, the police take all practical steps to identify who is responsible for the arrestee's welfare and inform them of the reasons for the arrest. A new note in the code of practice advises that a solicitor who is present in the police station in a professional capacity is not the 'appropriate adult' to accompany a young or mentally handicapped person whilst at the police station.

Finally note that as soon as the police officer making the enquiries of any person believes that a prosecution should be brought, and that there is sufficient evidence for it to succeed, the person should be asked if they have anything further to say. Unless the person has more to say, the officer should cease questioning in order to bring a charge.

Exclusion of Confessions

The above rules are intended to ensure the voluntary nature of statements made at the police station. Particular problems arise in relation to confessions made at the police station which the prosecution later wishes to rely on, but which the defence wishes to see excluded. Broadly there are now two grounds for exclusion, modifying the earlier common law test as laid down by the House of Lords in *DPP* v *Ping Lin* [1976] AC 574. The two grounds are oppression and unreliability. Oppression includes torture, inhuman or degrading treatment, or the use of violence (s. 76(8)) but could include anything 'which tends to sap ... free will' (see *R* v *Priestly* (1965) 51 Cr App R 1 per Sachs J). Note also the similarity of the wording to that in article 3 of the European Convention on Human Rights which may mean that case law from the ECHR may be relevant here.

Even if it is decided that conduct is not oppressive, the confession may be ruled unreliable nonetheless. Thus even if the conduct of the police in not allowing access to a solicitor is not thought to be oppressive (which it was in *R* v *Gowan* [1982] Crim LR 821) the court may use its wider discretion to decide that there was something said or done which in the circumstances was likely to render the confession unreliable (see s. 76(2)(b)). In *R* v *Mason* [1988] 1 WLR 139 the Court of Appeal went rather wider than this and held that a judge could refuse to allow evidence (in this case a confession) obtained by deceit, notwithstanding the conduct was not 'oppressive' nor the confession likely to be unreliable. In our example this might be the refusal to allow access to legal advice when it ought to be available, as happened in *R* v *Samuel* [1988] QB 615, or, even more obviously, a statement that legal advice would be available following a confession. The latter illustration would have been said under the common law prior to 1984 to have been obtained by fear of prejudice or in hope of advantage (see *DPP* v *Ping Lin* [1976] AC 574).

Now the test is clearly wider and breaches of the code (for example) may amount to circumstances likely to render a confession unreliable. Once the issue of unreliability is raised by the defence, then the onus is on the prosecution to prove that the confession was not obtained in consequence of things said or done in such circumstances. This is a burden which is increasingly difficult to discharge, for the Court of Appeal has taken a dim view of breaches of the code, even though the formal view is that breaches must be 'significant and substantial' to justify exclusion of interview evidence (see R v Keenan (1990) 90 Cr App R 1). The courts are clearly vigilant to ensure that the codes are used to prevent allegations that the suspect has been 'verballed'. A good example is the recording of an off-the-record remark by the accused, in R v Scott [1991] Crim LR 56, who was not then shown the note or asked to sign it (cf. R v Younis [1990] Crim LR 425). Note that once a breach of the code has occurred, later proper procedures may be insufficient to overcome the prejudice (see R v Ismail [1990] Crim LR 109; R v McGovern (1991) 92 Cr App R 228; R v Canale [1991] 2 All ER 187). Nevertheless there is no universal rule that subsequent proceedings will be tainted — R v Gillard [1991] Crim LR 280.

REVISION

The above discussion is fairly lengthy, but then it needs to be. Problems on police powers can easily include a wide range of events and will generally include the following type of examples. X is stopped on the street, questioned, taken back to the police station, detained, questioned further and she confesses to a particular crime. Or Y is stopped on the street, searched, taken back to her flat which is also searched, and in which evidence of a criminal offence is found. In each example you are expected to discuss the legality of the police's action and the admissibility of the relevant evidence.

The safest way to deal with such problems is to draw up a checklist of the relevant powers. For example, ask yourself 'What are the powers of arrest?' and 'In what ways might the manner of the arrest render it unlawful?' Then if a constable in your problem says to a suspect, 'Come with me to the station', you can address yourself to the two questions of whether there was a power to arrest in the situation and whether the words of the constable amount to a lawful arrest. Thus if your checklist on manner of arrest contains three potential reasons why the arrest might be unlawful (in line with the text above) you can run through these and comment upon whether the words 'Come with me' amount to sufficient information as to (a) the fact of and (b) the reason for the arrest in line with s. 28 of the Act.

Note that the points raised here are not difficult, but the purpose of the checklist is not necessarily to provide you with the answer, but to ensure that your approach is thorough and logical. A good checklist should ensure that all relevant possibilities are considered. Once you have devised a checklist (or two checklists) on arrest, move on to search of the person, search of premises, seizure etc. Ensure that each checklist contains the powers under which, for example, a search would be lawful and the factors which might render that search unlawful.

When it comes to applying such checks to a problem question, ensure that you begin at the beginning. For example if a person is stopped whilst driving along in a car, and then arrested, it would be inappropriate to begin with the arrest. It is the stopping of the car which provides the first point of potential conflict between the citizen and the police, so that if you have covered the authority of the police to stop traffic (under, e.g., s. 4 of the 1984 Act) then this would be the initial point to consider when working through the problem. As we shall later see, you may not wish to deal with the points in chronological order in your answer, but it is vital that your essay plan covers the full range of possibilities.

This makes it obviously important to attempt some problem questions prior to the examination. This may be done in seminars where you can improve your technique by making a conscious effort to study the method which your tutor uses to analyse the problems. Too few students do this, since they spend much of the time concentrating upon the substance of the problem. Concentration upon the technique of answering questions is no less important. In addition to seminars, you can practise problem questions as part of your revision work on them in the library at first, with all the sources available to you. Then gradually restrict the time you allow yourself, but continue to use the books. As you begin to know the area better aim to complete the question in the time which will be allowed in the examination and without your books or notes. As was said earlier in this book, do not become too alarmed if there are certain problems from earlier exmainations which you cannot answer, since the emphasis may have changed over the years. This may be true in relation to the area of police powers which has altered dramatically following the 1984 Act.

Finally, some comment is necessary upon the Act. Find out if you are allowed a copy of the Act (and the codes) in the examination room — since this might shorten your revision process in line which what is said in previous chapters. Take care that you know whether you are to assume that all of the Act is in force (if appropriate at the time of your examination). Case law is highly significant in determining the meaning of certain provisions in the Act and you must be on the look-out for new cases. There is a danger that, under the rather more codified approach of the 1984 Act, the student will be tempted to say, 'Ah, this is s. 25' and fail to bring in case law which would make the answer more enlightening and more interesting.

THE EXAMINATION

Essay Questions on the Act

On a number of occasions, this book has stressed that you must look for recent developments in law as a likely basis for examination questions. It follows that the introduction of the Criminal Justice and Public Order Act 1994 may be a likely source of questions in examinations. Moreover, the codes of practice form an obvious area of questioning, since they will involve you in considering both statutory material, case law, and the codes themselves. This will seek to ensure that you have a good knowledge of how the codes interrelate with both statute and case law.

Of course, any question on the codes could be set in the form of a problem question. This is because it will generally involve the rights of the individuals in situations such as stop and search, search of premises, or questioning at the police station. Nonetheless, it is possible to set a question on the codes in their own right. This is because they form a basic body of good practice which will be vital to the suspect at the hands of the police. It follows that you may be asked within a particular area of police procedure to consider the rights of persons subject to investigation. It is not at all unusual for the examination question to be presented as one of balance — between the necessity of police powers to investigate serious crime, and the basic freedoms of the citizen which are likely to be curtailed by activities such as search or detention.

Let us take a very straightforward examination question of this type:

Of all the rights given to the suspect in relation to police investigation, access to legal advice may be the most significant. Discuss.

This question is not very tightly set, and on first reading may prove rather disconcerting. It may suggest to you that you should discuss the various rights available to the suspect, and rank the rights of the suspect to legal advice amongst the whole of these. Clearly, this would not be possible in the course of an examination. You could get nowhere near completing your litany of the various rights in the time available. It follows that this is a situation in which you can assume some knowledge on the part of the examiner in relation to the broad body of rights generally available to a suspect, and focus your answer on provisions relating to access to legal advice.

The law in this area was considered earlier in this chapter, and it is not intended to repeat the substance of these rights in advising now on the likely structure of an answer. Nonetheless, important case law has been emanating from the courts recently, and this has covered some significant areas relating to access to legal advice. Therefore, however you choose to answer this question, it is important that you cover recent case law.

One way of answering this question would be to deal chronologically with a typical detention and consider the issues of interrogation from the point at which a person is detained for questioning on the street. Remember that you must deal with lots of the background common law and various relevant sections of the Act as well as with the codes. Indeed, your starting-point might be the famous quotation by Lord Parker in *Rice* v *Connolly* [1966] 2 QB 414:

> The whole basis of the common law is the right of the individual to refuse to answer questions put to him by persons in authority, and to refuse to accompany those in authority to any place, short, of course, of arrest.

Formally, this is still the position, but certain inroads into this principle have been made by the general arrest conditions of s. 25, and stop and search powers in Part I of the Act and the 1994 Act. You could also consider the effect of the provisions of s. 51(1) and (3) of the Police Act 1964.

This is useful material in your answer, since it demonstrates that questions are likely to be put from the earliest stage of detention. Yet, you can point out, that even the revised codes impose no requirement to notify a suspect of his or her rights to legal advice in advance of arrival at the police station. You may wish to deal briefly here with the issues at stake. Clearly, the authorities believe that early access to legal advice, before anything has been said, may discourage suspects from giving an immediate reaction to the police when they are apprehended. Equally, of course, the street-wise villain may know of the right to access to legal advice, and choose to say nothing anyway.

The provisions of the code now state that the suspect should not be interviewed about the relevant offence except at the police station. You must point out the exceptions to this rule (which are considered above). You should make comment on how far these exceptions are likely to derogate from the safeguards of having legal advisers present. Given that there is no necessity to inform on arrest of the rights to see a solicitor, any questioning undertaken at this point will almost certainly be without access to legal advice. You may point out also that where interviewing is carried on before arrival at the police station, under one of the exceptions, it should cease once the risk allowed for by the exceptions has been averted.

All of this leads to an important body of case law which concerns the notion of an 'interview'. In the case of *R* v *Absolam* (1989) 88 Cr App R 332 there was a definition of interview:

> a series of questions directed by the police to a suspect with a view to obtaining admissions on which proceedings could be founded.

Several chapters ago, the point was made that a definition may be useful even if it is only there to knock down. The *Absolam* definition appeared inadequate in light of the views expressed by the Court of Appeal in the case, *R* v *Matthews* (1990) 91 Cr App R 43. The definition in the code of practice now makes it clear that questioning a person to seek an immediate explanation of facts or conduct does not itself constitute an interview under the codes. However, other questioning regarding involvement or suspected involvement in a criminal offence will amount to an interview. This definition would seem to support the decision in *R* v *Maguire* (1989) 90 Cr App R 115.

This definition of 'interview' is important not only in terms of rights of access of a solicitor to attend, but also in terms of other formalities such as recording and verifying the proceedings. Your knowledge of these formalities should be briefly indicated, even though they are not directly in point on the question of access to legal advice. In relation to access to legal advice, there are other obvious areas upon which you should comment. One is the question of delay in access to the legal advice. Here you should cover formal rights to delay access to the legal advice in the event of 'a serious arrestable offence'. You should make reference here to s. 116 of PACE especially in relation to the notion of 'serious' which is governed by the likely or intended consequences of the offence. You should also make reference to the fact that this section has been amended and extended in relation to offences such as the Drug Trafficking Offences Act 1986 and the Criminal Justice Acts 1988 and 1993, which contains powers to seize and confiscate the proceeds of crime.

Another significant area has been the access to the police station of persons who are not solicitors, but unadmitted clerks. The use of such persons has become more and more common, as legal aid solicitors, with criminal practices, have had less and less resources at their disposal. However, such clerks have sometimes found themselves barred from the police station. For example, this happened in *R* v *Chief Constable of Avon and Somerset, ex parte Robinson* [1989] 1WLR 793. That case seems to suggest that a blanket ban on solicitors' clerks would be likely to be overturned by the courts, but that the police were entitled to refuse access to a person who is not a genuine clerk, or whose visit the police believed would hinder the investigation of a crime given that person's past criminal record or associations. The presence of a legal adviser during an interview could be a mixed blessing. In *R* v *Dunn* (1990) 91 Cr App R 237 the presence of a clerk during the interview led the Court of Appeal to admit as evidence a confession notwithstanding apparent breaches of the code.

This serves as a significant reminder that you must deal with the consequences of a breach of the provisions relating to legal advice. This is, of course, that they may lead to evidence, even confession evidence, being excluded. This is so where the practices of the interviewing officer mislead not only the suspects but also their legal advisers (see *R* v *Beales* [1991] Crim LR 118). Breach of the law on exclusion of confessions is dealt with above, but see also *R* v *Moss* (1990) 91 Cr App R 371.

Police Powers: a Problem

Stephen MacQueen is standing in a bus shelter on which is carved in large letters: 'Saward was here'. PC Harris approaches and asks MacQueen whether he wrote the words. MacQueen, who is a little surprised, does not reply immediately and PC Harris asks him his name. 'Steve MacQueen' he truthfully replies. PC Harris tells MacQueen that he thinks that that is a very witty remark and says, 'You can come with me, son'.

They go to a flat, the address of which is given by MacQueen as his home address. Using a key provided by MacQueen, Harris enters it and immediately sees a large sign which reads 'Shepherd's Bush' which appears to be stolen from a nearby railway station. PC Harris takes the sign along with MacQueen to the police station. Here MacQueen is searched, and charged with theft.

Advise MacQueen.

If you are to advise MacQueen, then you ought to explore his remedies against the police and the admissibility of any evidence relevant to the charge of theft. In order to deal with both, it is necessary to deal in broad terms with the legality of the conduct of the police, and to follow carefully the questioning on the street, the detention and the search of both person and premises. If we begin by looking at the power to arrest, perhaps the only likely offence is the carving of the words on the shelter. At this stage you may not have studied criminal law, although you may have some inkling that there is an offence of criminal damage. But then you do not know whether such an offence is an arrestable offence. As is said throughout this chapter, it is unrealistic to attempt to learn, e.g., all of the possible arrestable offences — particularly in relation to those offences carrying sentences of over five years. In fact criminal damage is an arrestable offence (see s. 24(1)(b)), but if it is unrealistic for you to know this, all you can say is that if the offence is an arrestable offence it will be governed by s. 24 whereas if it is not, s. 25 may be applicable.

However, under s. 25 there would have to be a general arrest condition. Perhaps Harris has reasonable grounds for doubting that MacQueen answers with his real name in view of the fact that it sounded like the name of a well-known film actor (this seems to be the case here). Alternatively Harris may have reasonable grounds for believing arrest to be necessary in order to prevent MacQueen causing damage to property (e.g., by further defacing the bus shelter).

However, if there are prima facie powers to arrest here, it is not clear that MacQueen is arrested. You can talk about manner of arrest here in terms of the s. 28 requirements (and supporting case law such as *Christie* v *Leachinsky*

[1947] AC 573 and *Alderson* v *Booth* [1969] 2 QB 216 could be brought in to illustrate these requirements).

The legality of the searches may depend on the legality of the arrest. If MacQueen does not consent to the search of the flat, s. 18 may nonetheless allow this. However, you could point out that MacQueen was under no obligation to give his home address to Harris (simply a satisfactory address for service of a summons) or for that matter to answer the initial question as to whether he wrote the graffiti. Section 18 applies to search following an arrest for an arrestable offence, so again you must point out the relevance of whether the offence is arrestable. However, the arrest seems in any case to have been unlawful and this would render the searches, both of the premises and of MacQueen himself, unlawful (consider the search powers in relation to MacQueen, s. 54 would seem to be more appropriate than s. 32 here). Note that searching a person at the police station cannot simply be standard procedure for it has been said that in all cases there must be a good reason for conducting the search — see *Middleweek* v *Chief Constable of Merseyside* [1992] 1 AC 179.

Having considered the legality of the police conduct consider the remedies against the police. Usually the tort of trespass will be involved. In this case there is the trespass to the person inherent in the search of MacQueen, trespass to land if the entry on to the premises is unlawful, and trespass to goods if the seizure falls outside the ambit of the police's power. The detention without lawful arrest will constitute false imprisonment. These are the actions against the police which will usually be appropriate but be on the look-out for others, for example malicious prosecution (see *Wershof* v *Metropolitan Police Commissioner* [1978] 3 All ER 540). Also remember to deal with the possibility of complaints against the police at a depth appropriate to the coverage of this topic on your course.

Finally remember to deal with the admissibility of the evidence. It is not intended to repeat here what is written above, but you must show that you are familiar with the court's exercise of discretion allowed by s. 78. Finally a summary of your findings should prove helpful in a problem on police powers which may be long and complex. This should be included — but only if there is time!

CONCLUSION

Police powers can be a heavy subjet to prepare for examinations. It can be made much more simple by breaking the area down into a series of smaller units, and maintaining a checklist which can be applied to problems. It is also necessary to prepare for essay questions by knowing where the balance is drawn between police power and individual freedom, and by reaching your own informed opinion of where the balance should lie.

FURTHER READING

Card, R. and Ward, J., (1994) *Criminal Justice and Public Order Act 1994* (Bristol: Jordans).

Fenwick, H., 'Curtailing the Right to Silence, Access to Legal Advice and section 78' [1995] Crim LR 132.

Robertson, G., (1993) *Freedom, the Individual and the Law*, 7th ed. (London: Penguin). (Chapters 1 to 3).

Wasik, M. and Taylor, R., (1995) *Guide to the Criminal Justice and Public Order Act 1994* (London: Blackstone Press).

13 CONCLUSION

Because the notion of a constitution is central to all organised activity, constitutional law is a very wide-ranging subject. Dealing as it does with the nature and role of the principal organs of government and their relationship with the people, the syllabus includes a large variety of topics. Dalton and Dexter once described constitutional law as 'a subject which can range from Plato to the police'. This remark reminds us of two problems relating to the study of the subject. The first is that there is a vast area to be covered. Just as this book has selected various areas of discussion and analysis, so too your own syllabus will be selective. This leads to the second point which is that in making the selection a great deal may depend upon the perspective adopted upon the particular course. There may be much more emphasis on Plato than on the police. Your course may have a strong theoretical underpinning (or ought to have) or it may not. The emphasis may be a study of the political institutions, for example, or there may be a concentration upon civil liberties issues.

The possible permutations are enormous, and there is one lesson to be learnt from all this. Maintain an approach which is in tune with that adopted on your particular course. Textbooks on law may offer a coverage of the material which is likely to appear in any course, but they cannot bring to bear the particular viewpoint adopted in your classes. Nor can they necessarily provide the level of detail which your lecturer has included on certain topics. This is not to suggest that lecturers are capricious or whimsical in deciding which topics to cover. Constitutional law is a living subject and from time to time topics assume a particular importance usually in relation to political events. Good lecturers respond to this, if only because they wish to maintain the students' interest by placing the material in the context of contemporary issues.

In chapter 5 it was pointed out that issues of parliamentary supremacy assume particular significance in the light of political events. So too a variety of other subjects may become more fashionable over time. The attempts of the Thatcher Government to suppress the book *Spycatcher* gave prominence to such areas as official secrecy, contempt of court, and individual ministerial responsibility. Freedom of information is now a significant item in the manifesto of certain parties.

One important feature of such political controversies is that they cut across many of the areas of law as laid out in the textbooks. In the real world, legal problems do not fall neatly into compartments. Not only is it important, therefore, to take a lively interest in such developments, but it becomes essential to review them in terms of the legal topics which they knit together. These may form unexpected combinations. The decision to forbid trade union membership to the staff of GCHQ at Cheltenham in 1984 raised questions of natural justice and the exercise of prerogative powers. Not unnaturally, such questions are difficult to handle both in reality and upon the examination paper. Nonetheless the political ramifications of such events, and the controversy which surrounds legal decisions in these situations make some form of inquiry in the examination quite probable.

Use your initiative. Consider carefully where the emphasis has been placed during the year of study. Follow your course carefully. Attend lecturers and prepare for your seminars. All lecturers are at pains to ensure that they cover the material which is likely to appear on the examination paper. It may be that in a tutorial they will repeat the argument on a particular point in order to ensure that you understand it. This is not necessarily an attempt to offer hints, but, being conscientious people, they will generally want to satisfy themselves that they have put the students into the best possible position to make a success of the paper. Therefore, it is your course that you should rely on. Your hand-outs should form the basis of your revision. They may include subject-matter not covered in your textbook.

This is not to say that textbooks are redundant, although there is no single book which will guarantee a student success in law examinations. In a sense, the book most likely to offer this is a good textbook on the particular subject. All teachers hope that students will spend time reading cases, monographs and journal articles relating to the course which they are studying. At the same time, it is difficult to deny that if the student has a sound knowledge of the material contained in a major textbook, then that ought to provide a sufficient fund of information for examination purposes. A lack of detailed reading may show through, and it is usually possible to distinguish those students who have spent time studying the law reports from those who have ascertained the facts and a bare *ratio* from a textbook. In consequence examination answers based on textbook reading alone will be too shallow to provide much more than a bare pass.

Nonetheless, textbooks may provide sufficient information. What they fail to offer is any form of instruction on how to present that information in its best light in assessment. That is the aim of this book, especially because few tutors or law courses will seek to do this either. That this is the case is not so surprising. Within most law departments the tradition has been that of the three-hour examination as the assessment at the end of the course. The introduction of assessed course work during the year (especially within semesterised systems) has made some sort of assault upon this tradition, but in a 'core' subject such as constitutional law, the impact of other forms of assessment has been less marked. It follows that the examination plays the role of the one independent method of calculating the aptitude of the law student on many courses, and a major element on all of them. Hence the tradition of leaving the student to sink or swim at examination time — assistance being offensive to the notion of an objective process of assessment.

This might be fair if the only skill which the examination tests is aptitude for, and knowledge of, law. Yet most teachers would observe that there are certain students who fail consistently to reflect their progress in law, during the year, at the time of the examination. Others manage to hide massive deficiencies apparent throughout the year. It is not simply a case of one group of students being brighter than another. The qualities necessary for examination success are many and varied. Not all of them are vital components of a good law student or, for that matter, a good lawyer. In short, as a system of assessment, the examination is not very efficient, with the result that a student cannot rely simply upon a knowledge of the subject as a passport to success.

This book seeks to redress the balance. Nowhere does it say that there is an easy route through the law examination. What it does say is that if you are going to study law, you may as well direct your efforts towards achieving success as measured under the present system. There will be no rewards if you fail to work consistently throughout the year, but if you do work at your studies, you should seek to ensure that your efforts are not wasted. Thus in seminar preparation, you ought to remain aware that the types of questions which you are considering are the types which will appear on the examination paper. The notes which you make should be carefully prepared. They should be structured in such a way that they are easy to understand and to learn. They should contain headings, lists of major points, and be well spaced out. Each topic should be written up before you pass on to the next one. In this way, you do not have to begin to write notes for the first time when you should be revising them.

Above all, it is important to be able to face the examination with a degree of confidence. If you know that you have invested time in preparing answers to questions from previous papers, and if you know that you have covered a sufficient range of topics, from a set of well-prepared notes, there is little to fear. You should enter the examination room in a spirit of confidence that you will be able to prove your ability. Remember also, that no examiner wishes to fail a student, but all examiners need proof that the examinee deserves to pass. To that extent the examination is fair, if the candidate produces the evidence of a capacity to understand and apply the principles of constitutional law, then that candidate must pass.

The onus, therefore, is on you. This book contains a whole host of short cuts, hints and suggestions which should improve your examination technique, but many of these require the student's application. Notes do not write themselves. Hints concerning memorising of material are only useful to a student making the effort to remember. Working for examinations is not always easy, not least because revision is exceedingly boring. There will be many occasions therefore in the weeks before examinations when you will have to force yourself not merely to refuse an invitation for an evening out, but even to return to your room when you suddenly find you have wandered into the kitchen to make yet another cup of coffee which you do not really want.

Even a few weeks of revision may seem endless. The sun will shine constantly, and everyone that you know will hold a stream of parties which you wish to attend. At this time it is simply a question of how badly you want to pass. The sacrifice required is only short-term, and the rewards may last a lifetime. Try to maintain a sense of reality. A few weeks of restricted social activity are unlikely to lose you true friends, or cause you to suffer from any permanent personality disorder. Moreover, examinations are usually followed by long holidays in which you can more than make up for your previous inactivity.

No matter how few, or how many, weeks you have to go before the examination, therefore, sit down now and draw yourself up a timetable of work to be done. Be reasonable with yourself. There is no need to chain and padlock yourself to a desk. Producing too hard a programme will only lead to despair when you fail continually to meet its requirements. However, the programme ought not to be too easy either. A certain percentage of students underestimate the demands which successful law studies make upon their time.

A law degree is a valuable asset. You cannot expect it to come easily. On the other hand law is not so difficult an academic subject — it is possible to name a host of other subjects which are more challenging intellectually. In consequence, for the majority of law degree students who have met the entry requirements for their course, a law degree is readily accessible. Only two difficulties may stand in your way: you need to acquire a sufficient technique to cope with law assessments and examinations and you need to commit yourself to your studies. This book can assist you in overcoming the first of these difficulties. The second is very much up to you.

INDEX

TITLES IN THE SERIES